Trek *of*
Faith

Trek *of* Faith

By Peggy Tucker

ISBN 0-9672363-0-4

Library of Congress Card Number: 99-95203

Printed in the United States of America

This book is dedicated
in loving memory of my husband

Keith Douglas Tucker

He first introduced me to the beautiful lake country.

He taught me the history of the place.

We visited Old Town,

fished and swam in the lake,

saw the three Silver Lakes and the Gould Homestead.

In Girard we saw the house Uncle Lute Whiting built.

We took a canoe trip on Ottertail River

up to Phelps Mill.

He took our family of seven children there

every summer of our lives,

and we worshiped the Lord together

in the little white church in Clitherall.

He would want our children and their children

to hear the story of his grandparents

and their journey of faith.

Foreword

The people who enliven these pages were people of faith. They were pilgrims on a journey of hope, like so many before them, who moved out to a promised land in search of peace and the opportunity to worship God as their consciences dictated.

As one who traces my heritage back to those Minnesota pioneers, I marvel at the strength of their convictions and the courage that brought them through so many trials and tribulations. Their unique religious beliefs led them to separate themselves from their fellow citizens in southern Iowa. Later missionaries from the church led by "young Joseph" came to preach and convert many of the immigrants away from the church founded by Alpheus Cutler. It is all too common among groups, who having started out as brothers and sisters, to diverge along the way and later see themselves as adversaries. This story tells of the division that came, ensuing heartbreak, and the faith and love among the people that brought reconciliation.

The Tuckers, Goulds, Whitings, Fletchers, Murdocks and other families whose stories are told in this book shared a common belief in the Restoration Gospel, even though they came to see that Gospel in different ways. They were people with strengths and weaknesses, just as we are. Their joys and sorrows were real. Here, they come to life again and we see them as real people living out their faith.

The author is to be commended for sharing this story of long-ago events. As we prepare to enter the third Millennium, we can know and appreciate the struggles and the triumphs our ancestors experienced in the wilderness of western Minnesota in the late nineteenth century.

May we share their strength and determination.

RUSSELL R. FLETCHER
Executive Director, Outreach International

Contents

Acknowledgments

This work would have been impossible without the foresight of many people. These did what every family should do—that is, to keep a history of the main events of their families.

Hallie Gould compiled stories of the first white settlers of Ottertail County, Minnesota and had them printed in booklet form, calling it *The Old Clitherall Story Book.* Some of the information in this book was gleaned from that work. Hallie and her sisters, Maude Sherman, Ethel Tucker, Nina Tucker, Iva and Gladys Gould kept journals of their own and wrote them up as well as those of their parents. Gladys typed many manuscripts. Others were handwritten.

In 1975, many of these papers went into the hands of Frank and Norma Tucker, son and daughter-in-law of Frank and Ethel Tucker. They typed and retyped all the loose papers and made copies for all the relatives. Joyce McCarty, daughter of Nina and Orison Tucker, provided illustrations for their copies.

These papers were compiled in 1992, by Velma Sherman, daughter-in-law of Plin and Maude Sherman. Using her computer, they were organized, indexed and a genealogy added. It was given the name of *MINNESOTA PIONEERS, A History of the Founding of Ottertail County and Families of Gould, Sherman, Tucker, Whiting and Others.*

Other sources of information include Ottertail County Historical Society and Ottertail Power Company, as well as personal experience of the author in the land in which this story takes place.

Others who were of great help are Kenneth Tucker and Frank and Norma Tucker who read the manuscript and offered suggestions. And to all the relatives who have shared family photographs, thanks are due.

To Peggy Feagins must go credit for many hours spent in proofreading the manuscript several times, giving invaluable suggestions and corrections. Without her help it could not have been accomplished.

Ed McGuire gave good suggestions and invaluable help in the production of this book. Garry Hood's expertise is greatly appreciated in designing the cover.

Other sources as noted in the footnotes.

Many thanks to all concerned.

Preface

Minnesota became a state May 11, 1858. The land was offered to homesteaders and many took advantage of the opportunity. These people settled mainly in the southern and eastern parts. A few, however, began to venture toward the northwest. Some settlements were started and a fort raised in Ottertail County. This was in the area of the Young Drift Plains where, according to the geologists, the glacier moved along the surface, sometimes leaving large areas smooth, which became prairies. In other places, great gouges were scooped out, leaving holes which became lakes, of which there are more than 10,000 in the state. Where the glacier stopped and melted, it deposited its load of rock, soil and sand, forming hills. The prairies were mainly vast treeless plains, but groves of trees grew along the streams and edges of some lakes. Among these were ash, elm, sugar maple, oak, ironwood, basswood, some pines and white birch. Wild blueberries were abundant in the pine forests and red raspberries flourished along the edges of the woods. Hazelnut bushes and wild choke cherry trees also bordered the lakes.

Here the Indians had lived well. The wild game was plentiful, fish in the lakes were an ever present source of food and the wild berries, roots, hazel nuts and herbs made life good for them. However, with the continued westward push of the pioneers, their habitat became threatened. The Government signed many treaties with them and as many were broken. Some of the land was paid for with so many barrels of whiskey. Finally, many of the Sioux were moved to reservations in the more barren parts of the state. In 1862, when many men were away fighting in the Civil War, the Indians went to war against the white settlers. Part of the problem was the delay in the Indians' annuity money, which caused them to be short of rations, and thus short of tempers. But the trouble seems to have started when a party of four Sioux hunters stopped at the home of some white settlers. According to the report they made to their own people later, one of the Indians wished to take some eggs which he found in a fence corner near a cabin, but he feared to steal from a white man. His companions accused him of cowardice, and in blustering self defense he announced his intention of shooting the first white man he saw. He turned and fired at the friendly settlers, killing three men and two women.

Believing the whites would retaliate, the Sioux decided to get them first. The uprising was widespread. It is difficult to judge with any accuracy the loss of life during the Sioux outbreak, since no official count was made, but various estimates made by men who aided in suppressing the uprising place the number from 600 to 1,500. No other single Indian uprising in all the history of the country caused such a loss of life among the whites. Many settlers who had emigrated from eastern states abandoned their homesteads and refused to return to Minnesota

Ottertail County was left desolate and scarred. Many of the Sioux were then moved onto reservations in South Dakota. Of the three hundred warriors sentenced to death, all but thirty-eight were pardoned by President Lincoln, the others held as prisoners. The more peaceful Chippewa remained in northern Minnesota.

It was only three years later that another group of courageous pioneers entered the territory. These people, who are credited with establishing the first permanent white settlement in Ottertail County, came originally from Nauvoo, Illinois. Nauvoo, which is a Hebrew word meaning "beautiful place," was an industrious city built on the bend of the Mississippi River. It was built by a people with a deep faith in God and a belief that they had been commissioned to preach repentance and begin to prepare a righteous city for the return of

Jesus Christ. The church was called The Church of Jesus Christ, its founder having received instructions for its organization directly from Him, through revelation. It was patterned after the church Jesus established in Galilee, and because it was set up in modern times, they added the phrase, Latter Day Saints.

These people established schools and a college, all manner of industry. Because they were sincere and tried to keep the laws of God, they prospered. The city grew in numbers and influence in the state. It was the largest city in the state at the time, eclipsing Chicago. They believed that "all men are created equal," therefore they stood strong against slavery. Because of their influence politically, they encountered much opposition. Joseph Smith, their leader, and his brother were arrested several times on false charges and released when no foundation for the charges could be found. Finally, on June 24, 1844, they were given a warrant for their arrest and were to appear in court. As they left Nauvoo to go to Carthage, Joseph told his people, "I go as a lamb to the slaughter," knowing he would not return. While jailed waiting trial, the following day, a mob of masked men stormed the building and shot both Joseph and his brother, Hyrum.

Like sheep without a shepherd, the people were driven from the state. There was a mass exodus westward to what is now Council Bluffs, where they lived through the winter in their covered wagons. From there the main group continued west to the Great Salt Lake Valley. Another group followed a leader to Texas and others found their way to Wisconsin.

However, some were unhappy with the teachings they were hearing which were contrary to the original beliefs. About thirty families left the larger group to found a small village in southwest Iowa, with the intention to remain there until the son of the leader was old enough to take his father's place. Within a few years, however, a new church, called simply, The Church of Christ, was organized among them, under the leadership of Alpheus Cutler, who had been an active member of the original church. He believed he had been given authority to do that when he saw a sign of two half moons back to back. Mr. Cutler also said he had been shown in a dream a beautiful strip of prairie lying between two shining lakes, far to the north. There, he believed, was the sanctuary for their people. Although he died before his dream was realized, in the fall of 1864 a part of their group set out in covered wagons for the far north. Enduring unbelievable hardships, they reached Red Wing, Minnesota, in November. Deep snow and extreme cold made it impossible to go further. They rented rooms for the families, while some of the men, with an Indian friend, went on as far as Crow Wing. There, they made contact with a group of Indian chiefs, with the result that a treaty of peace was drawn up and signed by all concerned.

Early in the spring, traveling through unexpected blizzards, mud and rain, these sturdy pioneers reached Ottertail County. After fervently praying for guidance to find the place of Cutler's dream, they arrived on the shore of Clitherall Lake. It was indeed a place of beauty. A wide strip of prairie separated Clitherall Lake on the south from a larger lake on the north. The Indians had given it the name of *Ish-quon-e-di-winig* meaning "The Place Where Few Survived." The area had been the scene of a great battle between the Sioux and the Chippewa Indians at an earlier time. The English name was shortened to simply Battle Lake.

Living neighbors to the Indians, the people began at once to build log cabins, plow the prairie sod and plant crops and gardens. They were many miles from other towns, schools, stores. They took their wheat one hundred miles to a mill to be ground. The nearest post office was nearly as far. But with courage and fortitude, they founded a community to be proud of. It is among these people this story takes place.

CHAPTER 1

The Land Between Two Shining Lakes

Two men trudged wearily to the top of a rise in the prairie. Each carried a canvas pack on his back, a gun in one hand and an ax in the other. On reaching the crest of the hill, the younger man slipped the pack from his shoulders and dropped his tired body onto it. In spite of the ache in his shoulders and the pain of a blister on his foot, his face brightened at the view before him. A wide strip of prairie separated two beautiful shining lakes. Although there were still large chunks of ice floating in the lakes, a flock of wild geese began landing on the nearest one. They called loudly to each other, plainly glad to have arrived at their summer home. A few trees near the edge of the lake had a tint of green. It was a sure sign spring was close.

"Pa, you said it was pretty up here," he remarked, still taking in the beauty of the area, "but I could never imagine it like this. There must be all kinds of fish in the lakes and wild game to be had for the taking. What a great place!"

The older man removed his cap and ran his fingers through his brown hair. His tanned face showed him to be a man acquainted with all kinds of weather. There was a light in his eyes as he, too, surveyed the scene. "It's a great new country, Winfield," he said, "this northwestern part of Minnesota. We are fortunate to be some of the early ones to homestead here. Together we can carve our own niche in this part of the world."

George Gould and his older son, Clayton, had been in the area the summer before. George had filed a claim on a homestead and returned to Filmore County in southern Minnesota to prepare for the move. Clayton, however, had decided to stay and work for the settlers through the winter.

"How much farther to the Mormon settlement?" asked Winfield.

"This is Clitherall Lake on the south," answered his pa. "The settlement is on down the shore of the lake, just a little ways. We should find Clayton there someplace. Hopefully we can stay there tonight, and go on to the homestead in the morning."

As they topped the next hill, Winfield could see a little group of log cabins lined up along the lake, with smoke curling from their stick chimneys. A beautiful sunset, reflecting across the lake, made a gorgeous setting for the little village. As they neared the first cabin, a dog spotted the newcomers and promptly announced their arrival.

"Who goes there?" called a man from the doorway.

"George Gould here," came the answer, "we're looking for Clayton Gould."

"I think you'll find him at Henry Way's cabin, on down the trail about a mile."

Winfield groaned. His feet were wet and cold and his stomach empty. But he shouldered his pack and with gun in one hand and ax in the other set off behind his pa. He was relieved when he heard the familiar voice of his brother.

"Pa! Winfield! Am I glad to see you! We had an Indian scare and I was worried about you. Did you have any trouble?"

"Only trouble we had, Clayton," answered George, "was pulling our tired legs over these fifty miles. Sure is good to see a friendly face."

Another man came from the door of the cabin, offering his hand to George.

"Henry Way, this is my pa, George Gould," explained Clayton, "and this young stripling is my brother, Winfield."

"Glad to meet you both," exclaimed Henry good naturedly.

"How old are you young man?"

"I'm seventeen," he answered, feeling a little put out at Clayton's introduction.

"Come on in and spend the night. Clayton tells me your homestead is up by Silver Lake. Can't send you off up there in the dark."

Winfield thought he had never tasted anything so delicious as the beans and corn pone Mrs. Way gave him. The fire was drying his feet and the comfort made him sleepy. But he wanted to hear what the men were saying. He had heard so many stories about the Mormons, but these folks seemed like ordinary, friendly people.

"Yes, we had a rider come in from Ottertail warning of an Indian uprising," explained Henry. "Some of the settlers from outlying areas came in to Clitherall settlement for protection. But it was a false alarm. Actually, the treaty the Indians signed at Crow Wing, with the first of our folks who came in 1865, has never been broken by either the Chippewa or the whites. We are pretty good neighbors, but we are watchful. They can really make trouble if they get whiskey."

"If it has lasted three years, that is a good sign. I've wondered," questioned George, "why you people came up here among the Indians so soon after that massacre."

"You aren't the first to wonder that," returned Henry. "You see, our people had been persecuted, murdered and run off our land in Illinois among supposedly civilized citizens. Minnesota was a new state and had been opened up to homesteaders. We felt we could make a new beginning here." He added another log to the fire and then resumed. "But how we happened to come here to this place is another story."

"I'd be interested to hear about it," George offered carefully. "That is if you care to tell."

Henry had a far away look in his eyes as he continued. "I suppose you heard about the murder of the prophet Joseph

17

Smith and his brother Hyrum." It was more a question than a statement.

"Yes," answered George, "my family was still in New York. We had some contact with the Latter Day Saints up there. I remember my mother coming in the house so excited, telling us that the neighbors' little terribly sick girl had been healed by some Mormon elders. We were Baptists, so didn't have anything to do with their church, but I always felt sorry because they were treated so harshly."

"The public called us Mormons," corrected Henry, "because of the book by that name. But the name of the church was the Church of Jesus Christ of Latter Day Saints. But to continue, soon afterward we were all ordered out of Nauvoo and the state of Illinois. We set to work building wagons so we could haul our families and a few belongings. We established Winter Quarters in northwestern Iowa, and camped that winter, living in our covered wagons. However, quite a group of us decided there were too many wrong things being taught, things which had never been spoken openly while Joseph was alive. So in the spring we took our families and settled in southwestern Iowa. We called the place Manti."

"Did you continue to live in the covered wagons?" asked George.

"No," answered Henry, "we began at once to build log cabins and set up a few shops. We expected to stay there until Young Joseph was old enough to take his father's place. Later, Alpheus Cutler came to the community. He had been active in the priesthood in Nauvoo. In fact, he was the Master Builder of the temple there. Because he had the highest priesthood, he was chosen leader. He organized the church again, rebaptizing everyone. Cutler believed that he had been set aside by Joseph to be the prophet in an emergency. We were hoping and praying for guidance, and we accepted what he told us. He told us of a spiritual dream in which he saw a beautiful strip of land lying between two shining lakes, and felt he was supposed to lead the people there. Because part of his assignment in the original church had been to preach to the Indians, he felt that part of the country offered a golden opportunity to reach them. He died before he accomplished that, but the group decided to investigate."

"It certainly fits the description," said George. "As Winfield and I were coming in, we came to a spot where we could see both lakes."

Early morning found Henry Way hitching his mule to a light wagon. "Take this mule and wagon along with you George. He can pull up the logs for your cabin. By the way, on up the trail a ways you will see a hay stack. Take plenty for the mule, and if you like maple syrup, you can stop over at my sugar bush which is just a little out of your way. Boil down whatever there is in the troughs."

"We're sure obliged to you," said George, hardly able to believe this good turn of events. "When we get the cabin finished, Clayton will be going back for the rest of the family and our things. Hope to be able to repay your kindness."

The sun was shining and Winfield's adventuresome spirit was high. He was anxious to reach Pa's homestead and get started making it theirs. He was glad he could put his pack in the wagon and need only carry his gun. That set him to thinking about the kindness of those people. Some of his friends down in Filmore County told him those Latter Day Saints were a bunch of thieves. That was one reason Pa chose his claim nine miles farther north and west. Well, he had only seen one family. Maybe they are an exception, he thought.

They reached the maple grove without much trouble, and found the wooden troughs nearly full of fresh sparkling sap.

"This is the best weather for running the sap," remarked Clayton. "When it freezes at night, but gets warm in the daytime, it just seems to pump it up fast."

"It's real good of Henry to let us work it up," said George. "Winfield, you gather up some fire wood and we'll get this syrup boiling."

The men began pouring the sap into the big boiler. Soon the fire was blazing hot and the simmering began.

"It will take most of the night to cook down," said Clayton. "We can take turns keeping the fire going. In the meantime, maybe we can rustle up something to cook for supper. Winfield, why don't you take my fish spear and see what you can find at the inlet of that little lake? There should be plenty of bass."

"Never used one before," returned Winfield, "but I'll try." Silently he was thinking he would rather take his gun and go after a deer. But he took the spear from the wagon and headed for the lake. The sun was a bright red disk just above the horizon, as he carefully made his way over the bank. Suddenly, he saw it! A big buck lifted his head from the water, stood a second and with the greatest of ease cleared the bank in one bound and was gone!

"If only I'd had my gun!" he said aloud. "What a chance, what a wonderful animal! I'll never get another chance like that." Reluctantly he took the spear and eased down close to the narrow channel of the inlet. The fading light made it difficult to see if there were any fish. Soon, however, his eyes adjusted to the dancing lights of the stream and he could see some movement—a few panfish darted through. He waited. If he had to take fish he wanted it to be a big one. A mud turtle climbed out on a half submerged log. He wondered how turtle soup would be. He was about to return to camp when he saw a little fish jump from the water, a large mouth followed and in that instant the spear flashed out. There was a tremendous thrashing about, but the fish had met his match. Guess we'll eat good after all, thought Winfield. This is a big bass. Triumphantly he headed back for camp.

"Say, Kid, you did all right for a first timer!" exclaimed Clayton, as Winfield strode nonchalantly into camp. "Look, Pa, what this kid brought back. That bass will weigh six pounds or I'll eat it all."

"Well," returned Winfield, "you should have seen the one that got away." Then he told them about the big beautiful buck.

"That's all right Son," said George, "we can have this fish ready to eat in a little while. It would have taken us all night to dress a deer and cook a piece of it. We'll wrap that bass in some of these wet leaves and put it under the coals. You really did good."

Mr. Way had put up a three sided shelter where the heat of the fire would reach it. After the fish was devoured, Winfield got his blanket from his back pack and curled up in it where he could watch the fire. In imagination, he was staking out his own homestead and building a house for a beautiful young lady. He would raise the best crops and provide the best home of anyone around. His dreams were interrupted by the sound of his pa singing:

> "Mine eyes have seen the glory of the coming of the Lord;
> He is trampling out the vintage where the grapes of wrath are stored;
> He hath loosed the fateful lightning of his terrible swift sword;
> His truth is marching on."

Clayton's bass joined in the chorus and the woods rang with the music:

> "Glory, glory, hallelujah!
> Glory, glory, hallelujah!
> Glory, glory, hallelujah! His truth is marching on."

That's my pa, thought Winfield, he's the best man there is. I hope I can be as good. And in his heart he offered a prayer of thanks to God.

"Let the kid sleep," Winfield thought he heard Clayton say. "I'll take the first jag. You get some rest too, Pa."

CHAPTER 2

The Homestead

T ime's a-wasting, Kid. How about some firewood so we can cook some breakfast?"

Winfield opened one eye to find Clayton about ready to drip some water in his face.

"All right! all right!" he yelled, "I'm awake." Then he reached out and tackled his brother's legs, bringing him down. A good natured tussle ensued, and to Clayton's surprise, Winfield had him pinned.

"I give, brother, spare me," begged Clayton, pretending fear for his life.

"On one condition," answered Winfield. "Quit calling me Kid!"

"Agreed. My little brother has become a man!"

George cooked some corn gruel over the coals. Each took some in his tin cup and added drizzles of that delicious brown syrup on top.

"This is mighty good eating, thanks to Henry," said Clayton. "There's just nothing quite like maple syrup."

They poured the rest of the syrup into the tin bucket they had used to carry drinking water on the trip. "If we hadn't eaten so much," said George, "we would have had a gallon."

Camp was soon broken, the troughs replaced to catch more of that wonderful sap, and they were on their way. The mule even seemed anxious after filling up on the hay through the night.

"It won't take us long now," said Pa. "We only have about five miles to go. Less than that if we could go by boat. We have to go around the west side of big Silver Lake, past the center one and to the north end of the west one." There was no road, no trail, from there on. They followed the shore of the first lake in the chain of Silver Lakes, made their way across a narrow swamp between that one and the middle lake, and soon came out on the north side of West Silver Lake.

"Whoa, Mule. This is the end of the journey for today," said George, as he began to unhitch the mule from the wagon. "Clayton, you take the harness off, please, and put the tether rope on him. I want to show you boys how our land lies."

Winfield took off his coat and wool knit cap, and wiped the sweat from his broad high forehead. The south wind felt good. Then he watched as Pa pointed to the north, showing the rolling prairie, green with new grass; to the hollow where a grove of tall oak trees waved their arms in the wind, sending their few remaining brown leaves flying. Silver Lake made a beautiful boundary on the south. Its shining water blue with silver streaks where the sun touched the white caps.

"Our first job," said Pa, "will be to cut some of those straight oak trees and build us a house. The sooner we get that done, the sooner your ma and the others can come. I'm sure glad you fellows have grown so big and strong. I doubt I could do it alone. Let's eat a cold snack before we decide on a spot for the house. We'll try to get started first thing in the morning."

The ring of axes could have been heard for a mile around, but there were only the ears of the wild geese on the lake, the deer in the woods and all the other wild neighbors to hear. It was a solitary, but beautiful land. As the trees fell, they set to work stripping them of branches, and cutting them to length. Once ready, Winfield fastened a chain around one end of the log and hitched the mule to the other end of the chain. Coaxing the mule to pull the log was about the hardest part of the job, but he would finally yield and head slowly in the direction Winfield guided him. Using some of the brush, they built a makeshift shelter. They stretched over it the canvas tarpaulin they had used on the trip. Day after day they worked, sleeping on the ground at night, too tired to know their bed was cold and hard.

George wiped the sweat from his brow as he surveyed the pile of logs. "Well, boys," he said with a sigh of relief, "it looks as though we have enough logs. Now it's time to start notching them and begin to build. I think we'd better take a trip into Clitherall today for some supplies. We can take Henry's mule back at the same time. There just might happen to be some young fellow there needing work. If so, we could use one more hand at raising these logs. What do you think?"

"Sounds great to me," chimed in Clayton.

"As for me," answered Winfield, "I'd like to see some more of the Mormons. If there are any more like Henry Way, I'll begin to think those were all lies we heard down there in Filmore County."

Winfield enjoyed the walk. The time spent getting the logs had made a difference. The prairie grass had grown tall and green. The basswood trees along the lakes were putting out their pretty heart-shaped leaves. Here and there he discovered a wild goose already on its nest. Ducks were everywhere on the shining silver lakes. There were no neighbors between Pa's homestead and Clitherall. There were no weeds, only bluebells and mayflowers along the trail. Everything looked so new and clean.

"Pa," said Clayton as they came over the rise overlooking the blue expanse of Battle Lake, "Before long I want to see about a homestead next to yours, there on the west side."

"That's a nice eighty acres, Clayton," responded his father. "That would be great. And Winfield, yours could lay to the north. We can farm them all together. We could call our place, Gould Father and Sons Homestead."

"I have been meaning to ask you about that Pa," said Winfield, excitedly. "We better do it before somebody else moves in."

"Doesn't look too crowded right now," joked Clayton.

"Your mother's folks plan to come in the fall," said George, "but they want a place on middle Silver Lake, not too far from us."

After returning the mule and wagon, George went to the blacksmith shop. Clayton and Winfield wandered down the sandy road to the little store.

"This is Sylvester Whiting's place," said Clayton. "He has some stock set up in his home. We'll go in to see what he has."

Winfield looked around the store room with interest. There were a few pairs of shoes on a shelf, some bolts of cloth, some tools and barrels of flour, sugar and cornmeal.

"Can I help you boys?" Mr. Whiting was dipping up some flour for a lady.

"We're down from the homestead," answered Clayton. "This is my brother Winfield. We have been pulling up logs for the cabin. Have you seen Alma Sherman?" Just at that moment, the door opened and in walked a good looking young man with a friendly smile.

"Thought I saw you come in here Clayton," he said. "Where have you been?"

"Hey," exclaimed Clayton, "I was just asking about you. Alma, this is my brother Winfield. We have been helping Pa get the logs up for our cabin. How'd you like to come and help us raise them? Winfield will feed you good on fish. He's quite an expert."

"Sounds like a good deal," answered Alma, as he reached to shake hands with Winfield. "How do you like this part of the country?"

"I think it is the greatest place on earth. Never saw any place so beautiful. I'm planning to take a homestead north of Pa's." That thought was on Winfield's mind most of the time, even though he was happy to be busy helping Pa. He liked the looks of this friend of Clayton's. He was shorter than himself, with a stocky and muscular build. We'll be glad for his muscles when we get started raising up those logs, he thought.

George, having finished his business, came in the store. Mr. Whiting's friendly face made him welcome. He came around the counter with an uneven gait, seemingly lame in one leg.

"You must be George Gould," exclaimed the store keeper. "My name is Sylvester Whiting, but they all call me Uncle Vet. We're glad to have more settlers coming in. If there is anything I can do for you just name it."

"The folks here have already been a big help," answered George. "These boys are going to help me raise the logs for our cabin. Your blacksmith, Ed Fletcher, is loaning us an ox team to break some ground with. We could use some corn-meal, though. Then we'll be on our way."

On the way back, Alma was telling the news. The county had just recently been organized. "'There being so few in-habitants at the time, this district was attached to Douglas County for judicial purposes. Three commissioners were ap-pointed, viz.: Chauncey Whiting, Sr. of Clitherall, E.J. Lacy and Andrew Johnson of St. Olaf. Marcus Shaw was appointed clerk and, in course of time, Charles Sperry appointed pro-bate judge.' They were thinking about asking for Clitherall to be the first township."[1]

"Seems to be a lot of Whitings here," said George. "Are they all related?"

"Yes," returned Alma. "You see there were five Whiting brothers in the group that left Nauvoo. Chauncey is the old-est. He has a tin shop up the road and a big spread north of town. He is also head of the church here. Edmund went to Utah. Almon, he is the chair maker. You met Sylvester, he's a good old guy. The other one is Francis Lewis. We call him

Uncle Lute. He and his family went back to Iowa to bring Aunt Net's mother up here. They are supposed to be back sometime in June, they're first-rate folks. And by the way, Winfield, you should meet Lu and Em. They are lots of fun to be with."

"Is there a school in Clitherall?" asked Winfield.

"Yes," answered Alma, "they built a log building that doubles for school and church. They hold school when the kids aren't needed at home, or when the snow isn't too deep. There is usually a term in the fall, one in the spring and one in the summer."

"I went to school down in Filmore County. But I'd sure like to get some more learning."

Work on the cabin was interrupted often by sudden spring rains, but at last it was taking shape. It was slow hewing out the boards for the door and window frames. Finally all was ready for the shingles.

"Since we only have one tool for making the shingles," said George one morning, "I think, Clayton, you might as well go back to your uncle Fred Sherman's for Ma and our things. Winfield and I can get the roof on while you're gone. I'll give you money to buy the windows and door to bring back when you come."

"All right, Pa," answered Clayton. "Alma says he will go with me. Uncle Cassius said we could take his oxen and wagons. I'm sure Ma is anxious. We'll take our time going, but hurry back," he finished with a grin.

"I'll look for you back in a week," assured Pa, ignoring that last remark. "It's only about fifty miles down to Holmes City."

———————⇒►●◄⇐———————

The oxen plodded slowly as the plow dug into the sod and turned up the damp earth. Winfield had plenty of time to daydream as he followed, calling out "Gee" or "Haw" to guide them in a straight way. The plow was a primitive affair. The plowshare had been brought north with the pioneers. But the apparatus to which it was fastened was a result of pioneer genius. It had a large beam about six feet long made of wood, with a piece framed into the back end of the beam to fasten the plowshare to. There were four half-inch rods bolted above the share to take the place of a moldboard, and a wooden axletree about four feet long. To this was fastened the plow with two wagon wheels attached to the axletree and a gauge made out of wood, so arranged that one could set it at a range of depths. There was no need for Winfield to hold the plow, as it performed its task quite well by the power of the oxen. The main problem was the stones, big round stones were turning up so often, he was stumbling over them.

Finally, in desperation, he left the oxen standing and went to find Pa. "Pa," he said, "there are so many big stones plowing out of the ground, what shall I do with them?"

Pa left his work to walk over the plowed ground. "I see what you mean, Winfield. We had better get them off the field. Suppose we make a pile of them in the center of the field. That way it won't be too far to carry any of them. Do what you can now, but later, we may need to use a slip to haul them. The soil looks good, Son."

"I'll soon have enough ground broken for a garden," said Winfield, "and won't Ma be happy if she can begin to plant seeds when she comes." The happy thought called forth a shout of encouragement to the humble oxen. "Come on, now, let's put a little speed into this business!"

While Winfield and the oxen were plowing, George was making shingles. He had cut some blocks of oak logs each about sixteen inches long. With what was called a frow, he cut slices from the logs, thinning them down at one end with a knife. He had covered the roof with small poplar poles, flattened on one side. Once this was accomplished, they were ready to start putting on the shingles.

"Well, Winfield," said George one morning, "we have just about enough time left to get these shingles on that roof before Clayton gets back here with your Ma."

"I think Ma will be pleased with the cabin, Pa," answered Winfield. "We can carry water from the lake, but I'm concerned about the floor. What are we going to do about it?"

"Only thing we can do, Son, is smooth out the ground and cut some of this nice blue grass and lay on it. That will be clean and sweet smelling. You may have to haul it out each day for her, and bring in fresh, but it will do until we have time to make the puncheon floor. Before we do that, we need to dig a deep cellar for storing our vegetables and dig a well. The floor may have to wait until fall."

They worked diligently fastening the new shingles to the smoothed side of the poles, and soon the work was finished. That night they slept under a real roof for the first time since they arrived at the homestead. Just in time, too, for they were awakened in the night to the sound of thunder and the swish of rain against the new shingles.

"Hey, Pa," said Winfield sleepily, "that's sure sweet music. The rain will start those seeds sprouting I planted yesterday. I hope Clayton gets here soon with Ma and the rest."

"The Lord has been good to us," responded George. "We owe Him many thanks. I think we might go down to Clitherall to the little church come Sunday, since we don't have one of our own."

Winfield was drifting off to sleep, but he wondered if those Whiting girls were back from Iowa and if they would be at the church.

CHAPTER 3

Winfield Meets the Whitings

The log building was filled when Winfield and his pa stepped inside. They found space on a rough bench just inside the door. Winfield felt as if every eye in the place were fastened on him. His home-spun shirt was soiled around the collar and his trousers needed a patch on the knee. Soon, however, the service began and all eyes were turned on the preacher. Winfield glanced around the room. One thing was plain. All the men were on one side and the women and girls on the other.

"Brothers and Sisters," the preacher's voice broke through Winfield's reverie. "The gospel of Christ is not only spiritual, but also temporal. I will read in your hearing from the Holy Bible, Acts Chapter two, verse forty-two through forty-five, speaking of the early Saints after Jesus had ascended into heaven:

"'And they continued steadfastly in the apostles' doctrine and fellowship, and in breaking of bread, and in prayers. And fear came upon every soul: and many wonders and signs were done by the apostles. And all that believed were together, and had all things common; and sold their possessions and goods, and parted them to all men, as every man had need.'

"You see, it was because they had all things common that they had the spiritual blessings. It is a commandment!" Here the preacher's voice rose to a high pitch and his fist came down on the table with force. "We must be obedient and pool our resources."

Winfield could see Pa was listening to every word. He was sitting up straight on the edge of the bench. We'll be coming back to hear more, thought Winfield. Just then there was a commotion on the women's side of the church. Two girls had their heads down and the sound of stifled giggles could be heard above the preacher's words. The preacher paused, cleared his throat and looked squarely at the two girls. They immediately sat up, their lips held firmly to prevent further disturbance. But Winfield noticed their backs continued to quiver. Wonder what was so funny, he thought, I'd like to get acquainted with them.

"George Gould?" asked a tall, fine looking man as they began to file out of the building.

"That's right," answered George, "and this is my son Winfield."

"My name is Francis Lewis Whiting. I just returned with my family this week. We spent the winter in Iowa. Sylvester said you were in the store. My wife and I would like for you and your son to come to our home for dinner."

"That is really kind of you, Mr. Whiting, but I don't want to put you out," returned George. "What do you think, Winfield?"

Winfield was beginning to put the pieces together. This must be the father of those two girls. Alma had said they were lots of fun. He didn't want to seem too anxious, so he said quite casually, "It's fine with me if Mrs. Whiting doesn't mind."

Mr. Whiting motioned the two visitors to a log bench outside the door of the cabin. "We'll visit out here while Jannette and the girls prepare the meal," he said, "how do you like our June weather?"

"It's different from southern Minnesota," exclaimed George. "It stays so cool. Now that we have the roof on our cabin, we don't mind the rain too much. The rest of my family should be coming in any day now. They will be bringing the door and windows plus our furniture, then we will begin to feel at home."

"By the way," resumed George, "I was interested in the sermon. Henry Way was telling me that your group was separate from the Utah Mormons. Do your people practice all things common?"

Oh, oh, thought Winfield. We're in for another sermon. He was hoping to hear the call for dinner any time. But Mr. Whiting had taken the cue and turned a serious face to Pa.

"Some have dedicated their property to the church, but not all. It is hard for some to be obedient. But I believe the day will come when all will obey this principle and there will be no rich and no poor among us. It is the Lord's plan for Zion."

One of the girls appeared in the doorway. "Pa," she called, "Ma says to come to dinner."

When they were all seated at the long table and Mr. Whiting had returned thanks, he proceeded to introduce his family, while Mrs. Whiting served the plates. "This is my wife, Ann Jannette, but everyone calls her Aunt Net; Grandmother Burdick, Jannette's mother; Emma, our oldest; Lucia, our second. Next is Ella, then Art and little May." As they were introduced, each one smiled shyly, except Lu. She looked at Winfield, grinned and said, "Pleased to meet you." Winfield's heart gave a jump, and he felt his face flush. He immediately turned his attention to the food Mrs. Whiting had put on his plate. However, as he ate, he glanced from one to the other. Mrs. Whiting was a pretty lady, slim and rather tall. Emma had a round face and her hair was done in a high pompadour. Lu had dark sparkling eyes and rosy cheeks. Her hair hung in two dark glossy braids. Ella was so shy he tried not to look at her, but Art, about eight he guessed, was so full of energy he could hardly sit still to eat.

The meal was nearly over when a boy came running and stuck his head in the door. "Uncle Lute, there are two covered wagons coming over the hill!" he called excitedly. "Who do you think it is?"

Winfield excused himself, saying, "It might be Clayton with Ma. I'll go see, Pa."

He followed the boy around the corner, past the schoolhouse and sure enough, an ox team was just coming around the bend of the little sandy road. "It is my folks!" he called to the boy, and he broke into a run. "Clayton! Ma! I'm sure glad you got here!" He climbed up to give his ma a hug and to greet his sisters in the back of the wagon. "Where is George?" he asked, turning to Ma. Although the children sometimes made fun of their simple half brother, they truly loved him.

"George is riding with Alma," answered Ma, "they should be here soon. Where is Pa?"

"He is at Uncle Lute Whiting's house. They are first-rate folks. They invited us to dinner after church."

What a joyous reunion the family had. Aunt Net invited the newcomers in to rest and have some food. There were more introductions, handshakes and hugs. At last Alma came driving the other team with the cow plodding along behind. "Little George" was clinging to the wagon seat, as though afraid he might fall off.

"This is the rest of my family," said George. "You already know Clayton. This is my wife Eleanor, my oldest son whom we call Little George, daughters Eleanor and Emma." Eleanor and Emma started talking to the Whiting girls. They discovered that Eleanor Gould and Lucia Whiting were both thirteen. Emma Gould was ten and Ella was eleven.

"We seem to have two Emmas," suggested Mrs. Gould. "My Emma's middle name is Luella, what is yours?" she asked, speaking to the older of the Whiting girls.

"My full name is Emma Lucine," she answered, "but everybody just calls me Em."

"That makes it easy," answered Mrs. Gould, "and to put an end to the confusion in our family, they call me Eleanor and my daughter, Norie for short."

By the time all had eaten, they were visiting as if they were longtime friends. George thanked the Whitings for their kindness and decided it was time for them to go on to the homestead and get settled.

"Norie," Winfield called to his sister. "Do you want to ride with me in Alma's wagon? He needs to go to his home. I'd like your company."

"Sure," answered his sister, as she climbed nimbly up to the wagon seat. Her blond braids, tied with blue ribbons at the ends, reached halfway down her back. She was a well developed young lady for her thirteen years. "I'm anxious to hear all about our new home. It sure is pretty around here. Is it pretty where you built the cabin?"

"Oh, yes, Sis, the cabin sits on a hill overlooking Silver Lake. The meadows are full of wild mayflowers, the basswood trees are blooming, and just wait till you get a whiff of their beautiful scent—sweetest perfume in the world!"

"Have you caught any fish from the lake?" asked Norie.

"We have practically lived on fish," answered Winfield, "and I discovered a great way to cook them. There's a clay bank over west of the cabin. I took some of it to our camp and soaked it up enough to work with. When I catch a big fish I wrap it in clay and lay it in the coals. It bakes up great without any watching. When I peel off the baked clay, the skin and scales come off, too. Of course, now that we will have a stove, I guess you and Ma will want to cook them other ways."

The oxen plodded along steadily, if not swiftly, and the cow, tied to the back of Pa's wagon, kept pace. The miles went by quickly while they visited. He told her about the school in Clitherall, hoping they could attend sometime. He told her about the young people he had seen at the church. "You know what people were saying about the Mormons, down in Filmore County? Well, these people all seem to be like the Whitings you just met. They have helped us out a lot. But they're not Mormons, they are called Cutlerites because their leader was named Cutler. The real name of their church, though, is True Church of Christ."

"You seem to have learned a lot in a short time, Win," said Norie. She had called him that since she was just a little girl. "I would like to get better acquainted with those Whiting girls."

"Well," rejoined her brother, "so would I!"

It took some time to unpack the wagons and move things into the cabin. All helped carry and unpack, even Little George, who was no stranger to work. When the beds were made, the stove set up, and the table laden with some food, it did look homey. The sweet smell of the drying grass that covered the floor made it even nicer. Winfield watched as Pa took Ma in his arms. "Welcome home, my dear!" he said as he gave her a kiss. "It has been lonesome around here without you."

"You picked a lovely place, George," she said, smiling up at him. "The cabin is a nice size. I'm sure we will be able to make a good home here. I have a good feeling inside about it. There will be much hard work ahead of us, but if we all do our part, we'll be fine. Now, suppose you bless the food, George, so we can eat. It's getting dark."

When supper was over, Winfield built a fire in the fireplace. The nights were chilly even in June, and since there were no doors or windows on the cabin, the fire also discouraged the mosquitoes. George took his flute out of its case and ran his hand lovingly over it as though he had missed having it these weeks.

"Come on, everybody," he coaxed, "let's have a sing-a-long." He began to play softly an old familiar hymn. Little George began to sing quietly as he lowered his body awkwardly to the floor beside his father. George was small for his twenty-six years, and though he was loved by all the family, his mind had not developed past that of a child. He had a love of music, however, and could sing in harmony with the others. Clayton, too, joined in with his bass and soon Ma and the girls were harmonizing with them, until their sweet music filled the little cabin:

"Never be discouraged, trust the Father's word,
In the time of trial let his voice be heard;
Trusting in his promise, though the waiting long,
He will surely bless us; praise him with a song.

"Praise him, trust the Father's word,
Praise him, let his voice be heard;
Praise him, though the waiting long,
Praise him, praise him with a song."[2]

Winfield finally joined in the chorus. He thought the others could all sing better than he. But he knew the words by heart, too, and was caught up in the spirit of the occasion. It reminded him of the days when he was small and they all lived in a nice house in Wisconsin, how they used to sing in the evenings after Pa came home from his shoe shop. He remembered the pile of gold coins on the table the man gave Pa when they sold the house. They were good memories. However, deep in his heart Winfield believed he was really home at last and he was happy.

The following days were filled with activity. The doors and windows had to be placed in the cabin. The garden had to be planted and more ground plowed for planting grain. The girls had discovered wild strawberries ripening at the edge of the woods, and what a treat they were, topped with maple syrup and Bossie's good cream. Winfield made a fishing pole from a young sapling for Little George. For though there were many things he could not do, he could catch fish about as good as anyone.

Sunday mornings George and Winfield usually walked to Clitherall to the Cutlerite church service. The horses needed their rest after a hard week's work. Often, they were invited to dinner with Uncle Lute and Aunt Net, as most of the people called Lewis and Jannette Whiting. They were becoming the best of friends. After dinner, George and Uncle Lute would discuss religion. But Winfield was spending more time with Lu. She was such fun to be with. He really liked her a lot. They would take walks along the lake, or sometimes go as far as Cemetery Hill, where the view was magnificent. One Sunday, however, it was raining. The girls were busy helping their mother, so Winfield became absorbed with the talk about religion.

"Tell me, Lewis," asked George, "what are some of the basic beliefs of your church?"

"First of all," began Uncle Lute, "we believe with the Apostle John, that Jesus was born 'not of blood, nor of the will of the flesh, nor of the will of man, but of God.' The sixth chapter of Hebrews names the six principles. These are often illustrated as a ladder reaching to salvation, that is: repentance, faith toward God and Christ, baptism, laying on of hands for the baptism of the Spirit, resurrection and eternal judgment."

"But," returned George, "the Hebrew letter says leaving the principles, and not laying again the foundation, etc."

"True," returned Lewis, "but the writer was talking to believers who had already been baptized and received the gift of the Holy Ghost. There should be no need to preach that over and over, but go on keeping the other commandments, continuing in faith, unto perfection. Our beliefs are basically those of the Lord Jesus, as he taught the people in Galilee."

"There is nothing in that to cause persecution," remarked George thoughtfully. "What caused the Christian people to turn against your church?"

Lewis ran his hand through his black beard. "I suppose," he said, "it went back to the founding experience which Joseph had. He claimed to have had a vision at a time when Christians believed God didn't speak any more; that all they needed was in the Bible. They didn't understand about the apostasy."

"What do you mean by the apostasy?" asked George.

"Paul warned the Saints," said Lewis as he reached for his Bible and turned the pages until he found what he wanted. "He said this, 'For I know this, that after my departing shall grievous wolves enter in among you, not sparing the flock. Also of your own selves shall men arise, speaking perverse things, to draw away disciples after them.'[3] And back in Jude 3 and 4 it says '...it was needful for me to write unto you, and exhort you that ye should earnestly contend for the faith which was once delivered unto the saints. For there are certain men crept in unawares, who were before of old ordained to this condemnation, ungodly men, turning the grace of our God into lasciviousness, and denying the only Lord God, and our Lord Jesus Christ.' And if you read the twelfth chapter of Revelations you will see the prophecy of the church, as the woman, having to flee into the wilderness, and her child, which I believe was the Kingdom, being caught up to heaven. History tells how the church was changed after it was made the state religion. The ordinances were changed. Baptism was not done by immersion, but by sprinkling. There were no more gifts and blessings. The Lord had withdrawn the authority of His church and priesthood from the earth."

"So you're saying," asked George, "that Jesus' church was no longer on the earth? There were plenty of churches teaching about Him."

"That is true," returned Lewis, "but at the time of Joseph's vision, they were all teaching different creeds, and even fighting among themselves over converts. That was why he couldn't decide which church to join. He was just a boy, younger than Winfield. But he wanted the truth. When he read James 1:5, he went into the woods, taking God at his word, and knelt, praying as he had never done before. He had a terrifying experience with a spirit of darkness, but his cry for Jesus' help brought relief and a marvelous light from heaven. In the light he saw two personages. One pointed to the other, saying, 'This is my beloved Son, Hear Him.'[4] Joseph asked which church he should join. He was told to join none of them, that their creeds were the precepts of men, and that there was a work for him to do."

"I begin to see," said George, as he stood up, "why he wasn't too popular. It kind of has the hair standing up on the back of my neck. I'll have to study about that a bit. We had better be going, Winfield. Thanks again for dinner, Lewis, we may see you next week."

George was quiet on the way home. Winfield, too, was busy thinking over what Uncle Lute had said. He couldn't keep from wondering if indeed that boy had actually seen Jesus and heard him talking. He made up his mind to look up James 1:5.

Winfield was always aware of the changes of nature. July had brought in wonderful warm days; days when the sky seemed bluer and bigger; days when the twilight lingered long past supper time. It brought mosquitoes, also, and mayflies, insects which bred in the shallow, weedy parts of the lake. They appeared in great hordes, covering bushes, buildings or people. They had no bite, but their presence in the water made it almost impossible to catch fish. They were only around a week or two. In spite of the nuisance of the insects, it was a great time and place to be alive. The long days gave ample time for the field work, and the sun's heat made the crops grow fast. And always, when the day's work was done, there was the reward of a swim in the clear cold water of the lake.

Those summer days were filled to the minute with activity and they slipped quickly by. The corn was ready for the roasting stage. "Ma," suggested Clayton, "the Indian women dry some of the fresh corn. It tastes real good. Suppose we find out how they do it. There are some families camped around the end of the lake, we could go and ask them about it."

"All right," returned Ma. "You and Winfield pay them a visit. Take them a big armful of the corn for a present."

Before they reached the camp, they saw some of the squaws picking red raspberries. They looked startled as the boys approached, but at Clayton's friendly "Howdy," they stood waiting.

"We brought you some corn," said Winfield, offering his armful.

"Mun-dam-in[5] good," said one of the women, quietly.

"Ya, corn good food," said another, as she bowed graciously, taking the corn.

"Can you tell us," said Clayton, "how you dry the corn?"

Taking one of the ears, the squaw who spoke last held up an ear in the shuck. "Put corn in hot akik[6] short time." She then stripped down the shuck, leaving it attached, and held the ear up. "Hang in tree to manomin days."

"When is manomin days?" asked Winfield.

"The moon when manomin ripe," she answered.

"The month of rice gathering?" asked Clayton.

The woman nodded. "We bring makuk of manomin for your wigwam."

"Thank you," said Clayton, as he put his armful of corn on the ground beside her. "We would like some rice, and we will try drying some corn."

Ma thought their recipe sounded simple enough. When they had finished heating and hanging the corn, it looked as though corn was growing on the tree. They tied the ears on the tips of the branches so the coons couldn't reach them.

Summer merged swiftly into autumn. The crops were ripe and ready for harvest. It was time to dig the cellar. Clayton and Winfield worked together shoveling the sandy soil, until they had a hole so deep that Winfield could barely reach the ledge with his hand. They knew the frost line would reach several feet into the earth. Some of the prairie grass hay they had stacked in the summer was put in the bottom of the hole, ready for the vegetables to be laid on. A cover was made of saplings on which hay could be placed when the bin was full. Later they would rock the walls and build steps.

Clayton went to the village and found some Indian women who would help with pulling the turnips and rutabagas, and picking up the potatoes as Winfield dug them out of the ground. The women came, quiet and shy, their babies strapped on their backs. They worked willingly, taking their pay in vegetables. Emma and Norie liked to watch them from a distance, but had a certain feeling of fear because of stories they had heard. Ma made big kettles of vegetable soup or stew, and the Indian women were so grateful they became quite friendly.

At last great piles of potatoes lay ready, some to be sold in the village, the rest for storage. Big dark green warty squash with their bright orange flesh promised delicious winter meals. There was a good supply of corn for the bin the boys had erected. Ma and the girls had dried onions, chokecherries, wild blueberries and red raspberries during the warm dry summer days. They had even dried some mushrooms, large white puffballs that had appeared in the meadow north of the house. Finally, the storage cellar was full and covered. And the corn they had hung in the tree was hard and dry.

One day Norie and Emma were shelling the hard kernels from the cobs and placing them in cloth bags. "Look," said Emma, "there come some Indians, shall we go in?"

"No," said Norie, "they are squaws. They look friendly."

The women approached slowly. Norie stood up and said, "Hello."

"We brought manomin for your wigwam," said one of them. "You dry corn? Look good job."

"You told our brothers how to do it, didn't you?" asked Norie, excitedly. "They said you promised to bring some rice. Thank you. Emma, go get Ma."

Eleanor came quickly, smiling at the women. She motioned to the bags of corn the girls had shelled. "We followed your recipe and the corn turned out fine. Thank you."

The women handed Ella the birchbark box-like container full of hulled wild rice. "This is too big a gift," said Eleanor. Picking up one of the cloth bags, she proceeded to pour half of the rice in it, and handed the box back to the woman.

The squaw shook her head. "You keep all, makuk, too."

"Girls," said Ma, "go to the cellar and get two nice squash for them, please."

The girls soon returned with two big warty green squash and handed them to the women. Their smiles showed their pleasure. "Good trade," said the oldest one, "we go put in akik and make i'ckode'."

As they walked briskly away, Ma smiled, saying, "I think they are going to camp and put their squash in a kettle and build a fire. We had a lesson in Indian language, didn't we, girls?"

That evening Ma fixed a wonderful supper. Winfield had brought in a squirrel, so she made a stew with lots of vegetables and some of the wild rice.She also baked a big squash drizzled with maple syrup.

"George," she said when they were seated at the table, "I have been thinking how the Lord has blessed us. We have plenty of food for the winter and hay for the horses and the cow. We even have enough vegetables to share with my folks. I'm so glad they have moved in close to us. I just want to say thanks to all of you who have worked so hard and to the Lord who has blessed your efforts."

"It has taken the combined efforts of us all," returned George. "Suppose we make this our Thanksgiving dinner. Doesn't matter that it's a little early. I'll start our thank you prayer and each of you tell the Lord what you are thankful for."

Winfield listened to the prayers, his own heart bursting with pride to be part of such a wonderful family. When it was his turn, he said, "Dear Heavenly Father, I want to thank you for this nice land you brought us to, but most of all, I thank you for the Ma and Pa you gave us. I praise you, amen." Pa had to get out his big kerchief to wipe his nose, and Ma suddenly thought of something she needed to get from the cupboard.

After supper, Pa took out his flute and began to play all the hymns of praise they could think of, everybody singing with enthusiasm, even Winfield.

The following day, was threshing time. Uncle Lute came early with his new-fangled threshing machine. It was pulled out into the field where Pa and the boys had cut the wheat with the tool called the cradle, and tied bundles of it into shocks. Winfield and Clayton loaded the shocks on a wagon and hauled them to the thresher. Alma Sherman and Lurette Whiting, who had come to help, put the bundles into the hopper. One horse was hitched to each of the four long poles which were fastened to the center machine. As the horses walked in a circle, the machine turned around, crushing the straw and sending the grain out into the trough. It reminded George of a carousel he had seen years ago in New York. It was hard work, but all hands worked with a will. Norie and Emma were so interested they stood and watched for a while.

"Norie, Emma," called Ma from the edge of the field, "You girls come in here and help with the dinner."

Winfield, Ella, Iva, and Nina in the field by West Battle Lake.

"But I want to watch," answered Norie, "it's so interest-ing!"

"You can watch again after dinner. Come on, right now!"

Reluctantly, the girls followed their mother to the cabin, but not until Lurette, who the fellows all called Ret, had caught a good glimpse of Norie's long braids and cute turned up nose. Later, the men all filed in to eat the rabbit stew, baked beans and hot biscuits with chokecherry jelly. Norie took another pan of biscuits out of the oven and put them on the table in front of Lurette. He smiled up at her. "Did you make those?" he asked.

"Of course!" she answered. "Em and I also picked the choke cherries and helped Ma make the jelly. Why do you ask?"

"Why—uh," he stammered, "I just wanted to congratulate the cook. They are delicious."

Norie turned away, but Winfield noticed her face was a lovely blush pink color. I'll have to check on this fellow, he thought. He seems to have his eye on her. I'll ask Clayton about him.

CHAPTER 4

What Cassius Found in a Barn

The frost had tinged the leaves with color and the geese were gathering for their long trip south, when Uncle Cassius came to the house one evening. "George," he said, "I've been working down by Clitherall for Hyrum Murdock. What do you suppose I found out in his barn in the hay?"

"Can't imagine, Cassius," returned George, "unless it was a snake."

"Worse than a snake," said Cassius with a sly look as he took a dog-eared book out of his pocket. "It's an old Book of Mormon. Don't tell anyone about it. I thought we'd read it and find out for sure what these people are about."

"Lewis Whiting has told me quite a bit about their church," answered George. "He seems sincere enough, but he has never talked very much about the Book of Mormon. I guess we can tell if there is something contrary to the Bible. Go ahead and read some of it to us."

"Well," offered Cassius, "the first few pages are missing. I already read some. It claims to be a record of a people who came to this continent from Jerusalem during the first year of Zedakiah's reign. My Bible puts that at about 600 B.C. Anyway, this man Lehi had to slip out at night, taking only his family and some provisions, because the Jews were trying to kill him. Seems he was some kind of prophet and had told them they had to change their ways or the city would be destroyed. It says they camped in tents and traveled beside the Red Sea. I was interested in this part," and Cassius began to read from the worn book.

"'And it came to pass that the voice of the Lord spake unto my father, by night, and commanded him, that on the morrow, he should take his journey into the wilderness. And it came to pass that as my father arose in the morning and went forth to the tent door, to his great astonishment, he beheld upon the ground a round ball, of curious workmanship; and it was of fine brass. And within the ball were two spindles; and the one pointed the way whither we should go into the wilderness.'"[7]

"It seems this ball was a kind of compass, but it also had words on it sometimes. They supposedly followed its directions until they came to the sea and a place where there was 'much fruit and wild honey.' Then it says, get this, 'And it came to pass that the Lord spake unto me, saying, Thou shalt construct a ship, after the manner which I shall shew thee, that I may carry thy people across these waters. And I said, Lord, whither shall I go, that I may find ore to molten, that I may make tools to construct a ship...?'[8] Can you imagine digging the ore, melting it and making tools. Do you really think it could be done?" asked Cassius with an unbelieving look in his eyes.

"Well, does the book say he got it done?" asked Winfield.

"Yes, it says he made the tools and then his brothers called him a fool for trying to build a ship." Cassius scanned the pages. "Seems like this Nephi had two older brothers who didn't like him very well. They weren't going to help with the ship, so Nephi preached to them about Moses and the Children of Israel, and what happened when they were disobedient. The brothers got mad and were going to try to drown him, and it says: 'And I said unto them, If God had commanded me to do all things, I could do them. If he should command me that I should say unto this water Be thou earth, it should be earth;...And now, if the Lord has such great power, and has wrought so many miracles among the children of men, how is it that he can not instruct me that I should build a ship?...And it came to pass that the Lord said unto me,

Stretch forth thine hand again unto thy brethren, and they shall not wither before thee, but I will shock them, saith the Lord; and this will I do that they may know that I am the Lord their God.'[9] He did that, and it made believers out of them, so they helped him build the ship."

"Sounds like an interesting tale," said Clayton, "although a little too miraculous."

"I'll have to admit," said Cassius, "there's nothing so far to make me suspicious. Only makes me wonder about the Lord speaking to him, like it says."

"Keep reading it," said George, "and come back and tell us more about it soon. It is only fair to investigate it fully. It can't hurt us to read it. The next time I see Lewis, I'll ask him about the book."

With the harvest over, the men began getting the wood supply for the winter. They had cut up the limbs left from the logs for the cabin as they worked, so quite a bit was accumulated. But they were facing at least eight months when there would need to be fire for heating, as well as for the cook stove. The chinks between the logs were filled with clay from the clay bank, and the house made as tight as possible. A shelter was also built for the horses and the cow. There remained one thing needed for the house, that was the floor which had been put off in the spring until the work was done.

One evening as they finished their supper, George cleared his throat in a manner he had of calling the family's attention. "When I was down at the village today," he said, "Uncle Vet told me the new term of school was starting this week. What do you think, Eleanor, about the girls boarding with someone in the village so they can attend?"

Everyone looked at Ma. Ma looked at the girls. "What do you think, girls, would you want to do that?" she asked.

"I would very much like to, Ma" said Norie excitedly. "Please, Ma. I can work for my board."

"Couldn't you teach me at home, Ma?" asked ten year old Emma. "We brought our books from Pilot Mound school."

Winfield was looking from one to the other. More than anything he wanted to attend this term of school. He knew the spring and summer would be such busy times he could not hope to go then. And when the weather turns bad, he thought, they won't have school. He stole a quick glance at his Pa. Clayton noticed the look and spoke up quickly.

"Didn't you say, Pa, that you plan to start laying the floor right away? We'll need all the strong backs we have to saw, smooth and haul those logs for the puncheon floor."

Anger flared a moment in Winfield's heart. Leave it to Clayton, he thought. It's not fair. He doesn't care whether he gets an education or not, and doesn't want me to, either.

None of this was lost on Pa. He reached out and laid his hand on Winfield's shoulder. "Son," he said, "I really want you to have the advantage of more education. But I don't see how I can spare you right now. Maybe you can go in at the middle of the term. I'm sorry."

Winfield got up, took his cap and jacket from the wooden peg by the door. "I'll go water the horses," was all he said. He knew it wasn't right, but he wanted to punch Clayton in the nose. He was deeply disappointed. After all, he thought, I'll soon be too old to go to school. There are so many things I need to learn about. He went to the make-shift barn, unfastened the horses and led them down the hill, through the grove of oak trees to the edge of the lake. While they drank he lifted his eyes to the western horizon. The last faint color from the setting sun still clung to a big puffy cloud, giving it a pink lining. As he watched, a loon gave his lonely call and flew tranquilly across the lake. The horses raised their heads, water dripping from their soft lips, and turned as if to say thank you. The peace of the scene calmed his feelings. A strange sweet sensation came over him. It's almost like God is speaking to me through his beautiful creations, he thought. It's not really Clayton's fault. I know Pa needs my help. Somehow, everything will work out okay. Though the disappointment lingered, his anger abated. He patted the horses on their strong necks, sprang easily up on Mike's back and rode back to the barn.

The decision was made to let Norie board with the Shaw family during the week to attend classes. Emma was to study at home and help Ma with the work. Winfield made up his mind to study on his own, evenings. They had a few school books and they had the Bible. He worked hard with Pa and Clayton hewing flat the logs for the floor and laying them down, during the daytime. But evenings were his time to study. He chose the Geography book to study first. By candlelight, he reviewed the names of the continents, the oceans, the major rivers. He studied about South and Central America.

"Look, Ma," he said, as he showed her a picture. She put down her knitting and took the book. "It shows a pyramid built by an ancient people in Mexico. It says they had an advanced civilization and that there are many ruins of buildings the archeologists hope to uncover some day. They have only known about these things a few years."

"How interesting," remarked Ma, "I thought there were only savages on this continent before the white people came."

Ma took up her knitting again. It wasn't easy by candlelight, but the family must have warm mittens, scarves and socks. Winter had begun and it would be long and cold. "Now that the floor is finished," she remarked, "maybe you can go to school. I understand Zeruah Sherman is the teacher. She and her mother also weave cloth. The next time someone goes to the village, I need to send for some homespun to make the girls each a dress."

They were startled by a knock at the door. "It's just me, Cassius," came a voice. "If you'll lift the latch, I'll come in."

Emma ran to open the door. "Come in, Uncle," she said.

"Say, there's a real bite to that wind tonight," he said, "I wouldn't be surprised if we get a snow."

"Glad you came, brother," exclaimed Eleanor. "How is my mother? She was feeling bad when I was there last."

"She is better," replied Cassius. "We have all been interested in reading that book I found in Hyrum's barn."

"What do you think of it by now?" asked George.

"I'll tell you what," said Cassius, and he had an incredulous look in his eyes, "I have never been so interested in any book in my life! Its teachings go right along with the Bible, and the story is more interesting than a novel. You really need to read it. I'm sorry I was so skeptical of it at first." He shook his head. "The people were Israelites," he continued, "that kept the law of Moses. When they got rich and prosperous, they forgot God, and then their wars and troubles began. The Lord sent a prophet to warn them of impending disaster unless they repented."

"How about polygamy?" asked George. "What did you find about that?"

"Listen," returned Cassius, "and I'll read what it says about polygamy and married life." He pulled the book from his pocket. It was even more dog-eared now. He began to read. "'Behold, David and Solomon truly had many wives and concubines, which thing was abominable before me, saith the Lord. Wherefore, thus saith the Lord, I have led this people forth out of the land of Jerusalem, by the power of mine arm, that I might raise up unto me a righteous branch from the fruit of the loins of Joseph...Wherefore, my brethren, hear me, and hearken to the word of the Lord: For there shall not any man among you have save it be one wife; and concubines he shall have none: For I, the Lord God, delighteth in the chastity of women.'"[10]

"That is pretty plain," said George. "Evidently that doctrine was from some other source."

"Something else," remarked Cassius, "their prophets told plainly about the coming of Christ, and that He would be crucified and rise again and ascend up to heaven; that it is only through his name that we can be saved."

Winfield's curiosity was aroused. "Uncle Cassius," he asked, "when you were here before, you told about them building a ship to cross the sea. Did it tell whether they built the ship, and where they went?"

"Well, they did build the ship and stocked it with all the seeds they had brought with them, and all kinds of food. It says they were on the water many days and then they arrived at the promised land. Now you're going to ask me where was the promised land. All I know is the Cutlerites say the book was found in New York, so we have to assume they landed someplace on North or South America."

Winfield's excitement increased. He picked up the book he had been reading and found the picture of the pyramid. "Does it say anything about them building cities?" he asked.

"Oh, yes," answered Cassius. He flipped through the worn pages of the book. "Here it says, 'And there began to be much peace again in the land; and the people began to be very numerous, and began to scatter abroad on the face of the earth; Yea, on the north and on the south, on the east and on the west, building large cities and villages in all quarters of the land.'[11] And it tells later on that they built many temples."

Winfield showed his uncle the picture in his geography book. "See," he said, "these were built by an ancient civilization in Central America and Mexico. Do you suppose it was the people this book tells about?"

They were all quiet for a while. "For my part," said George, finally, "I intend to read the book for myself and investigate this new religion."

Winfield was quiet, but his mind was racing. How much he wanted to know about the world, and about God and Jesus.

He wondered if a lifetime would be long enough to study and learn all the things he wanted to know.

CHAPTER 5

"Announced by all the trumpets of the sky, arrives the snow, and, driving o'er the fields, Seems nowhere to alight: The whited air hides hill and woods, the river and the heaven, And veils the farmhouse at the garden's end. The sled and traveler stopped, the courier's feet delayed, all friends shut out, the housemates sit around the radiant fireplace enclosed in a tumultous privacy of storm."
—*Ralph Waldo Emerson*

True to Cassius' prediction, a blizzard came in that night. The wind howled around the little cabin for three days. The whirling snow made it impossible to see more than a few feet. The wind managed to find its way through tiny cracks, the cold crept into the house and into the bones of its occupants. When the horses needed feed or water, or when more wood was needed for the fire, two went together, George and Winfield or Clayton and Winfield, making sure that no one got lost in the blizzard. They had seen the gravestone on cemetery hill of the man who had frozen to death the winter before. He had managed to go within a mile or two of the village. His body was not found until the following spring.

During the shut-in daytimes, Ma helped the girls with their knitting, heard them read from the Wilson Reader or taught them how to make corn bread, stew and hot biscuits. Clayton and Winfield worked at shaping long poles into skis. They swept up the shavings and added them to the fire. Little George helped keep the boiler on the stove full of melting snow. And all the while, the wind roared and the snow whirled and isolated the little cabin from the rest of the world.

In the evening, George found his book of poems by John Greenleaf Whittier and while his family sat around the roaring fire, he read to them. "We're not the first," he said, "to know a blizzard fierce. This poet must have lived in such a clime as ours for this is how he wrote in the poem he called 'Snowbound.'

> "The sun that brief December day rose cheerless over hills of gray,
> And, darkly circled, gave at noon a sadder light than waning moon.
> A chill no coat, however stout, of homespun stuff could quite shut out,
> A hard, dull bitterness of cold, that checked mid-vein the circling race
> Of life-blood in sharpened face, the coming of the snow-storm told.
> The wind blew east; we heard the roar of Ocean on his wintry shore,
> And felt the strong pulse throbbing there beat with low rhythm our inland air.
> Meanwhile we did our nightly chores—brought in the wood from out of doors,
> Littered the stalls, and from the mows raked down the herd's-grass for the cows:
> Heard the horse whinnying for his corn; and, sharply clashing horn on horn,
> Impatient down the stanchion rows the cattle shake their walnut bows;
> The gray day darkened into night, a night made hoary with the swarm
> And whirl-dance of the blinding storm, as zigzag, wavering to and fro,
> Crossed and recrossed the winged snow: And ere the early bedtime came
> The white drift piled the window-frame, And through the glass the clothes-line posts
> Looked in like tall sheeted ghosts.

"'Shut in from all the world without, we sat the clean-
   winged hearth about,
Content to let the north-wind roar in baffled rage at pane
   and door,
While the red logs before us beat the frost-line back with
   tropic heat;
And ever, when a louder blast shook beam and rafter as
   it passed,
The merrier up its roaring draught the great throat of the
   chimney laughed;
The house-dog on his paws outspread laid to the fire his
   drowsy head,
The cat's dark silhouette on the wall a couchant tiger's
   seemed to fall;
And for the winter fireside meet, between the andirons'
   straddling feet,
The mug of cider simmered slow, the apples sputtered
   in a row,
And close at hand, the basket stood with nuts from brown
   October's wood.

"'What matter how the night behaved? What matter how
   the north-wind raved?
Blow high, blow low, not all its snow could quench our
   hearth-fire's ruddy glow.'"[12]

On the third evening of the storm, the door suddenly flew
open and three blanketed figures came in, snow whirling with
them into the room.

"Indians," whispered Norie in Emma's ear. "Let's go to
the loft, I'm scared!"

George rose quickly. "Come, warm yourselves by the fire,"
he said. "It is good you found our cabin in this storm."

The Indians sat cross legged in front of the fire, stretch-
ing their hands out to the inviting warmth. "We lost in

storm," said the tall one. "We need food."

Eleanor was already busy dipping up bowls of cornmeal mush which she gave them, along with big slices of bread. They ate in silence and then stretched out on the floor in front of the fire, wrapped in their blankets. An odd, over-powering smell began to permeate the room. Eleanor looked quizzically at George. He shrugged and nodded toward the three on the floor. Winfield thought he would lose his supper and wondered how long they would stay. But it was plain, they intended to spend the night.

"Let's have our Bible reading," said George. "Come down girls, while we read." Reluctantly, they came, Emma climb-ing on Pa's lap, and Norie standing beside Winfield. Little George was only curious about the three on the floor, peering into their faces.

George handed the Bible to Winfield. "Read the first Psalm," he said. Winfield turned quickly to the place. He had read Psalms many times, and tonight, he welcomed the as-surance the scriptures always gave him.

"Blessed is the man that walketh not in the counsel of the ungodly, nor standeth in the way of sinners, nor sitteth in the seat of the scornful. But his delight is in the law of the Lord; and in his law doth he meditate day and night. And he shall be like a tree planted by the rivers of water, that bringeth forth his fruit in his season; his leaf also shall not wither; and whatsoever he doeth shall prosper. The ungodly are not so; but are like the chaff which the wind driveth away. Therefore the ungodly shall not stand in the judgment, nor sinners in the congregation of the righteous. For the Lord knoweth the way of the righteous; but the way of the ungodly shall perish."[13]

"I'll sleep with the girls," said Ma and hurried them up to their bed. Little George climbed to his corner of the loft. Winfield heard their whispered prayers and added one of his own in silence for the safety of the family.

"I'll take the first watch, Pa," he said, "and keep the fire going. I need to study anyway."

"I'll sleep with one eye open," answered Pa. "I think they will sleep till morning, but it will be just as well to be watchful. Wake one of us when you get sleepy."

Winfield took his gun from its rack over the door, laid it on the table beside his book and tried to settle his mind on his reading. Using the index, he found a chapter on the American Indians. "It is believed," the book said, "that these people came across from Asia on the Bering Strait at a time when there was a land bridge between the continents." What does that do, he wondered, to the story Cassius was telling us, about those people building a ship and crossing the ocean? And what about these people here in our house? Are they any relation to the ones in the story? When this storm is over, I want to talk to Uncle Lute. Maybe he can loan me a Book of Mormon, or tell me some of the things I want to know. He cautiously stepped around the Indians put a big log on the fire and blew out his candle. Then just as quietly, he went to Clayton and roused him. "It's your turn to watch," he whispered.

The cold had crept through Winfield's blanket. He roused enough to pull it tighter around him. Something is different, he thought. Without opening his eyes, he listened. It's the wind, the wind has stopped! With one eye open, he looked toward the window. Beautiful frost etchings covered the glass inside. Outside, the snow reached to the middle of the window, but beyond he could see the faint light of dawn and what he believed to be blue sky. The storm was over at last. I sure overslept, he thought. He was out of bed quickly, shivering with the cold. He pulled his woolen pants over his long underwear, put on his homespun wool shirt and wool socks Ma had made for him. Pa and Ma were up. Soon the fire was bright and roaring up the chimney. The cook stove, too, was hot and the big black teakettle beginning to sing.

The Indians were awake and seated cross-legged in front of the fire, seemingly waiting for breakfast. They talked and laughed among themselves in their own language, pointing now and then to the string of bright red hot peppers hanging over the stove.

Ma put the food on the table, motioning to them to come and eat. Winfield knew she was hoping they would leave as soon as they had eaten. The stack of cakes disappeared quickly and one of them looked at Ma. "You good cook, like more." While the two men ate more, the squaw moved toward the stove. When Ma turned her back for a moment, she reached up and pulled one of the red peppers from the string, put it in her mouth and sat back down. Winfield watched her face turn red and tears stream from her eyes. He nudged Clayton. He nearly laughed out loud at the sight. She made no other sign that any thing was wrong. The other Indians watched her soberly, wonderingly, but no one attempted to steal another one! They soon gathered their blankets around themselves and, without a word, opened the door and walked out into the snow.

"That poor squaw!" exclaimed Winfield. "That pepper must have nearly burned her mouth up. Talk about stoic Indians, she was that."

"Served her right for stealing," rejoined Clayton, laughing.

"Once she had done it," suggested Ma, "there was not much to be done. Water only seems to make it hotter. At least she knows what they are now. I'm sorry everybody," she continued as she held out empty hands," but the pancakes are all gone. There is some boiled wheat on the stove. That will have to do this time. I'll make you some rose hip tea and throw in a red pepper to keep you warm today."

"Not hot pepper, Ma!" complained Emma.

"Never worry, I won't make it too strong," said Ma. "It does help keep a body well. It was the Indian women who came to help with the harvest that told me about the rose hips. There are so many wild roses growing on the hill, and their seed pods are large. They said they always picked them in the fall to use in soups and pemmican. It was an old doctor back in Wisconsin who told me red peppers were good medicine."

Pa, Clayton and Winfield bundled up and started shoveling paths. Their wool scarves covered their faces, except for their eyes. Everywhere they looked there was a fairyland of white. The glistening prairie seemed to stretch forever, only the upper branches of the oak trees showed above it. There was no sign where the lake began and the shore stopped. It was majestic, almost frightening beauty.

The weather grew milder after a few days. Clayton got on his skis and went off to the village. Henry Way had sent word by an Indian that he had work for Clayton. With the other skis, Pa helped Winfield improvise a sled. They cut some slender branches from the trees and fastened them across the skis with rope. It wasn't the best, but it would do. Norie was anxious to visit Lu and Em, and Ma needed some supplies.

With Norie bundled in blankets, Winfield drove the horse and they made their way across prairie and lakes, it was all the same, until they came at last to the Whiting house. It was none too soon, for both were getting cold. Mrs. Whiting welcomed them in, took their coats and pulled two chairs up close to the heating stove. The Whitings had been able to bring a heater with them when they returned from Iowa. Most of the families depended on fireplaces for heat.

"We have been wondering about you folks." said Mrs. Whiting. "Have you been all right during the storm and awful cold?"

"Yes," answered Winfield, "but it wasn't easy. We never had quite so much winter before. We had a surprise visit from three Indians one night. They just walked in and demanded food, and made themselves at home in front of the fire. We were a little uneasy, but no harm was done."

"A funny thing happened, though," spoke up Norie. "While Ma was cooking them breakfast in the morning, the squaw snatched a red pepper from Ma's string. She popped it right in her mouth. Pretty soon tears began to stream down her face. I guess she didn't know what they were, but she sure knows now. By the way, is Lu here?"

"No," Mrs. Whiting hesitated and then continued, "She is out skiing. She should be back soon. Ella and Em are here. Girls," she called, "you have company."

"I need to get some supplies," said Winfield. "I'll stop back by to pick Norie up. He said hello to the girls, pulled on his wraps and went out the door. He really wanted to find Lu before going to get the supplies. He led the horse up the road toward the store. There had been enough sleds along the road to pack the snow down smooth. He tied Mike to the hitching post and was about to go in when he saw two skiers gliding down toward him. It was Lu, all right, with that happy-go-lucky Ed Anderson. I've been away too long, he thought.

"Hi, Winfield," called Lu, waving her ski pole. "Haven't seen you for a while."

"It's been a little cold for that trip. I stopped at your house. Your Ma said you were skiing, but she didn't say who with." Then turning, he continued, "How are you, Ed?"

"I'm doing fine since the blizzard quit," answered Ed. "By the way, some of the gang are having a party next Saturday. Better come down if it doesn't snow again."

"Can you come to the spring term of school when it starts?" asked Lu.

Winfield shook his head and turned his face away. "I was planning to, but Clayton is going to work for Hyrum again. Pa needs me to help on the place." There was a knot in his throat big enough to choke him. Here was Lu keeping company with somebody else, and he couldn't even be part of the school. It did seem like fate was against him. But he forced a smile. "I'll try to make it to the party, and if I get to Lu's house first..." He didn't finish but he gave Ed a knowing look and went into the store.

With the sled loaded, he left Mike tied and walked up the road to the Whitings. He was still upset over Lu and Ed, but he wanted to see Uncle Lute. Besides, Aunt Net was so good to him his spirits were always lifted when he left. Their place was like a second home to him.

"Yes, Winfield," said Aunt Net. "Lewis is in the bedroom studying. Here, have a bowl of hot soup and a biscuit while I get him."

Ella was seated close to the stove, reading. She looked up and smiled at him.

"What are you reading, Ella," he asked.

"I'm studying my grammar book," she answered. "I have trouble with adjectives and adverbs and such. If I work on them now, I might be ready by the time the spring term starts."

Winfield thought he had never heard that many words from her before. She was always so quiet. Perhaps it was because Lu was so out-going that made Ella seem so quiet. He noticed the fine line of her forehead and the sincerity in her eyes. She is just as nice in her own way, as Lu is in hers, he thought, as he finished his soup. She is serious for a girl of twelve.

Lewis emerged from the bedroom, ducking his head as he came through the doorway. "Hello, young man, I'm glad to see you survived the blizzard. How are your folks?"

"Everyone is all right," answered Winfield. "Pa said to tell you hello. He also wondered if you have any copies of the Book of Mormon for sale. We would like to read some in it this winter."

"We have a few left," replied Uncle Lute. "We brought all we could with us. You are welcome to a copy, without charge. I'm just glad you are going to read it."

"Pa gave me some money to pay for it, I'm sure you can use it for the church," and Winfield placed some coins on the table. "These long winter evenings give plenty of time for reading. Thanks, and Pa will let you know how he feels about it."

"Bundle up, Norie," he said as he tweaked her ear. "We need to get started. I'll go get the sleigh. Be ready when I get back." He nodded to Ella, and thanked Aunt Net for the soup. "I may be down Saturday to the party," he said. "I'll see you then."

On the way home, he had time to mull over his mixed feelings: Lu and Ed; Ella and school and now the possession of a whole Book of Mormon. What would be the outcome of it all, he wondered. Did the Lord have a plan for him to follow? And if so, how would he know it? There was a desire emerging in his heart to find and do the Lord's will.

CHAPTER 6

Winter 1868–1869

The winter days grew short. It almost seemed the sun had hardly begun to shine before it was declining in the west. Pa and Winfield bundled up each morning to feed the horses, milk the cow, and bring in enough wood to fill the big wood box. When the weather permitted, they took their guns and walked across the lake to the basswood grove, where the deer sometimes bedded down. They were able to keep the family in meat. Most of the time, there was a deer hanging from the big oak close to the cabin. Sometimes, the cry and howl of wolves was heard as they stretched, trying to reach the meat in the tree. It was a wild and lonely place. Even Cassius, their only close neighbor, didn't come visiting in the evenings now. The cold was just too brutal.

Supper was over one evening, and the family seated in a circle close to the fire. Pa had started to read from the Book of Mormon. "Cassius' book," he said, "was missing the first few pages. It says down here on the title page, 'Wherefore it is an abridgment of the record of the people of Nephi, and also of the Lamanites; written to the Lamanites, who are a remnant of the house of Israel; and also to Jew and Gentile; written by way of commandment, and also by the spirit of prophecy and of revelation. Written and sealed up, and hid unto the Lord, that they might not be destroyed; to come forth by the gift and power of God unto the interpretation thereof; sealed by the hand of Moroni, and hid up unto the Lord, to come forth in due time by the way of Gentile; the interpretation thereof by the gift of God.'" He stopped reading aloud, scanning the page to himself. "What do you know, it says part of it is a record of people who were scattered at the time the Lord confounded the language of the people, when they were building a tower to get to heaven. Norie, you get the Bible. Let's check to see just what it says about the confounding of the language. I think it is Chapter 11 in Genesis."

Norie found the place and began at the sixth verse. "'And the Lord said, Behold, the people is one, and they have all one language; and this they begin to do: and now nothing will be restrained from them, which they have imagined to do. Go to, let us go down, and there confound their language, that they may not understand one another's speech. So the Lord scattered them abroad from thence upon the face of all the earth: and they left off to build the city.'"

"Well, that is interesting," commented Ma. "Part of this is supposed to be a record of some of those scattered people. I wonder."

"Yes, it is interesting, but the test will be in the reading," said Pa. "It goes on down here to say, '...which is to shew unto the remnant of the house of Israel what great things the Lord hath done for their fathers; and that they may know the covenants of the Lord, that they are not cast off forever; and also to the convincing of the Jew and Gentile that Jesus is the Christ, the Eternal God, manifesting himself unto all nations.'"[14] Suddenly, the horses began to whinny nervously.

"Pa, shall I go see if they're all right?" asked Winfield. "It isn't like them to make a noise at night."

"Yes," said Pa, "but take the gun, and be careful."

Winfield quickly pulled on his coat, checked the gun to make sure it was loaded and went out, quietly closing the door. He could hear the horses stamping and straining at their ropes. There was only a half moon, but with the snow as a reflector, it gave quite a bit of light. He made his way to the barn behind the house. He spoke quietly. "There now, Mike, Molly, what's got you so worried?" He patted their necks, checked their ropes and turned to go. There in the path he saw something big and black. He caught the glint of big white teeth and heard a low, fierce growl. Surprise held him spellbound for an instant. Then the thing reared up on hind legs and headed straight for him. A bear! Raising the gun, he fired without really sighting. It was still coming. I couldn't have missed, he thought. There was no time to reload. Turning the gun, he clubbed the bear's head and let out a scream. The bear fell, but as he did his long sharp claws caught Winfield's leg. He felt the warm blood sliding down his leg.

"Winfield!" Pa called and came running. "Are you all right?" Then he saw the black monster on the ground. "No wonder the horses were worried. I heard you scream, did he hurt you?"

"I screamed to scare him away. He kept coming after I shot, so I clubbed him. He clawed my leg on the way down."

"You go in and have Ma check you out. I'll drag him over close to the house."

Winfield was feeling dizzy from so much excitement by the time he got to the door. Ma was there holding it open for him. "You are hurt, boy! lay down here by the fire and let me see." With her sewing scissors she finished cutting his trouser leg open. "Norie," she called "bring me a basin of water and a clean tea towel, quickly."

"It's a mean scratch, dear" she said as she cleaned the blood away, "but not real deep. What happened?"

"It was a bear, Ma. I shot but he kept coming so I hit him over the head and he fell that close to me."

Ma leaned over and kissed his forehead. "I thank the dear Lord he only hurt you with one claw!"

By the time Ma had him bandaged, he was beginning to feel normal. "I have to go help Pa skin that bear before the wolves come. Get me a knife and a dishpan. Norie, you bundle up and bring some coals in the bucket. We'll need fire for light as well as warmth."

"Wait," said Ma, "Let me wrap your leg with some twine to hold your pant leg together."

The bear was finally skinned and as much meat saved as they could. They filled the dishpan and the washtub. The skin had to be brought in. When tanned it would make a wonderful rug. They pulled the carcass far from the house and left it for the wolves. The meat would be put out to freeze in the morning.

When all was finished, Pa called them together. "We have had two blessings tonight," he said. "That was a close call for Winfield. I sincerely believe the Lord intervened. The bear was not mortally wounded. When I started to drag him, He raised his head. I had to be quick with the knife. And besides that, we have enough fresh meat for many days. Let's kneel and thank the Lord for his watch care." As the prayers ascended, a wonderful feeling of peace and love descended into Winfield's heart. It was fostered by the faith that, even here in this wild frontier, God was near. Somehow, they would survive the long cold winter.

A few evenings later, the topic that had been interrupted by the bear was resumed. Pa had been reading to himself, but he called the family together. "There is an interesting part in this story. I want to read it to you and see if you can tell me who this prophecy is talking about. Nephi had a vision in which he saw many things that would happen from their time up to the time of Christ and even until his people would be destroyed by the Lamanites. Then it says: 'And it came to pass that the angel said unto me, Behold the wrath of God is upon the seed of thy brethren. And I looked and beheld a man among the Gentiles, who was separated from the seed of my brethren by the many waters; and I beheld the Spirit of God, that it came down and wrought upon the man; and he went forth upon the many waters, even unto the seed of my brethren, who were in the promised land. And it came to pass that

I beheld the Spirit of God, that it wrought upon other Gentiles; and they went forth out of captivity, upon the many waters. And it came to pass that I beheld many multitudes of Gentiles upon the land of promise; And I beheld the wrath of God that it was upon the seed of my brethren; and they were scattered before the Gentiles, and were smitten.'"[15]

"That sounds like my history lesson," said Emma. "Could it mean Columbus and the Pilgrims?"

Winfield was quickly searching through his geography book. "It tells in here about Columbus wanting to make that voyage, here it is. It is a quote from his *Book of Prophecies*. Let me read it to you.

"'It was the Lord who put into my mind (I could feel His hand upon me) the fact that it would be possible to sail from here to the Indies. All who heard of my project rejected it with laughter, ridiculing me.

"'There is no question that the inspiration was from the Holy Spirit, because He comforted me with rays of marvelous illumination from the Holy scriptures, a strong and clear testimony from the 44 books of the Old Testament, from the four Gospels, and from the 23 Epistles of the blessed Apostles, encouraging me continually to press forward, and without ceasing for a moment they now encourage me to make haste.'"[16]

"Such a convincing confirmation of Nephi's experience," remarked Pa thoughtfully. "I am so glad you two young people can see that. The book becomes more interesting the farther we get into it."

⟫•◦•⟪

It was the day before Christmas. Pa had ridden Molly to the village on a secret mission. Ma had said she and the girls would spend the day preparing the food for Christmas dinner. "I do wish," she had said, "that we could visit Cassius and the folks, but I suppose it is just too cold for the girls to be out." Winfield saw Pa give him a sly wink, as he said, "It depends on what the weather is like in the morning," and then he had climbed on the horse and headed for Clitherall.

Winfield was doing the evening chores, when he saw Pa coming. What a wonderful surprise he was bringing for Ma and everybody! A bright red sleigh! Molly even looked proud to have the privilege of bringing it home. Right up to the door she took it and stopped with a loud whinny, as if she were calling everyone to see. The door opened and Ma threw up her hands. "George, where on earth did you get that? Is it for us?"

"Merry Christmas, Eleanor. I hope you like it. How would you like to ride in it to see your mother tomorrow?"

"Oh, George, It's just too wonderful!" And she ran to meet him and gave him a kiss, even though she had no wraps and the snow was over her shoe tops. "I have your supper ready, hurry in," she coaxed as she ran back to the warmth of the cabin. Norie and Emma scraped the frost from the window so they could watch Pa put it away. How exciting it was to think of riding over the prairie bundled in that pretty sleigh. Even Little George got up from his place by the fire to watch out the window.

There was much happy chatter around the table as they ate and planned their surprise visit to Grandma and Grandpa Sherman tomorrow. Ma had a bear roast in the oven baking slowly to be finished in the morning. There was a big kettle of mixed vegetables. Norie and Emma had made a mince-meat pie, with some of the dried berries and venison. And to top off the list, Ma had made a loaf of hazelnut bread, brightened up with dried red cranberries.

Before bedtime, Pa gathered them around the fire. He read the Christmas story in the Bible, and they talked about how the angels went to the shepherds and told them about the Baby Jesus. "What a wonderful thing, the miraculous birth of Jesus," said Pa. "And so like Him to choose to be born in humble circumstances. If he had been born to a rich family, the poor people might never have had an opportunity to know him. The ways of God are past finding out."

―――――――♦‑◦‑♦――――――――

Winfield stretched to wake himself up. Pa was stirring up the fire, and singing softly as he worked. What a great way to wake up he thought, as he listened to the words and music.

"To us a child of hope is born, To us a Son is given;
Him shall the tribes of earth obey, Him all the hosts of
  heaven;
His name shall be the Prince of Peace, Forevermore
  adored,
The wonderful, the Counselor, The great and mighty
  Lord;
His power, increasing still, shall spread, His reign no
  end shall know;
Justice shall guard his throne above, and Peace abound
  below."

He was out of bed in a flash, taking a bundle from his box of clothing—his gift for Ma and the girls. When they were all up they exchanged their gifts. Ma had knit wool vests for Pa, Winfield, Clayton and Little George. For the girls she had knit hoods with scarves long enough to wrap around their faces and necks. Winfield proudly presented Ma with a bolt of cloth. "Uncle Vet said it was enough to make you and each of the girls a dress," he said. "I hope you like it." Norie and Emma had mittens for Pa and Winfield that they had knit themselves. And for George, Pa had bought a magazine with interesting pictures. Even though he could not read, he loved to look at the pictures.

Breakfast was hurried and chores done quickly. Everyone dressed in their best. Ma wrapped the hot sadirons ready to go in the sleigh at their feet. The food was packed in the basket. When all was ready, Pa and Winfield went out to harness Molly and hitch up the new sleigh. It was a tight fit, but all were excited and anxious to be off over the hills and through the woods to Grandmother's house.

The ride seemed almost too short, so swiftly did Molly pull the new sleigh over the hard sparkling snow. Jacob and Rhoda Sherman and their son Cassius had built their cabin about two miles from the Gould home, a distance easily covered with the horse and sleigh, but an uncomfortable one for Eleanor to walk in the snow and cold to see her mother and father. Hence, all were overjoyed to be together on Christmas Day.

The women put their food together, making a bounteous feast. Cassius told of tracking a big buck, from which the delicious roast they were eating was taken. Of course Winfield had to tell the story of the bear. Eleanor had brought some rutabagas and a big squash from storage for her folks, since they had not arrived in time to raise vegetables.

Finally, everyone had eaten all they could possibly hold. While Eleanor and her mother, with the girls' help, cleaned up and put the food away, the men built up the fire. The conversation turned to the Book of Mormon.

"We have been reading that Book of Mormon," said George, eyeing Jacob to get his reaction. "What do you think of it?"

"Well," returned Jacob, "I'll admit we went into it to prove it terribly wrong. To our surprise, we found it full of teachings similar to the Bible. The people that came from Jerusalem brought with them a set of brass plates that had the books of Moses and the prophets down to Isaiah. Their prophets taught that Christ was to come."

"I just read the Christmas story in the book," said Cassius, "can I tell it to you?"

"Sure," said George, "we haven't read anything like that yet."

Picking up the book to refresh his memory, Cassius began. "There was a Lamanite man that went to prophesy to the Nephites..."

"Wait," said Winfield, "I just found out the other day who the Lamanites and Nephites were. There were four brothers who came with their parents out of Jerusalem, plus another family who had some girls. Anyway, two of the sons didn't want to leave and made all kinds of trouble. The oldest was named Laman. The youngest was Nephi and he was the best one. He believed his father and tried to obey God. Later, after they reached the promised land, and the father died, Laman and some of the others tried to kill Nephi, so he and those who would go with him, left and went farther north. After that there were two groups, the Lamanites and Nephites. The Lamanites seemed to always be the bad guys."

"That's right," returned Cassius, "but at the time this Samuel, who was a Lamanite, went to prophesy to the Nephites, they had become more wicked than the Lamanites. It was a long time after they had reached the promised land, nearly 600 years. What he told them was if they didn't repent, destruction would come. But the most important thing he said was that the Messiah would be born over in the land of Jerusalem in five years. He said there would be a sign so they would know when it happened, here on this land. There were to be two days and a night of light. When the night came there would be no darkness."

"How could that be possible?" asked Norie who had joined the group.

"We'll get to that," said Cassius, "let me finish. There were still some righteous people and a man, also named Nephi, who tried to teach the people. Those who believed Samuel were happy and watching for that sign to come. But when the five years were nearly over, the unbelievers began to persecute the believers. They finally set a day when they were going to put them all to death if the sign hadn't come. Nephi went out and prayed all day long that the Lord would spare his people. That night the sun went down, but it didn't get dark. There were great lights in the sky all night to keep it light as noon day! It says the people were so astonished they fell down to the earth. I guess they thought the destruction Samuel told them of was about to come to pass—the tables were turned."

"Think what a happy time it was for the little group of believers," exclaimed Eleanor who had also joined the group to listen to the story. "So this was the first Christmas Eve in the Land of Promise. Oh, I hope this is true."

"This Samuel also prophesied of the Messiah's death," added Cassius. "He said there would be a sign for the Nephites of three days of darkness when that happened. I don't know about that yet."

"Yes," said Jacob, "we all hope to be able to know whether it is true. For if it is, it gives us such wonderful hope, knowing that God was mindful of other people far from Jerusalem."

"It's been a wonderful day," said George. "We need to go, but you have inspired me to go on reading that book. Thanks again for a very happy Christmas Day. We'll be seeing you more often now that we have the sleigh."

New Year's Day came and went, as the snow continued to pile high on the little cabin. Week after week it was the same. Each family isolated for the most part from each other except for special occasions when the weather grew mild and there was no threat of a new blizzard. Twice Winfield took the sleigh and went to get his grandparents to come and spend the day with them. But Grandfather was not well some of the time, and needed to stay close to the fire. Often Winfield went with Pa and Cassius on hunting trips, when the meat supply grew low. But the long dark evenings were spent close to the fire. Winfield alternated his study between the school books and the Book of Mormon. Ma continued to help the girls with their school lessons so they would not be too far behind when the next school session started.

A few times Winfield took the sleigh to Clitherall and the young people would have ski races, or go skating if the ice were clear of snow. Sometimes they would all pile into the sleigh and ride over the countryside, singing happy songs. Clayton would join them, with his new girl friend, Delia Sherman. Alva Murdock often came and he and Winfield had a friendly rivalry going over who got to skate with Lu. But Winfield always tried to include Ella in the fun whenever she was with them. Ed Anderson had switched his attentions to Lu's sister, Em.

One day, after a trip for supplies, Winfield and Pa stopped in to visit Uncle Lute. Aunt Net welcomed them in and offered them some lunch, which they gladly accepted.

"That cold sure does increase the appetite," said Pa. "How much longer can we expect this cold to go on. I supposed when March came we would see some relief?"

"We may get some mild days in March," returned Uncle Lute, "but the ice doesn't go off the lake until about the end of April. And the danger of a blizzard is still with us through the first of that month. Winter is king here for a long time, but when spring does come, it is worth celebrating."

"The long dark evenings have been good for study," said Pa, leading to the subject he had been wanting to talk about. "I have finished reading the Book of Mormon. It is a wonderful story, if it's true. The possibility of Jesus appearing to the people after his resurrection, would certainly be a second witness, supporting the Bible. Is there anything in the Bible that in any way speaks about the possibility of Jesus going outside his own country?"

"We know," answered Uncle Lute, "Jesus did not go outside Palestine during His life on earth. However, He did say something about 'other sheep.' In John 10, Jesus was talking about laying down his life for the sheep. Then He said, 'Other sheep I have, which are not of this fold: them also I must bring, **and they shall hear my voice;** and there shall be one fold and one shepherd.'"[17]

"He was talking about the Gentiles, there, don't you think?" asked George confidently.

Uncle Lute handed Winfield the Bible. "Will you look up Matthew 10, the fifth and sixth verses."

Winfield quickly found the place and read: "'These twelve Jesus sent forth and commanded them, saying, Go not into the way of the Gentiles, and into any city of the Samaritans enter ye not. But go rather to the lost sheep of the house of Israel.'"

"Now turn to the 15th chapter and verse 24."

Once again, Winfield turned to the place and read: "'He answered and said I am not sent but unto the lost sheep of the house of Israel.'"

"Well," said George, thoughtfully, "it does sound as if He were going to some other group of Israelites, and they were to hear His voice."

Winfield was becoming excited. "One of the first things we learned about the Book of Mormon," he ventured, "was that the people were Israelites who came from Jerusalem and were from the tribe of Joseph through Menassah. And after Jesus was crucified, according to the book," he went on, "the people *heard his voice* during the three days of darkness."

"It sounds logical," George said, "but there are other questions still unanswered."

"I'd like to hear about Joseph finding the record," spoke up Winfield. "How did he know where to look?"

Uncle Lute stroked his beard and sat deep in thought for a few minutes. "I think we talked about the first vision Joseph had when he was allowed to see the two personages and his question was answered about which church to join. He was not quite fifteen at that time. Three years went by while he led a normal young man's life, except for the fact that he knew he had seen a vision. He had told one of the revival preachers of the day about the wonderful vision, only to be ridiculed and treated with contempt. One night, however, as he knelt by his bed, praying for forgiveness, a wonderful light filled his room and a personage appeared in it. The messenger told him he had been sent by God with the glad tidings that the covenant which God made with ancient Israel was about to be fulfilled, and the preparatory work for the second coming of the Messiah was soon to commence. He told him about the early inhabitants of this land, where they came from and how part of them had finally been destroyed because of wickedness. He told him there was a record of those people engraved on metal plates and showed him in vision where they could be found. Joseph recognized the place as a high hill not far from his home near Palmyra, New York. The messenger introduced himself as Moroni."

"Does that mean," asked Winfield, "the one that wrote the last part of the book?"

"It does, indeed," said Uncle Lute, smiling at his inquisitor. "It is such an intriguing and wonderful story. The Lord has his own way of doing things. He wanted that record to be safe until the right time for it to be found. But back to the story. Moroni visited Joseph three times that same night, telling him the same things each time, evidently so that he would not forget anything he was told.

"The following day he went to the place and found, part way up the hill, the rounded top of a stone protruding from the ground. Digging away the soil around the edges, he pried the stone up and found beneath it a stone box. In the box was the stack of thin metal plates held together by metal rings, a strange item which turned out to be the Urim and Thummim and a breast plate. Of course, he was excited and reached his hand to pick them up. However, the angel forbid it, and told him he was not prepared to handle such a responsibility. He was instructed to meet him there again the next year at the same time. This he did. In fact for three more years he went to the place where Moroni met him and counseled him further, telling him that men would try to get them from him, but he must protect them at all cost."[18]

"Let me interrupt," broke in George, a look of concern on his face. "I have always understood that when angels appeared to people in the Bible, they were the spirits which God created to be with Him; those who never had lived on earth. I'm not sure about this one you call Moroni, who according to the book, was a person who lived on earth at least 1,400 years ago."

Uncle Lute reached for the Bible, handing it to George. "Do you remember reading about the transfiguration of Jesus? Turn to Matthew 17 and read verses 1 through 3."

George found the place and began to read. "And after six days Jesus taketh Peter, James and John his brother, and bringeth them up into an high mountain apart, And was transfigured before them; and his face did shine as the sun, and his raiment was white as the light. And, behold, there appeared unto them Moses and Elias talking with him." George studied the book before him.

"How long had it been since Moses had died, do you think?" asked Uncle Lute.

"Well," George admitted, "I must have read those verses a hundred times, but evidently with blind eyes. Moses must have been dead for at least 1,400 years at the time of Christ.

"Yes, and do you see what a wonderful blessing it was for Jesus to see their spirits and talk with them, knowing his own death was imminent? As the Psalmist said, 'The Lord is good; his mercy is everlasting; and his truth endureth to all generations.'"

"Also," resumed Uncle Lute, "when John would have worshipped the angel which was showing him concerning the marriage of the lamb and other things, in Revelations 19:10, the angel said to him '...see thou do it not; I am thy fellow-servant, and of thy brethren that have the testimony of Jesus;'"

"So what you are telling me," said George finally, "is that the man Moroni who wrote the last on the plates and hid them away, came all those years later as a spirit to show Joseph Smith where he buried them. Is that right?"

"So the record tells us. Can you think of a better way for it to happen? But don't take my word for it," said Uncle Lute. "Read the 10th chapter of Moroni when you get home. You will find a promise written there that you may know the truth."

George got to his feet, shaking his head. "You certainly have given us plenty to think about, Lewis," he said as he extended his hand. "Give us time to absorb this and we will return for the answer to the other questions. To be very honest, I hope this strange story is true."

That night, Winfield lay awake far into the night. Over and over his mind played out Uncle Lute's words. Could it be true that angels still ministered to people? Is God really interested enough in people to send angelic messengers? Supposing the Indians that we see up here are indeed the descendants of the Nephites and Lamanites. Do they know who they are? And what of the great pyramids in Central America?

Finally, feeling a desire to talk to his Heavenly Father, he quietly pulled on his shoes and wrapping his blanket around himself Indian fashion, stepped out into the still, cold night. A great boom resounded from the lake and echoed from the woods, as the ice expanded and sent a great crack across its surface. In the north, he saw a display of brilliant moving waves of color as though a giant curtain were being pulled to display a drama. Overcome with emotion, he knelt in the snow, oblivious to the cold, for a wonderful warmth had filled his whole being. His words could not adequately say what was in his heart, but he worshipped as he had never done, sensing his own unworthiness, and asking the Lord to guide him in understanding.

CHAPTER 7

Spring 1869

Gradually the days grew longer and the sun's rays had a certain warmth. Little trickles of water turned into little rivers and headed for the lake as the snow began to retreat. Pa and Winfield were busy preparing basswood troughs for gathering maple sap. It would soon be time to tap the trees on the south side of Silver Lake. They must build the wooden boiler, and erect a temporary shelter. Norie and Emma were boarding during the week at Shaw's so they could attend classes at Clitherall. But there was no way Winfield could get away, just as he had predicted. By the time the sap was through running, it would be time to prepare the ground for crops. A feeling of frustration and resentment was working in his mind.

One evening after the family had retired, Winfield heard his father and mother talking. "You know, Eleanor," said Pa, "Lewis has finally answered all my questions. I feel satisfied that the Book of Mormon is what it claims to be, a record of the ancient inhabitants of America. You know, he told us Joseph used the odd glasses, called the Urim and Thummim, to translate the strange characters engraved on the plates. He said they copied some of the characters and the interpretation, and one of his friends took them to a man who knew about old languages. The man said they were truly a kind of Egyptian characters, but wouldn't give him a paper saying so unless he could see the original. When told it was sealed and he could not show it to him, he tore up the paper he had prepared."

"Yes," answered Eleanor, "and that is just what it says there in the 29th chapter of Isaiah. That is what confirmed it to me, besides the fact that the Urim and Thummim is mentioned in the Bible in connection with revelations from God."

"That is right," answered George. "Another thing I thought about, the last mention in the Bible of the Urim and Thummim is a long time before King Zedekiah. In fact, there is no mention of anyone actually using it after the time of David. That was at least 400 years before the reign of Zedekiah, when the record said those people left Jerusalem. So when Lehi brought the Brass Plates with him, do you suppose he could have brought that sacred item, also?"

"Where did Lewis say he thought the people landed on this continent?" asked Eleanor.

"He said they aren't sure, except that they think it was either in the north part of South America or in Central America. That is where those marvelous ruins are being found. The archeologists believe there are huge cities buried under the mounds and covered with jungle. So the main civilization was probably in that area. However, the book tells about migrations to the 'land northward.'

"So the Indians we see here are probably descendants of those early people?"

"We think so," answered George. "And since the white people, or Nephites, were all finally killed off, that left only the dark skinned ones the book calls Lamanites. It is those people that the book is especially for; to help them know they are of the house of Israel, and that God wants them to know about Jesus Christ."

"Isn't that one of the reasons the Cutlerites came up here?" Eleanor asked.

"Yes, they said Mr. Cutler's special mission was to preach to the Indians. It all seems to fit together so well. I have not had any special experience, but I believe I am ready to be baptized."

"We should join as a family, if the children are willing," said Eleanor. "I am willing. Let's talk to them in the morning."

They did not know that Winfield had heard every word of their conversation, nor how agitated his mind had become. He didn't want to break the family circle, but he did not feel he was ready for such a step. I want that special experience, he thought. I want to *know*. And so far into the night, the words he had heard and those he had read went over and over in his mind. At last, his decision was made and sleep came.

On a warm sunny afternoon in early summer, a group of people gathered on the shore of Clitherall Lake. Chauncey Whiting gave a challenge to the family gathered at the water's edge. Uncle Lute then waded out into the clear cold water, accompanied by George Gould. Raising his hand toward heaven, he said, "George, having been commissioned of Jesus Christ, I baptize you in the name of the Father, and the Son and the Holy Ghost. Amen." He laid him under the water and raised him up out of the water. Then one by one, the other family members took their turn. All except one. Winfield stood at the side, feeling as though he were a stranger, an outsider. But he could not do otherwise.

The busy spring work had begun and there would be no let up until after the harvest, except for Sundays, when everyone rested, including the horses. Often George and Norie walked together to the church in Clitherall. Sometimes Winfield went along, and he would walk Lu home. Quite often, the young people would gather in the afternoon around the big swing near the school. The young men would swing the pretty girls. Clayton and Dee were together constantly. In fact, he had made plans to build his cabin in the fall, for he had already asked her to marry him.

CHAPTER 8
School At Last, Fall '69

The fall work was nearly finished. The corn crib was full. The cellar was full of vegetables. The wheat had produced so well they had some to sell, and the wagon was loaded to capacity for the drive to the mill in St. Cloud.

"I'm leaving the family in good hands," said Pa as he patted Winfield on the back. "When I return, we will have a house raising for Clayton. After that it's your turn for a school term. You have waited patiently. I hear Will Corliss is teaching this term. That will be different, going to your brother-in-law. He got a good education down in Pilot Mound. I'm glad they have moved here."

"Thanks, Pa," returned Winfield. "I have been counting on this fall term. I can help some in the evenings. How far is it to St. Cloud?"

"Almost a hundred miles," answered Pa. "It will take me a good week. You can help Clayton get his logs ready. And by the way," he added, "you will get your share of the price of the wheat."

George left the next morning as the weather seemed to have turned into a dry spell—important, to be sure the wheat was safe. Ma had fixed him a basket of food and plenty of warm blankets in case of a cold snap. "I should be back a week from today," he said as he waved good-bye.

Winfield did the morning chores, except for the milking. Norie had taken over that job. She liked old Bossie and loved to smell the warm fragrance of the milk as the foam rose on top. She had brought home a kitten from Grandma Sherman's. It was such fun to watch it drink from the stream of milk as she squirted it into the kitten's mouth. Emma would strain the milk through a cloth and then pour both of them a cup of that fresh milk. It was also her job to do the churning when there was enough cream. Ma would make delicious cottage cheese from the thick clabbered milk. Besides these chores, Ma and the girls were busy sewing and knitting winter clothes.

After the chores were finished and Ma had a supply of wood for the cook stove, Winfield took his axe and headed west toward Clayton's spread. He could hear the ring of Clayton's axe on the still morning air. He stretched his long legs, covering the distance in a few minutes. Even after the last hay had been cut, the grass had grown tall and lush. The sky was suddenly filled with geese rising from the wheat stubble. They were wary of this tall two-legged being approaching. He loved the land and every creature that made its home there.

"Boy, am I glad to see help arriving," exclaimed Clayton, putting down his axe and straightening his back. "Seems like it takes me forever to get one log ready."

"Looks like you have quite a bunch ready," said Winfield. "We should be able to get enough logs up by the time Pa gets back. He said we would have a house-raising, then, for you." He watched Clayton rolling a log into position, and admired his ability. His shoulders had become broad, his waist and hips slim. He was the envy of most of the young men. Long gone was the animosity Winfield had once felt for his brother.

"Clayton," he said, "remember the day on the way up here, when we wrestled? I wouldn't tackle you now! Your muscles are too bulging and strong for me."

"Well, if we both tackle these logs, we'll get this job done. Dee and I are planning to get married about Thanksgiving time."

"Eleanor," said George, the morning of the house raising, "do you think you have enough food for all those men? Look out there. I had no idea so many would come to help."

"Between all of the women who are bringing food and what I have, you will see, there will be enough," responded Eleanor. "The women are being just as helpful as the men. It is wonderful the way they turn out to help. Dee and her mother are coming, as well as my brother Ben's wife, and I see Will and Roseltha are just arriving! Don't you worry about the food, George. We can handle this end, and from the looks of the crowd, the house will be raised before the sun sets."

Winfield joined the men. George took charge and assigned the different jobs. Lurette had brought his oxen to help pull up the logs to the building sight. Others, using a horse and slip, leveled the area. When the base was set, each log had to be notched to fit exactly the next one. There was much good natured banter and teasing, but all hands worked with a will. When the call came for dinner, the walls were well started.

"Well, Clayton," advised Ike, "if you're really in a hurry to marry that gal, we could jest start the roof now. Course you might bump your head when you tried to look out the winder."

"Now, Ike," returned Clayton, "I just think I prefer to get those walls up at least as high as my head."

They all walked back to George's house where the women had washbasins outside on a bench for them to wash up.

"Winfield," said George Hammer, "I never saw such a bunch of fellows as you got working here today."

"Why," asked Winfield, "What's wrong with them?"

"Did I say anything was wrong? It's because everything is so right that I'm wondering. I haven't heard a curse word all day, nor seen a bottle of whiskey. Why down in Filmore County, a get together like this was always the source of two or three fights, and several would get drunk and be no good at the job. It's truly amazing."

"Well," returned Winfield thoughtfully, "most of these people are religious and they aren't just religious on Sunday, either. They live it every day."

George lowered his voice. "That's not what we were hearing about the Mormons down home. Don't you remember? They were called every bad name in the book."

"I remember," replied Winfield, "I heard the same things, but there was no truth in it. At least, these people are tops."

As Eleanor had said, there was plenty of food, even though the hungry men went back time after time for more. There was discussion about the best way to proceed with the walls and the roof. Chauncey Whiting carefully offered his suggestions and George listened, knowing Chauncey had much experience. But it was George who explained how the shingles were made for his house and all agreed his method was best. So while the others worked on the logs that afternoon, George helped Lurette get started making shingles. He had been especially interested, because he planned to build his own house soon. Before the sun was half way down the western sky, the walls were indeed a little taller than Clayton's head. Clayton could handle the rest, with Pa's help.

The brilliant fall colors of the maples and the golden shimmering of the basswoods, reflected the morning light and sent shadows dancing over the forest floor. The prairie grasses waved gracefully in the breeze. Overhead, birds were gathering in large flocks, preparing for their southward journey. Scurrying swiftly through the fallen basswood leaves were tiny striped chipmunks, their cheeks bulging comically with their baggage of tiny nuts. As Winfield watched, he laughed at their antics. He felt as light and free as they looked. Young and strong, it seemed as if he could almost reach up and touch that blue sky. His keen mind was anxious to tackle the problems and lessons that lay ahead of him at the school. And as he looked around at the marvel of nature, he felt, too, the desire to learn all there was to know about the universe and especially about its Creator. And so this long walk to and from the school became part of that absorption of knowledge.

Will Corliss handled the students very well, Winfield thought. He was patient with the little ones, listening to their timid, hesitant voices reading from the Wilson reader. Youngsters, like Art Whiting, who found it hard to sit still, were given the job of filling the water bucket, or carrying wood for the fire. The older girls, Em, Lu and Norie, were teacher's helpers, tutoring the younger ones.

During the lunch hour, the older students congregated around the swing. Ed was giving Em his attentions. Lu seemed to enjoy letting Alva Murdock and Winfield take turns swinging her. Lurette, whom everyone now called Ret, had even proposed to Norie. She seemed to like him, but insisted she must get her education before she could think of matrimony.

One day, when the school was quiet, Winfield noticed that Ella was watching him. For a few minutes, their eyes were fixed on each other. Winfield felt as though there was a bond drawing them together. Her hair fell in long curls around her face. He found himself thinking how much he would like to hold her head on his shoulder. Quickly, however, he drew his attention back to his lesson, remembering the purpose he was there for. Nothing must be allowed to shift his mind from his desire to learn.

"Can you come on over to my place, Win?" asked Alva one Friday afternoon. "We can take Pa's boat out and catch some fish. There's a good spot just around the point."

"Isn't that where the Indians are camped?" returned Winfield. "We don't want to aggravate them."

"No, it's all right," said Alva, "there's plenty of fish for all, and they are friendly enough. We will just have to dig some worms for bait."

They were soon in the boat and headed down toward the point. Alva rowed while Winfield baited their hooks. As they passed the Indian camp, he could see about a dozen wigwams among the trees. Several curious children came out by the shore and stood watching as they passed. Some birch bark canoes were pulled up on the sand.

Just as they had the boat anchored and were putting their lines in the water, there was a loud barking of dogs, some shouting and an awful commotion.

"Those dogs must be after Pa's sheep!" exclaimed Alva "I better go back to help."

Winfield raised the anchor and Alva began rowing back. Suddenly, several sheep ran out into the water, a dog at their heels, then more and more. Alva tried to head them back toward shore, but their wool absorbed water so quickly they were beginning to drown. The boys waved their arms in an attempt to turn them, but to no avail. Rowing furiously, Alva beached the boat. They climbed the bank to find the dogs had killed several sheep besides the ones they had chased into the lake to drown.

Alva's ma and his brother Charley stood there holding sticks they had tried to stop the dogs with. The Indian men had finally caught their dogs after the damage was done, and Winfield could see them seated on the ground in a line, their faces sullen, evidently expecting retaliation.

"I'm going to kill every one of those dogs!" shouted Charley as he ran to the house to get his gun.

"No, Charley, No!" pleaded his mother, "they will kill you!"

"Let them try," he retorted.

They watched as Charley walked resolutely toward the Indian camp. "Please, God," prayed Rachel, "please don't let him shoot that gun. We've lost the sheep, don't let me lose my son."

There was nothing to be done but to wait and watch in terror. For many minutes, which seemed to the three watching like an eternity, Charley stood, gun pointed toward the tied dogs. One Indian man picked up his gun and pointed it at Charley. Finally, Charley turned and walked slowly back.

"Thank God," whispered Rachel.

They set to work then checking for wounded sheep they could help and some they could dress to eat. It was a grim task, but it was not their first tragedy, for trouble had stalked Hiram and Rachel Murdock from the time they arrived in Clitherall. They always had the fortitude to pick up the pieces and begin again.

"What are those squaws coming up here for?" asked Alva. "They are carrying pillows."

The women walked slowly until they were close to Rachel. One of them walked close to the bank overlooking the lake, held her pillow high over her head and with a knife, slit the cover from top to bottom. Opening it wide she let the west wind carry the wonderfully soft down far out over the blue waters of the lake. One by one each of the others did the same, until the water was white with the feathers. No word was said, but they turned their faces to Rachel as if to say, we are sorry. Rachel held her hand out to the closest one. "Go in peace," she said.

"Why did they do that?" asked Winfield.

"The down and feathers in those pillows represent many, many hours of work for them," answered Rachel, "plucking them from probably a hundred ducks and geese. It was their way of trying to show their sorrow for us."

During the weeks and months of the fall term, Winfield watched Lu and Alva, and considered Ella, quiet, studious and always pleasant. As he searched his heart, he knew it was Ella who was holding his attention. He began walking home with her from school, asking her questions about their English lesson. Soon he was also walking with her to and from church. When there was a party, she was his partner.

It was the winter of 1869, the second one for the Goulds on the northern prairie. At least they were better prepared this year, and knew what to expect. School term ended in

November. However, Winfield managed to wade the drifts down to Clitherall occasionally.

One cold December evening the young people had a skating party. They gathered at Hiram Murdock's place on Clitherall Lake. Alva, Hiram's son, had a big bonfire going down on the point. "The ice is perfect here," he had told the group, "smooth as glass and no snow on it."

They had races, they skated in pairs and some did fancy figure eights. Winfield and Ella skated hand in hand toward the north shore making a wide loop and doubling back.

"I have a baby sister," she told him. "She was born yesterday. Her name is Sylvia Cordelia. We are calling her 'Cordie' for short. I'll be busy helping Ma much of the time."

"You will be a good baby tender, I'm sure," he answered. He squeezed her hand and pulled her closer as they coasted. "Ella," he said softly, "you be prepared, I might kiss you good-bye tonight." She pretended not to hear and withdrew her hand, skating faster back toward the others.

All gathered around the warmth of the fire. Clayton and Ed had joined the group. He started up a song and they all joined in:

> "Of all the mighty nations in the east or in the west,
> Oh, this glorious Yankee nation is the greatest and the best;
> We have room for all creation and our banner is unfurl'd;
> Here's a gen'ral invitation to the people of the world.
> Then come along, come along, make no delay;
> Come from ev'ry nation, come from ev'ry way;
> Our lands, they are broad enough, Don't be alarm'd,
> For Uncle Sam is rich enough to give us all a farm.
> Yes we're bound to beat the nations, For our motto's 'Go ahead,'

And we'll tell the foreign paupers That our people are
      well fed;
For the nations must remember That Uncle Sam is not a
      fool,
For the people do the voting, and the children go to
      school."[19]

The skates came off and all went their homeward ways.
Winfield and Ella headed back down the snowy road toward
the village. When they came to her father's door, he put his
arm around her. This time there was no pretense, but as she
lifted her face to his, a quick gust of wind blew his scarf
between them. She kissed one side of the scarf and he the
other! They were both too excited to try again. He gave her
hand one last squeeze and left, with mixed feelings of embar-
rassment and exultation—she had been willing, and there
would be another opportunity. She was young, but he could
wait.

CHAPTER 9
Independence Day, 1870

When the school term ended that spring, Norie earned a third grade certificate to teach. She applied and was engaged for a school in the Norwegian town of Tordenskjold, which was near St. Olaf where some of her old school mates lived that she had known in Filmore County.

"We are all invited to the Fourth of July celebration in Clitherall!" announced Pa. "Will is organizing the all day affair. He wants a band and everything. All the ladies are to bring their most delicious food to share, Eleanor. I told him Clayton and I would do our best to be a band. He said Cy Albertson had a bass drum. Maybe we can make enough noise to seem like a parade."

"George Hammer and the folks from St. Olaf are going, too," said Winfield. "They're excited because most of them haven't been to Clitherall yet. George was saying they thought the Mormon men had horns and the women's noses looked like fish hooks. We decided to let them find out for themselves. When I saw George, he said he would bring Norie down for the day."

"Well, that's only three days away," replied Ma. "Emma, maybe Little George can help you pick some gooseberries so we can make some pies to take for the dinner. The peas are just about ready, too. If we can find a few new potatoes to go with them, that will be a treat. This is the first time we have had a Fourth of July celebration since we were in Filmore County, and here it is 1870."

The morning of the celebration arrived, calm and clear. The family climbed into the wagon along with the food and Pa's flute. Winfield drove the horses while Pa practiced playing

"The Stars and Stripes Forever." On the way they caught up with Cassius and Grandpa and Grandma Sherman, and all went on together. Clayton, Dee and the other young people were congregated by the schoolhouse. Clayton took charge. "Let's go out to welcome the folks from St. Olaf. Pa, you and Cy get in the front of the wagon, I'll sit behind you. We'll be the band. All you girls and as many others as can sing climb in."

"Wait," called Winfield, as he jumped from the driver's seat. "I'll get the flag from the school room."

He was back in a jiffy, "All set? Here we go," and the horses jerked the wagon to a start. Em proudly held the flag high, Cy began the rhythm on his big bass drum, and George, keeping time with his foot, played the flute with gusto. Clayton's drum sticks fairly flew over the snare drum, and the girls began singing "Yankee Doodle Dandy." Before the song was finished, they could see the wagons coming across the prairie. George led out with "My Country 'Tis of Thee," the drums and singers joined while the flag waved bravely.

As the music came to a fitting climax, all of the St. Olaf's people cheered and clapped.

"Look at their flag!" said Lu laughing, as they came close to the other wagons. "It looks like it went through the Revolution," and she continued to laugh.

"Now, Lu, don't make fun of that flag." It was Roseltha Corliss and there was a tremor in her voice. "I helped make that flag ten years ago, with my own hands, down in Filmore county. It stands for hard work and bravery."

"I'm sorry," answered Lu, "anyway, we are so glad you all came to the celebration, flag and all. We're going to show you a happy good time."

Norie was glad to be back with friends. Winfield took her to where Ma and Pa were.

"Tell us about your school," said Ma. "We have surely missed you."

"I like teaching the little kids," she answered, "but I got homesick. Then I got really sick, so that I could hardly eat. Mrs. Lacy said she knew a root that grew down by the slough which might help me. She made a tea of the root which I drank, and also gave me fresh buttermilk when she churned. Before long, I was feeling good as new."

"What was the root like?" asked Ma.

"It was yellow inside and the tea was very bitter, but I didn't mind, because it did help."

"Ask Mrs. Lacy to show you the plant," said Ma. "Perhaps we can find some here."

At that point, Ret came bounding up, took Norie by the arm and led her away, whispering in her ear, leaving the others to guess what he might be saying.

A stand had been set up back of the school close to the lake, in a little grove of trees. All began to gather in as "the band" struck up the martial music of "Stars and Stripes Forever." Grandfather Jacob Sherman stepped up on the stand and read the Declaration of Independence. There was a prayer and then Uncle Chauncey Whiting stood up to speak.

"It has been five years since the first of our people set foot on this beautiful land. It was because of the providence of God that we were able to overcome all the hardships and troubles to make our way here. He caused a heavy snow to melt overnight, after our earnest prayers, that we might be able to proceed on our way. He brought us safely through a forest fire when we thought we would all perish. And though many warned that the Indians might attack and put an end to our endeavor, they are, instead, our good neighbors. And after reaching the area, we still were unsure where the Lord wanted us to settle. Since we were accustomed to seeking His guidance in all things, we were again rewarded by His revealment that this strip of prairie, lying between two shining lakes, was the chosen land.

"Time has wrought wonders and indeed brought many changes. Towns and villages have been reared where the Indians had long roamed, the wilderness has become a fruitful field and the distant plains and fertile valleys like a well-watered garden yielding forth abundant harvests.

"We must be thankful for the nation that has made it possible for us to live in this free and beautiful land. This land of America is the land that the patriarch Jacob saw in his blessing of his son Joseph. 'Joseph is a fruitful bough, even a fruitful bough by a well; whose branches run over the wall,' he said, speaking to the time that his descendants would cross the ocean. 'The blessings of thy father have prevailed above the blessings of my progenitors unto the utmost bound of the everlasting hills; they shall be on the head of Joseph and on the crown of the head of him that was separate from his brethren.'[20] Our Indian neighbors are fulfillment of part of Jacob's prophecy, for they are from the tribe of Menassah, Joseph's son. The Lord led Columbus to this land, he brought the Pilgrims, and guided the founding of these United States. For it is destined, at last, to be the home of the New Jerusalem, the city of Zion, which will show to the world the only way to peace is through Jesus Christ, that all men might be redeemed. Let us continue to serve Him and uphold the laws of this great country. Thank you."

The clapping and cheers continued for many minutes, while Clayton did a finale on the drums. When the din and clamor ceased, Uncle Vet hobbled up on the stand. "Don't anybody leave," he called, "the ladies have prepared their most delicious dishes. All are invited to the feast."

Winfield took George Hammer under his wing, since it was George's first visit to Clitherall. When they had eaten all they could possibly hold, including half of a gooseberry pie, he introduced him to all the young people, as his friend and pal from way back in Filmore County. They were all gathered around the swing. Alva Murdock had won Lu's attention, at least temporarily, and Ed and Em were completely oblivious to what was going on around them. They had been married only a few weeks. Ret and Norie motioned to Winfield to follow them to the edge of the group.

"We thought you would like to be the first to know," said Ret, looking like the cat that ate the cream, "Norie has said yes. We plan to get married in October!"

"Well, Sis," answered her brother, "I guess Ma and Pa might also be interested in that news. We're glad for you, we have really been expecting it, you know. I'll get George, here to help me plan a good charivari."

"Now, Win," begged Norie, "be merciful. Maybe we just won't tell you when it happens. See you later," and off they hurried to share their news.

Leaving the swing, Winfield pointed out the new log church. "Pa and I helped build it, part time," he said. "The people had been meeting in the school. The church is built on the spot where Uncle Lute and the others first knelt to ask God if this was the place they should choose. The lower story is for the services, but the top floor is reserved for some kind of secret rituals."

They passed Ret and Ike's wagon shop. "Ret seems to be doing fine in his business," explained Winfield, "he has already built his log cabin."

"Where is Ella?" asked Winfield of Em. "I haven't seen her since before lunch."

"She is watching Art and little May for Ma," answered Em. "I think they are out by the lake looking for shells."

"Come on, George, you have to meet Ella," said Winfield, as he started off in the direction Em had pointed. "She is my pick of all the girls." They found her, shepherding the two younger children on the sandy shore.

"Ella," called Winfield, "I want you to meet an old friend of mine, George Hammer. He lives over by St. Olaf."

Ella washed the sand from her hands in the edge of the lake and turned around. "I'm pleased to meet you, George," she said as she straightened her dress and smoothed her hair. "How do you like our celebration?"

George made a gentlemanly bow. "Well, Miss Ella, I like it very much," he remarked. "I have seen more pretty girls here than I've seen for a long time. Win here has told me you are his pick of them all, and I can see why." At that she blushed that beautiful pink Win loved to see and smiled up at him.

"Will you meet me at the swing later," he asked, "when you are through watching the children?"

"Yes," she answered. "Ma was busy with the baby, but she said to bring them home soon."

Winfield and George joined a group of men who were playing horseshoes. Pa was there and Uncle Lute. Hiram Murdock was in charge of the game, making sure all was done according to the rules. Several Indian men stood watching the game in process.

"Hiram's place is on up the road about a mile," explained Win. "He owns the point where the Indians camp through the summer. The chief's son came to school the term I was there. I like him. Hiram's place is a stop for the stage drivers, and his wife serves meals for them and the passengers. They have had a time. Their house burned, but they got it built back."

"Uncle Lute's store is there on the corner," commented Win, "and finally we have a post office here, in his store."

It was soon time for the folks from St. Olaf to start back. Winfield said good-bye to George and Norie and headed for the swing to find Ella. She was there, as promised, visiting with some of the other girls. He pushed her high, and watched while the wind and excitement brought the roses to her cheeks. He felt proud to be her friend.

"It was sweet of you to watch the children for your mother," he told her, as they walked toward her home. "You really are my pick of the girls, like I told George. Remember that night I tried to kiss you and the scarf got in the way? This time there is no scarf to bother." He gathered her in his arms, turned her face up to his and gently pressed her lips with his.

"Oh, Winfield," she whispered, "we shouldn't." But she clung to his hand as they walked the remianing distance to her cabin.

CHAPTER 10

Uncle Theodore and the Boat

Winfield had taken his sister Emma to Clitherall so she could attend the fall classes. After making sure she had everything she needed, he stopped in Uncle Vet's store to visit a bit. During the conversation, Uncle Vet happened to mention that Theodore Sherman wasn't too well.

"I'm sorry to hear that," returned Winfield. "I have been meaning to get over there to see Uncle Theodore and Aunt Sarah. It is just such a long walk around the lake to the point where they live."

"Well," said Uncle Vet, "if you want to go, why not take my boat and row across the lake? You're welcome to it. I seldom get time to use it any more, anyway."

"Say, if you're sure you don't mind," came the enthusiastic answer, "I'll just do that. Ma would sure appreciate hearing from them directly."

The weather was fair with a gentle breeze in the north, making the trip across the lake a nice change for him. He pulled the boat up on the shore and made his way up the hill to his uncle's log cabin. His cousin, Rhoda, met him at the door.

"So good of you to come, Winfield," she said. "Pa will be glad to see you. He's not too well, you know."

"So I heard, over in Clitherall," he answered. "I borrowed a boat from Uncle Vet and rowed across the lake."

Uncle Theodore greeted his visitor from the cot in the living room. "I'm not much count any more," he said as he made an effort to sit up. "Those old injuries I got in the Civil War keep flaring up. I keep hoping I'll feel good enough by spring to do some farming."

"I have some soup left from lunch," interposed Aunt Sarah. "Have a chair and I'll dip you a bowl."

While he ate, Uncle Theodore told again the graphic story of being in the cavalry; how he was thrown from the saddle with his foot caught in the stirrup and was dragged over the frozen ground. Winfield listened to the painful story and wished there might be something he could do to help. He talked to him about his brother, Cassius, and their mother, Rhoda. He was so engrossed in the visit, he had failed to notice the change in the weather. The gentle breeze had turned into a fierce gale.

"You're going to have a time rowing back across the lake in that storm," cautioned Anson. "If you want to leave the boat here and walk around the lake, I'll take the boat back to Uncle Vet when the wind changes."

"If you think you can do that for me, Anson, I think I will walk. I'd never make it against those waves." He said good-bye to his uncle and the others and set out for the long walk around the shore of Clitherall Lake. He was not sorry he had gone. His visit was appreciated, and he made up his mind to find a way to help them if he could.

It was several weeks later that he discovered the boat had never been returned. He was on his way to Sauk Center to get supplies for a store in Ottertail City. His honesty and desire to always make things right told him the trip could wait a while. He left the team and wagon by Uncle Vet's store and set out to walk around the lake to the Sherman house. He stopped long enough to speak to Uncle Theodore, who seemed weaker than ever, before pushing the boat off the sandy shore and climbing in to row it back across the lake to Uncle Vet.

However, misfortune was his partner again that day. The boat had dried out while beached all those weeks. Water began to seep in the cracks, fast! There was nothing in the boat with which to bail it out, but he felt if he rowed very fast, he could reach the other shore before taking in too much. The farther he went, the more water came in and the deeper the boat rested in the water, allowing the waves to splash over the side, adding to the already bad situation. Using every ounce of strength he could muster, the boat still began to sink some distance from the shore. Finally, Winfield stood up, riding it down, down to his knees, to his waist. He was about to shed his heavy overcoat and prepare to swim in the icy water, when the boat rested on the bottom. Well, he thought, I guess it could have been worse. Struggling with his boots and heavy clothing, he managed to wade to shore.

"Uncle Vet," he said apologetically, as he stood there with icicles forming around the bottom of his coat, "I really did try to return your boat, but had to leave it in the bottom of the lake about 50 yards out. I think the wind will bring it to shore. If not, I will sure pay for it. I guess Anson forgot about the boat and took off on a hunting trip."

"Winfield!" exclaimed Uncle Vet, "you are more bedraggled looking than an old wet hen. Come in here and dry up before you catch pneumonia."

"Thanks, but I'll go on to see if Will and Roseltha will let me spend the night with them and dry out my clothes. I will have to make that trip to Sauk Center tomorrow. After this, though," and he shook his head, "I'll think twice before I borrow someone else's boat."

CHAPTER 11

The Promise

The world was alive with the sights and sounds of spring-time. Birds were busy choosing their mates and building nests for their brood. Ducks, geese and loons were loudly marking their territory by the lake shore. The prairie was alive with bluebells and mayflowers, and the basswood trees had filled the air with an almost intoxicating fragrance.

"Ella," said Winfield as he guided the horses with one hand and pulled her closer to him on the wagon seat with the other, "this is my fourth spring here and it seems like each one has been the most beautiful, but this one tops them all. Perhaps though," he mused, "it could be because I have a beautiful young lady beside me."

"It does seem to make the world look brighter," she returned, smiling at him, "when one is in the company of a friend."

He had come to take her to his parents' home to spend the day. The trail had become a well-traveled road during these years. There were new houses along the way, especially beside Battle Lake, where a new village was forming.

Ella pointed to a small white frame house with flowers blooming beside the steps. "I have never seen that one before," she said. "Isn't it pretty?"

Winfield pulled the horses to a stop so they could see it better. "Yes, Ella. I would like to build one like it." He turned to face her and continued. "Would you share it with me as my wife, if I did?"

She looked into his eyes for a moment, surprise, wonder and admiration all there. "Oh, Winfield, you are so good and kind." She hesitated. "But I'm not sure I'm ready. I still need another year of school and Ma needs me to help with the little ones, but..."

"Ella," and his voice was tender, "I will wait however long it takes for you to be ready, if you will just say yes."

"Then Winfield, the answer is yes." And there in the old lumber wagon they promised to be true to each other for the rest of their lives.

Life continued much the same for those two, except for the singing in their hearts. Ella put her time into tending her little sister, practicing being a little mother. She knitted and sewed things for her hope chest, when there was time, and took over some of the cooking.

Winfield opened up more of his land and planted wheat. He helped Pa plant a big patch to truck garden, and sometimes made the weekly trip into the village with the vegetables and melons to sell to the villagers. There was always the tall prairie grass to cut, cure and stack for hay for the winter. That meant swinging the big cradle day after day during the summer, and again when the wheat and oats were ready. It was hard work and sometimes he felt a pain in his side and had to rest a while. But his singing heart kept him going untill the work was done.

CHAPTER 12
The Blizzard of 1873

The Goulds had been saddened by Jacob Sherman's death in the cold winter of 1870. More sadness came to them that fall. Roseltha's husband, Will, died of pneumonia. Roseltha brought her little girl and came home to live for a while. Pa and Ma tried to help her through her grief. They read the scriptures together evenings, building faith in the promises of eternal life. Time and their kindness helped and she began to help Ma with the housework. Emma was developing into a fine young lady who was taking an active place in the household work, and going to school when she could.

"Roseltha," said Winfield, one bright January morning, "would you like to go to Clitherall with me?"

"Yes," she answered, "I'll stop in with Norie and see how things are going with her and Ret."

"We'll come back before night, Ma," said Winfield.

He hitched Molly up to the sleigh and they started happily out. The weather had warmed overnight until it felt almost mild. The sleigh skimmed lightly over the snow while they talked of many things. She talked to him about Orris Albertson, who was so kind, and smart, too. "He's planning to open a store in the Battle Lake village soon," she said. "He has asked me to marry him, what do you think, Winfield?"

"He is a good man. If you really care for him, I want you to be happy." He was quiet a moment. "Since you have confided in me, let me say Ella has promised to marry me, but we will wait a while."

"She is a dear girl, I'm glad for you, and her."

They had been so engrossed in disclosing their secrets, they had failed to see the clouds rolling up behind them. Suddenly, however, snowflakes began swirling around. Winfield looked back at the sky and urged Molly faster.

"We'll soon be at Ret's place, Roseltha," he shouted over the roar of the rising wind.

She pulled the wool robe around her, trying to shut out the cold, and the sting of the wind-driven snow. By the time they reached Ret's door, it was difficult to see very far.

"Winfield, you can't go on! Come in and wait it out," shouted Ret, as he helped Roseltha in the door.

"I'm just going as far as Uncle Lute's," he called back. "I'll be all right."

It's only another half mile, he thought, I know every step of the way. But the blinding snow soon hid every landmark and his sense of direction failed him. He tried to turn Molly, but she pulled at the bit. Realizing she might know by instinct where to go, he loosened the reigns, pulled his coat over his head and prayed for the Lord to get them to safety. The cold was numbing his hands and feet. Still Molly struggled through the storm. Where is she taking me, he wondered? Peering out he was able to make out a dark shape ahead. Almost instantly, the sleigh struck something hard and Molly stopped. Climbing out of the sleigh, he felt along a log wall until he found a door. It's a barn, he thought. "Thank you, Lord!" he cried aloud. Feeling back along the wall, he unhitched Molly and led her through the barn door. In the semi-darkness, he found a stall and tied her, taking the bit from her mouth. He found the grain bin and dipped a double handful for Molly. A horse whinnied near-by. Going closer, he put his hand on the horse's neck. "You are Uncle Lute's horse!" Figuring carefully, he estimated the number of steps it would take to get from the barn to the house, and the direction he knew he had to go. Concentrating on going straight, he closed his eyes, bowed his head against the wind, counted his steps and finally bumped his head on the house.

The door opened to his frantic knock, and he nearly fell into Uncle Lute's arms. Quickly, Lute helped him to a chair by the fire. "How did you find us in this awful storm?" he asked as he pulled Winfield's snow packed boots off.

"I didn't," he answered. "The Lord and Molly did!"

Having been warmed and fed, Winfield began to feel better. But the storm still raged and the wind howled fiercely. It seemed as if the roof would be torn from the house. The wind found its way through tiny crevices, making it impossible to keep the house very warm. At times, lightning flashed and great peals of thunder shook the walls. For three days it continued without let-up. When the animals needed tending, Winfield and Uncle Lute tied scarves around their faces so that only their eyes were uncovered. Ropes were attached to their waists and the other end to the house, so they could not get lost. Walking was accomplished by using all their strength against the wind, and forcing their legs through the deep snow.

"I hope neither man nor beast is without shelter in this storm," said Uncle Lute. "Nothing could survive long in this."

"Cassius was at Town of Maine the day I came here," said Winfield. "He planned to get home that day. I sure hope he waited. It caught me by surprise. It was such a nice morning, who would have thought this was on its way."

One evening the family gathered around the stove for Bible reading. Aunt Net sat in the rocking chair holding baby Lester. Art, the teenager, sat on the floor whittling. Ten-year-old May had been reading a story to little sister Cordie. Winfield and Ella were seated together on a low bench. Perhaps that was what prompted Uncle Lute's question, or perhaps it had been on his mind anyway. But looking at Winfield, he said in a kind voice, "I have often wondered why you were not baptized when the rest of your family was. If you still have questions I'll be glad to answer them."

Winfield sat deep in thought. He had a great respect for

this man who had befriended him and his family. And now that he was planning to ask for his daughter in marriage, he wanted all the more to please him. Suddenly, a fearful thought came to him. Suppose Uncle Lute refuses to give his consent unless I join his church? I could never join unless I know it is the Lord's will, even if it meant...But he could hardly think of the consequences.

"You remember telling me about Joseph Smith reading James 1:5?" he asked finally. "I memorized that verse. 'If any of you lack wisdom, let him ask of God, who giveth to all men liberally, and upbraideth not, and it shall be given him.' But I add part of the next verse, 'But let him ask in faith, nothing wavering...' I have been asking, but no wisdom has been given yet. I need to *know* where the truth lies. Maybe my faith is still wavering. But I believe God led Molly to your barn door in answer to my prayer. He will yet answer this bigger question. When he does, I will come to you."

"I will be waiting, and praying with you," answered Uncle Lute.

At last, the wind died down, the clouds left the sky and the sun shone. Though it was bitterly cold, without the wind it was bearable. Winfield hitched Molly to the sleigh and headed back to Silver Lake. But it was hard going, with drifts so deep in places they would have to go around. He stopped at Ret and Norie's for Roseltha, but hurried on to see how Ma and Pa had fared in the storm.

"We were so worried about you," said Ma as she hugged each one. "But there is still one missing," and there were tears in her eyes.

"Who is missing?" asked Winfield, looking at Pa.

"Your Uncle Cassius, Winfield. He was to come back from Town of Maine the day of the storm."

"I will go and organize a search party." Winfield had thought about Cassius. "It was such a nice morning. Ma, fix me up some food, and a hot stone for my feet. I'll hitch up Mike and let Molly rest."

"Take time to warm up and eat," urged Ma.

"I'll eat as I go, Ma, there is no time to lose. The cold is so bitter."

"Wait, Winfield," said Pa. "I need to go with you."

Many brave men joined in the search, spreading out on the vast prairie between Ottertail City and Silver Lake. He had left the city the morning of the storm, they were told. But there was nothing to mar the frozen white sea of snow. He had not reached any of the few houses that were scattered over the area. At last, there was nothing to do, but to give up the search and return home with the sad news.

"It isn't fair, Pa," said Winfield almost angrily, "God could have saved him, same as he got me to shelter. Why didn't he? Grandma needs him. It just isn't fair!"

"There are many things we don't understand, Winfield. But this much I know, our Heavenly Father is a just and loving God. He doesn't think about death as we do. He knows the physical body is only a temporary home for the eternal spirit of man. Remember the words of Paul, in 1 Corinthians, second chapter, ninth verse, I think, '...eye hath not seen, nor ear heard, neither have entered into the heart of man, the things which God hath prepared for them that love him.' I believe Cassius, the real personality of the man we knew, is in Paradise, enjoying those wonderful blessings that we have only a hint of."

Winfield was quiet awhile as they slid homeward behind Mike. He wanted to believe what Pa was saying. But it was all so vague in his mind. And it hurt, awfully, to think of Cassius out alone in the storm, unable to find his way to shelter. It was hard to realize his body would probably not be found until spring, when he could be laid to rest with their final good-bys.

Tears came to Winfield's eyes, as he went to his grandmother. "I'll try to help in his place, Grandma," he said, as he gave her a hug. She patted his back and tried to smile through her tears.

"You're a good boy, Winfield. I'll be happy if you can come often."

Winfield was true to his word, going often to see Grandma Sherman. He made sure she had plenty of wood for the fires, and helped with the chores. In a few days, Emma suggested to Ma that she could go and live with Grandma through the cold weather. And so it was arranged and Grandma was glad to have her. The blizzard of 1873 was recorded as the worst in history.

Mild weather began a slow melting in early April. One morning there was a knock at the Gould door. George opened it and invited in two of his neighbors, Eric and Anton Glende.

"Good morning," he said as he shook their hands. "How are you?"

"We're fine, George," returned Eric, "but we have some news for you." He hesitated, but then continued. "We made a trip to Town of Maine yesterday. We think we found Cassius' body out there on the prairie. We knew you would want to know."

"Yes, of course," answered George, "we were planning to go out today looking for him. We really appreciate you telling us. If you will go to show us where he is, Winfield and I will get ready and start immediately."

It was a sad task that day, but it was good to at last be able to give Cassius a proper service and burial. His body was put to rest on "The Hill" in Old Town, with the other pioneers. The government provided his grave stone because of his service in the Civil War.

CHAPTER 13

Pain and Pleasure, 1875

It was too early spring for working the soil. Instead Winfield was busy cutting logs for his cabin. Ella was teaching the school at Clitherall. But they had set a date to be married in the fall. He was excited and searched the woods for the straightest, strongest oak trees to make a perfect house for her. He wished for Clayton to help him, remembering when they had worked together on his house, and how strong Clayton had been. But Clayton and Dee had moved to Far West, Missouri. Word was reaching them, however, that they were lonesome for the lake country and might be returning soon.

One day as he lifted a log into place on the wall, there was a sharp pain in his side. For a few moments he was doubled over in pain. Realizing he needed help, he went in search of his old friend George Hammer. Pa is too busy, he thought. I'll get George to help. And so with George's help, the walls were up and the roof on, before planting time. In between field work, he put the finishing touches on the cabin.

"Weather looks good for haying, Winfield," said Pa one June morning. "I think the rain is over for a while. Can you help me today? We'll cut the field over next to the slough."

"Sure, Pa," he said, smiling. "The grass has grown fast this spring, There should be plenty."

However, he had swung the scythe only a few times when he felt that same pain in his side. He would rest a while, then try it again. Finally, he had to sit down.

"What's the matter, Son," asked Pa, "don't you feel good?"

"No, Pa, I get this sharp pain in my side. I think I hurt it some way while I was lifting logs for the cabin. But surely it will be all right. I'll keep trying."

He did keep trying, and by stopping at intervals he managed to cut about half as much as Pa. That night, however, the pain came back. Day after day, he worked as he could, resting often, suffering with the pain and feeling so useless.

"Winfield," said Ma one morning, "you must do something about that trouble. Suppose you go on the train to your Uncle Jim's in Wisconsin. He can examine you and find out what the problem is. He has been a doctor for many years and has had much experience. I will write and tell him you are coming. Please go."

He laid his head on his arms on the table. He knew he had to have help. But how could he leave when there was so much work to do? And most of all, how could he leave Ella? "I'll talk to Ella, Ma," he said finally. "Maybe she can help me decide what to do."

"All right," returned Ma, "better go today."

The walk gave him time to think things through. Suppose, he thought, that I should get to Uncle Jim's and he can't help me. Suppose I die before I can ever get back. Finally, he knelt there along the trail and prayed, asking the Heavenly Father for help and guidance. After that he felt a little better, less depressed, so he could talk to Ella without making her feel so bad.

He found her in the garden picking peas. He helped her finish the job and then asked her to sit down beside him on the bench outside their door. "I need to talk to you, Ella," he began. "I've been having this pain in my side. It is bad enough that I can hardly work. Ma wants me to go to Wisconsin to my Uncle Jim's who is a doctor, and let him examine me. I want to get well, but I don't want to go so far from you. What shall I do?"

She turned a worried face to his. "How bad do you think it is?" she asked, "I mean," and she bit her lip to keep it from quivering, "do you think it is life threatening?"

111

"Sometimes, in the night, the pain is so severe I can hardly breathe. I don't know, dear, I wonder myself."

They were both quiet for a time, their arms around each other. The happy plans they had made for the fall were eclipsed by this sad state of affairs. Winfield had a plan in his mind, but he wasn't sure it was the right thing to suggest. The more he thought about it, though, the better it seemed to him.

"I know you had planned for a nice wedding in September," he said finally, breaking the silence. "But I have been wondering, well, if maybe we could be married before I go to Uncle Jim's." There it was out. "Of course," he continued, "there is the possibility I may never come back. And Ma said it wouldn't be right to send both of us to board with him. Honest, Ella, I just don't know what to do." He drew her close and kissed the tears away from her cheeks.

Looking up into his face, she managed a weak smile. "Let's do it," she whispered. "After all, I would rather be a widow than an old maid, but surely God will help you get well."

"Oh, Ella, thank you for being so understanding. I love you more every day. Will a week be long enough to get ready? If so, let's plan on the 7th of July. Ma will write to Uncle Jim to tell him when I will be going. And maybe it won't take long until I will be better and we can begin housekeeping in our little new house." Suddenly he remembered there was someone else he needed to talk to. "I will go and find your father, Ella," he said, "I need his permission."

He found Uncle Lute out by the barn. His heart was beating harder than usual as he approached. Once again he was wondering if permission would be granted. He began by telling Uncle Lute about his trouble and that his folks wanted him to go to Uncle Jim.

"I know your uncle Jim, he practiced here for a little while. He should be able to help you. I sure hope so."

Winfield struggled for words to continue. "I don't like to leave when there is so much work to do, but I am unable to help much. I suppose it is better to go now and try to be well in time for the harvest. I, uh, I really came to ask your permission to marry Ella." He looked down at his hands, gathering courage to continue. "We would like to be married before I go to Uncle Jim's."

Uncle Lute stood the pitchfork against the barn and turned a serious face to Winfield. "You have come to be almost like a son to me," he said. "We have known each other seven years, and in all that time I have never seen anything but a true gentleman in you. The only thing that stands in the way, is the fact that you and Ella are not united in religion. Married life is not easy. But if a couple has taken the Lord into their marriage and pray to Him together, He can be a peaceful bridge over the times of trouble."

"I understand," Winfield began, "and I plan to continue to study the books and pray for a testimony. I want very much to do the Lord's will."

"I have thought about you and Ella, and knew you were planning to be married in the fall. I had intended to give her a heifer as a wedding gift, but because you are considered a gentile, the church forbids it. But, I cannot forbid this marriage." He reached out his hand for Winfield's. "Go with my blessing and may you be returned to health and come back to make a good home for my daughter."

"Thanks, Uncle Lute," and Winfield took his hand, but threw the other arm around the shoulders of this good man. "I intend to provide the best home for Ella that is possible to have."

Plans were made and the word traveled fast throughout the countryside. The day arrived and neighbors, relatives, and friends came from as far away as St. Olaf and Oak Lake. Dressed in their best but sober attire, they gathered around the home of Uncle Lute and Aunt Net Whiting. Some of the Sherman relatives came across Clitherall Lake in a boat. Those that could not find room in the house, stood outside and waited. There was an air of quiet expectancy among them, as well as concern. Both Ella and Winfield were loved and respected, and the uncertainty of their future gave a serious turn to the celebration.

Art, proud to do his part, brought four chairs and placed them in a row in the big room. The people found seats as much as possible and Calvin Fletcher, Cutlerite Elder, stood waiting in his place. Uncle Lute and Aunt Net were seated next to George and Eleanor. They had all looked forward to this marriage, but today their happiness was tinged with apprehension, and in each heart was a prayer that all would be well.

Winfield ducked his head as he came from the bedroom. He remembered watching Uncle Lute do that and realized he had grown to the same tall height. Briefly, his mind went back over the few years to the good times he had enjoyed in this home and the first time he had seen Ella, young, shy and unpretending in her almost childlike manner. Oh, Lord, he prayed silently, please let me live to love and care for her.

He took his place beside one of the chairs, followed by his friend, Allie Whiting. Presently the door opened at the head of the stairs and his sister, Emma, lovely in her own right, came down the steps and took her place as bridesmaid. Ella followed, the picture of quiet loveliness in her soft gray gown, her long dark curls falling over her shoulder. He took her hand and led her to her chair.

"You may be seated," spoke elder Fletcher to the four of them. "And now, the groom's father will say a few words."

"I welcome you ladies and gentlemen to this important occasion," George began, but his throat was tight with emotion. "I have felt for some time that these two were ordained for each other. Their courtship has been good to watch. Ella is a wonderful, saintly girl, and I feel honored to have her as a daughter-in-law. I would say to you, Winfield, that you must love her as your own body. Protect and provide for her. Together, you must invite the Lord to be part of your marriage, consulting Him on every decision. The principle of salvation is based on repentance, forgiveness and keeping our covenant to the Lord until the end, and in no other situation in life are these put to greater test, than in marriage. But neither is there any situation in life in which the rewards are as great when the principles are employed faithfully. You will come in time to learn that the joy that follows reconciliation is well worth the pain that brings its birth. There will come times of doubt, times of trouble, but if you are both true to your covenant, the clouds will pass and there will come times of joy and happiness. May God bless you as your lives merge and become one."

George took his seat beside Eleanor, and Elder Fletcher stood. He, too, cautioned them to make the Lord part of their partnership, and urged Winfield to embrace the faith that Ella had. He then read from the small black book in his hand. "Winfield and Ella, do 'you both mutually agree to be each other's companion, husband and wife, observing the legal rights belonging to this condition; that is keeping yourselves wholly for each other, and from all others, during your lives?'"[21]

"We do," came their affirmative answer.

"Winfield, you may place the wedding ring on the third finger of the bride's left hand in token of the everlasting love you hold for her."

He took from his pocket the plain gold ring, and slipped it on her finger.

"Winfield and Ella, I pronounce you husband and wife, in the name of the Lord Jesus Christ, and by the laws of the country and authority vested in me. May God add His blessings and keep you to fulfill your covenants from henceforth and forever. Amen."

Morning came too soon. Winfield caressed the dear head that still slept on his shoulder. "Dear, precious Ella," he whispered. "How can I go away and leave you? It is only possible because of the hope that Uncle Jim can help me return to you well and strong."

She stirred. "Oh, Win." Tears slipped from her closed eyes and he kissed them on her cheeks.

"We must be brave," he said as he held her close, "and believe that all will be well. I will pray for you every day and do everything Dr. Jim says. Surely it will not be long."

After a hurried breakfast, Winfield hitched the horses to his two-seated buggy. Ma packed some food and they started on the fifty mile journey to the train station. Pa drove, with Ma beside him, and the newlyweds consoled each other in the back seat. The day was fair and the ride pleasant and they were thankful for this day together.

But the end of the journey was finally reached. Winfield kissed Ma's cheek, hugged Pa and held Ella in a long embrace. Lifting her chin he smiled at her. "Remember the scarf?" he asked.

She smiled through her tears and nodded, as he kissed her tenderly. "I love you very much, Ella, and I plan to come back as soon as possible."

"I love you, too," she whispered. "I will pray for you."

CHAPTER 14

Strange News from Home

Dr. Jim Wendell laid aside his stethoscope and was quiet for some time. Finally, he turned a worried face to his nephew. "Winfield," he said at last, "your condition is serious. You have a greatly enlarged vein that could rupture at any time. However, since you are young it may heal itself, if great care is taken. I will give you medicine to cause your heart to beat slowly to aid in the healing. You must be very careful, but slow walking is permitted. I will write to your father and explain the problem."

It was not good news, but there was some relief to know what the trouble was. He made up his mind to keep quiet and be patient. He spent some time in the doctor's office, listening and learning. But often he lay to rest on the couch. Day after day went by and he felt no improvement. His heart ached to be home with Ella. He sent letters to her and to Pa and Ma. But the mail was slow. He wondered if he would ever again be able to work his farm. He sent many earnest prayers heavenward for Ella's safety, and for health for himself.

"Good news, Winfield," said Dr. Jim one evening. "Two letters came for you today."

His face lit up with the first real smile they had seen, as he took the letters. He excused himself and went to his room. One was in Ella's handwriting and the other in Pa's. Ella's letter was full of homey things she and her ma were doing, and how much she missed him. He hung on every word and read it over twice. Pa's letter had news of the crops. Clayton and Dee had returned from Missouri. Norie and Ret had asked about him. And lastly he wrote that a Josephite missionary was holding meetings at their house and over in Becker County where Henry Way and the Andersons lived.

He wrote back to Pa asking about this new church, but the answer came before his could have reached Pa. "Dear Son," he wrote, "I want to tell you more about what is going on here. The missionary I told you about is Apostle T. W. Smith. He tells us that God had spoken to two different men, neither knowing of the other, asking them to denounce all who claimed to be prophets and that He would call upon the seed of Joseph to take his father's place. These men finally came together and through much prayer received light and guidance. The Holy Spirit blessed their meetings and more people were gathered together. They united in fasting and prayer for several days and the Lord spoke through one of the brothers, telling them to organize. Angels were seen by some, and many spoke in tongues which were interpreted, telling them how to proceed.

"These men visited Young Joseph, telling him of their experiences and all that had transpired. After much prayer, and assurances from the Lord, in 1860 Joseph Smith III, went to the conference at Amboy, Illinois. He told them, 'I came not here of myself, but by the influence of the Spirit...I have come in obedience to a power not my own, and shall be dictated by the power that sent me.'[22] He told them he had received spiritual manifestations which had guided him toward acceptance of leadership of the group.

"Proceeding carefully, doing nothing until guided through the gift of prophecy, the church was again organized according to the pattern that had been given at the first. And, Winfield, the Holy Spirit has confirmed the truth of Brother Smith's words to me. Your mother and I, as well as Clayton and Dee, Emma and others of your friends, have been baptized. Never before, either in the church of my youth or with the Cutlerites, have I witnessed such marvelous manifestations of the Holy Spirit.

"We love you and are praying for your recovery."

Winfield showed the letter to Uncle Jim. "I really feel like I need to be there," he said. "Do you think I would be just as well off at home if you sent the medicine with me?"

"That depends," answered his uncle, "on whether you can be quiet and careful, once you are back on the farm."

"I promise to do that," was the excited answer.

It took two days for Winfield to walk the fifty miles from the train station to Clitherall, keeping a slow but steady pace and resting occasionally. He stayed the first night with strangers, and the second with his friend George Hammer. Weariness was taking its toll, but as he came near to Uncle Lute's place and saw Ella running to meet him, weariness was forgotten.

"Oh, Winfield, I didn't know you were coming," she exclaimed, as soon as he let her lips free to speak. "I'm so glad and happy. Are you better? Can we go home to our own cabin home?"

He held her tight. "It will take time, dear Ella, but I will be better. I promised Uncle Jim I'd be careful. We will have to be patient. I'm not able to do hard work, and it is harvest time. But I can help you get our home prepared. We must just have faith."

Uncle Lute and Aunt Net were happy to see him. "When Ella gets her things gathered up," said Uncle Lute, "I'll take you home." In the meantime, Lute began to answer some of the questions in Winfield's mind.

"Yes," he said with a sigh, "there has come a division in our colony. Some are very bitter about what has happened. T.W. Smith and his wife are fine people. They stayed with us while he preached here. He went out in the field and worked like the rest of us, and Mrs. Smith helped Net with the housework. His sermons were strictly with the scriptures. But Alpheus taught us *he* was the one anointed. So many have gone with other leaders, and all are in apostasy. We must be careful!"

Ella and Uncle Lute shared all the other news with Winfield as they made the ten mile trip to Silver Lake. When the happy greetings were over, Ma put dinner on the table and insisted Uncle Lute stay to eat. They talked of many things, but no mention was made of the one thing uppermost in all their minds. Only as Uncle Lute was leaving, Winfield overheard Pa say to him, "Lute, please don't let this come between us. I respect you for holding to what you believe to be right. But," and he reached out to shake his hand, "I hope to receive the same from you."

The next few days were happy ones for the newlyweds. Their little cabin was only a short distance west of Pa and Ma's house. Together they planned how to arrange it. They made a trip to Clitherall for a few things. They bought two chairs from Almon Whiting's chair shop. Ella chose some brightly colored cotton cloth from a bolt in Uncle Vet's store for curtains. And Winfield insisted she get cloth for a new dress. They went on up the sandy road to Hiram Murdock's for one of his brooms. He bought some smooth boards for shelves and they hurried home, with the wagon full of their treasures.

The cook stove was already set up in one end of the long room. When Ella's dishes were put neatly on the new shelves and the chairs set beside the table Winfield had made, the kitchen was Ella's pride and joy. Pa came and helped Winfield make the bed frame. They cut four posts from a basswood tree for legs and drilled 2" holes for the rails, which were cut from ironwood trees. They wove strong bed twine across the rails both ways. Ma helped put fresh straw in the tick from Winfield's bed. When it was all together, Ella proudly spread it with the wedding ring quilt she had made while Winfield was gone.

CHAPTER 15

The Answer

Sunday came, and they went in the buggy to the Cutlerite service. But Wednesday evening, all the Goulds and Shermans met at Grandma Rhoda Sherman's house for prayer service. Winfield listened to their testimonies and longed to have one of his own. He prayed earnestly and often for forgiveness and knowledge of the truth. He studied the Book of Covenants, hoping to find answers. As he read in that book, he became sure the Latter Day work was of God. "Search these commandments," he read, "for they are true and faithful, and the prophecies and promises which are in them shall all be fulfilled."

He found there warnings of those things to come if the people continue in wickedness:

"Wherefore the voice of the Lord is unto the ends of the earth, that all that will hear may hear; prepare ye, prepare ye for that which is to come, for the Lord is nigh; and the anger of the Lord is kindled,...for they have strayed from mine ordinances, and broken mine everlasting covenant; they seek not the Lord to establish his righteousness, but every man walketh in his own way, and after the image of his own god, whose image is in the likeness of the world, and whose substance is that of an idol, which waxeth old and shall perish in Babylon, even Babylon the great, which shall fall."

And also there, the reason for calling Joseph Smith:

"Wherefore I the Lord, knowing the calamity which should come upon the inhabitants of the earth, called upon my servant Joseph Smith Jr., and spake unto him from heaven, and gave him commandments, and also gave commandments to others, that they should proclaim these things unto the world;

and all this that it might be fulfilled, which was written by the prophets; the weak things of the world shall come forth and break down the mighty and strong ones, that man should not counsel his fellow-man, neither trust in the arm of flesh, but that every man might speak in the name of God the Lord, even the Savior of the world; that faith also might increase in the earth; that mine everlasting covenant might be established; that the fullness of my gospel might be proclaimed by the weak and the simple, unto the ends of the world, and before kings and rulers."[23]

He could see, then, that just as God had spoken to Isaiah and told him to warn the people of Jerusalem concerning their wickedness, or Jerusalem would be destroyed, he had called Joseph to warn the people of this day that the coming of the Lord is near and we must be prepared and repentant, keeping the commandments and covenants. Oh, he thought, if I could just know the Lord can forgive me, and let me know which of these two churches is right.

It was time to dig potatoes and Winfield went out to help. He dug a while, but the pain soon returned and he had to stop. Deeply depressed, he turned to go to the house.

"Winfield," called George, "I want to tell you Apostle Smith is coming today. We will have a prayer meeting over at Clayton's tonight. Try to bring Ella and come."

"Thanks, Pa, I will be there. Sorry I'm no help here."

Ella declined to go to the meeting. Winfield kissed her good-bye and headed through the trees toward his brother's house. The twilight shadows lay long across the grass. The beauty of the hour lifted his spirits a little, but he wished Ella had come with him. He entered the house as the others had begun a hymn, and sat near the door. Pa, who had been ordained an elder the same day he was baptized, and another man, whom he supposed was Apostle T.W. Smith, sat behind the table. He was a kind-faced man, Winfield observed, and when he stood to read the scripture, there was a ring of conviction in his voice.

"We meet in the name of our Lord and Savior, Jesus Christ," he said. "to worship the Father in His name and testify of His goodness to us. I want to read from the Doctrine and Covenants, Sec. 76: 3, which is the testimony of Joseph Smith and Oliver Cowdry: 'And now, after the many testimonies which have been given of him, this is the testimony, last of all, which we give of him, that he lives; for we saw him, even on the right hand of God; and we heard the voice bearing record that he is the Only Begotten of the Father...'"

Winfield sat quietly, listening to the prayers and testimonies of those he knew so well, tell of their happiness since they had received a remission of their sins, and how the Holy Spirit had blessed and guided them. But the depression he had felt earlier in the day continued to press his spirit. Why, he thought, aren't my prayers answered? They have all been in vain.

Just as those thoughts were passing through his mind, the lady whom he supposed to be Mrs. Smith, stood up and began to speak in a strange musical language he could not understand. Then she began speaking in English, to several of the young people in the room, and turning around, she looked him straight in the eyes and said to him, "Verily, I say unto you, your prayers have *not been in vain*, and if you will continue to pray and seek in the right way, you shall receive that which you so much desire."

Her words sent a thrill through him from top to toe, and gave him hope. But, he wondered, have I not been seeking in the right way? Instantly a scripture came into his mind. It was the words of Peter at Pentecost, when the people were convinced that Jesus was indeed the Christ and they cried out, "Men and Brethren, what shall we do?" He answered them, "Repent, and be baptized, every one of you in the name of Jesus Christ for the remission of your sins, and you shall receive the gift of the Holy Ghost, for the promise is unto you and your children, and to all that are afar off, even as many as the Lord our God shall call."[24]

That, he thought, is the answer I have been needing. Oh, Lord, thank you. I will be obedient this very night. With that he stood, trembling, to his feet.

"Those words," he began, "have answered my many prayers. The Lord knows I have been crying to Him to forgive my sins. If you think He will do it, I am ready to obey and would like to be baptized this night," and he sat down.

Brother Smith stood up. "The Lord is pleased with your decision," he said. "You will be making a covenant to obey the commandments and walk in the footsteps of Jesus to the best of your ability. It is good, when a married person goes into the waters of baptism if both can go at the same time. However," and he looked at Winfield with a kind, assuring smile, "I feel sure that if you live faithful, the time will come when your companion will also obey the gospel." The meeting closed, and he ran home to change his clothes.

"Ella, honey, the Lord spoke to me through Sister Smith!" he exclaimed, his excitement making him less cautious than usual. "It was wonderful, and I am going to be baptized, tonight! Come with me, please?"

"No, Winfield, wait," she returned alarmed. "Surely there's some mistake. Let's talk about it later."

"But, Ella," his enthusiasm dampened, "the people are already on the way to the lake. Pa and Ma, Clayton and Dee and all the folks." While he talked he was changing his clothes. "I feel I must do this," he said. "It is what I have been praying for so long." He took her hands in his and looked her straight in the eyes. "Once more, please come."

"No, I will not!" she answered angrily as she jerked her hands away. "I think it's wrong," and she threw herself on the bed sobbing.

Saddened, but determined, he turned and went out the door. He knew the Holy Spirit had put those words in Sister Smith's mouth, and had brought those scriptures to his mind. He had to obey.

The folks were singing hymns while they waited and as he approached them, some of the good feeling began to come back. Brother Smith offered a prayer and Pa led Winfield into the water. In the fading light he saw the tears of emotion in Pa's eyes as he whispered, "I'm so happy for you, son." Then in a firm clear voice he said, "Winfield, having been commissioned by Jesus Christ, I baptize you in the name of the Father, Son and Holy Ghost, Amen."

As the cold water rushed over his body, he felt as though it was actually washing away the dirt of his years of wrong and selfish thinking and he stood straight and tall, feeling clean enough even to walk into the Savior's presence.

As they all walked back through the woods, Brother Smith started up the hymn he had written and all joined in until the woods rang with the joyful sound and echoed back from the hills. Clayton's bass and Pa's lovely tenor could be heard blending with the other voices.

> "Lift up your heads, ye heirs of glory, cast aside your doubts and fears:
> He who called you to His kingdom, soon will reign a thousand years.
> What if the hour of pain and sorrow bring to your eyes most bitter tears?
> God will wipe tears from all faces, in that day of thousand years.
> The budding fig tree tells that summer with it's ripening harvest nears,
> So the times as plainly teach us the Day's at hand, a thousand years.

Come Jesus, come and reign victorious: come with
   prophets, martyrs, seers,
Come and take us home to Zion: Come and reign a thou-
   sand years.
Chorus:
   "A thousand years, children of Zion, Glorious day
      so long foretold;
   'Tis the morn of Zion's glory, sung by saints in days
      of old."

Tenderly, he touched Ella's hair. She was still sobbing.
"Please listen to me, dear," he whispered. "It was such a
wonderful experience, I want to share it with you." But she
pushed his hand away and the sobbing continued until at last,
exhausted, she slept.

Morning came and the peace and joy of the night before
was replaced with a feeling of gloom as he watched Ella going about her work, quiet and unresponsive to him. Doubt
crept into his heart like a dark cloud. Perhaps I should have
waited, he thought. I can't bear to see her unhappy like this.
I must find relief from this awful doubtful feeling. He left the
house and walked out among the big oak trees. He climbed to
the top of the hill from where he could see Silver Lake shining in the early sunlight. There he knelt and humbly plead
with his Heavenly Father. "If I were right," he prayed, "in
going ahead against her wishes, Lord, please take away this
heavy doubt and gloom and bring again the peace and joy I
felt last night."

As he continued to pray, the scriptures he had read in the
books kept coming to his mind. Jesus had told his disciples,
"I will send you another comforter, and he shall bring all
things to your remembrance, whatsoever I have told you."
Brother Smith's words came to his mind also, "If you are
faithful, she will yet obey the gospel." Comforting thoughts

were bringing back the good Spirit. Then, suddenly, a voice, plain as any voice he had ever heard, said, ***"Your companion is honest in heart and she will yet be one with you."***

Oh, joy surpassing anything the world can give! He was filled with the strong warm wonderful feeling the Holy Spirit brings. Words of praise and gratitude flowed freely, prompted by that Spirit. How long he praised he knew not, for time was not a part of the experience. He felt as if he had tasted a little bit of heaven, and knew now that he could go home and love Ella and be patient, and someday she would understand.

After breakfast, Winfield went to Pa's house where Brother Smith was waiting. "Winfield," said Brother Smith, "we are acting in accordance with instruction from the church, and in accordance with the scripture in Acts 8:14–17, where Peter and John went to Samaria to confer the Holy Ghost to those who had been baptized in water." Then he and Pa laid their hands on his head for the prayer of confirmation and the bestowal of the gift of the Holy Ghost, as the scriptures show. Again, Brother Smith counseled him to be patient and his companion would eventually choose to enter the kingdom.

"I must start husking the corn today, Ella," said Winfield, as he put on his jacket. "I'll be in at noon for some lunch. Do you need anything before I go?"

"No," she answered rather coolly, "but thank you."

He went out with the team and wagon and worked steadily all morning, pulling the ears of corn out of the husk and throwing them into the wagon. The thought came to him that the twisting motion usually made him wince with the pain in his side. He stopped and touched the spot with his hand. It hurt if he pressed, but movement didn't bother. He worked until sundown that evening, and felt he had accomplished a good amount of husking. But he felt sure he would pay for it in the night, as the day's work always brought on the pain when he lay down. However, he slept soundly and when he awoke, he found the soreness was all gone in his side.

"Ella, something very good has happened," he said as he put his arm around her as she washed the dishes. "I worked all day yesterday, and there is no pain in my side this morning, nor soreness."

She dried her hands and turned to him. "I'm glad," she said, and some of the ice was gone from her voice. "I hope it doesn't come back."

He didn't tell her what he was thinking, but he thought she knew. This was only the third day since he was baptized. I am sure this is a blessing from the Lord, he thought. I will continue to do the necessary work, but avoid heavy lifting. Out in the barn, he prayed, thanking the Lord for this blessing.

Some time later, without thinking, he lifted a log that had fallen across the trail. At once, he felt that old pain return to his side. He was in the depths of despair. For several days he said nothing to anyone. Finally, faith returned. He determined to ask the elders for the anointing of the oil and laying on of hands the next time there was a meeting. It was nearly two weeks later when a group of the Saints met. At the close of the service he told Pa about the pain and asked for the laying on of hands. Pa and Jed Anderson placed their hands on his head, anointing him with the oil. As part of the confirming prayer the words, "According to your faith, be it unto you," were said. At that, Winfield was sure he would be healed, for his faith was strong. He went home, assured that he would be able to do the work of his farm, and so it was. Through all the days of wheat harvest, wood cutting, digging their root cellar, he had no more pain.

Cutlerite log church, built 1870

Interior view of the log church

Barn built of logs from the old church, circa 1909, by Orison Tucker, located at the junction of Highway #210 and Old Town Road, between Battle Lake and Clitherall, on the Stabnow farm.

Winfield Gould

George Gould, father of Winfield Gould

*Winfield and Ella Gould with daughters,
Ethel, Nina, Gladys, and Iva, 1897*

*Winfield and Ella's
older children,
Maude, Leon,
Hallie, and Winnie*

Lewis and Ann Jannette Whiting (Uncle Lute and Aunt Net)

Daughters of Lewis and Ann Jeanette, left to right, Cordie Murdock, Em Anderson, Mary Anderson (May), Lucia Luisa Murdock (Lu), and Ella Gould

Abner and Emily
Tucker
with sons
Frank and Orison,
1890

Ella Gould and her daughters,
Maude, Iva, Gladys, Nina, Ethel, and Hallie

Present day Cutlerite church (True Church of Jesus Christ), Clitherall, Minnesota

Present day Josephite church (Reorganized Church of Jesus Christ of Latter Day Saints), Clitherall, Minnesota

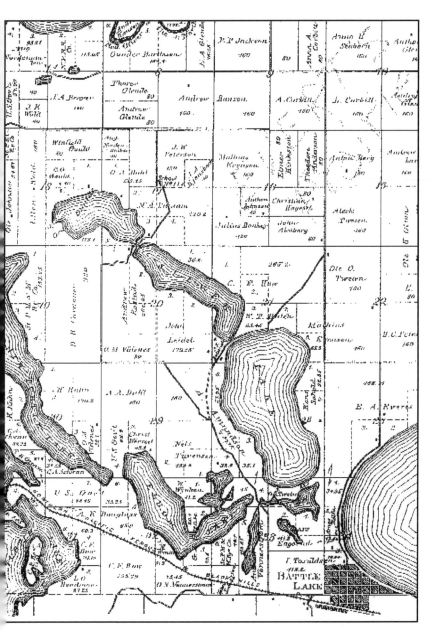

A section of Everts Township showing the three Silver Lakes and the Gould properties at the north end (Everts Prairie}.

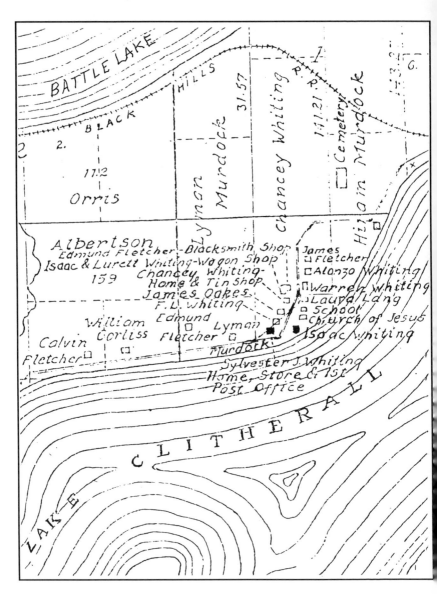

Map showing Old Town Clitherall and the land between Lake Clitherall and Battle Lake.

136

CHAPTER 16

April 7, 1876

It was a mild day for April, although the snow still covered the ground. The sky was dark in the north and Ella wondered if another blizzard were on the way. She was tending their few precious hens, hoping they would soon begin laying eggs. Suddenly she sat down the bucket of water and bent over double as a pain pierced her abdomen. Oh, she thought, can it be time? Hastily she finished her chores and walked down the hill to Mother Gould's house.

Eleanor saw her coming and welcomed her in. "How are you, Ella?" she asked. "Have you had any signs that it's time for the baby?"

"Yes, Mother Gould, that is why I'm here. I think it is time and Win is gone. Can you come?"

"Well, you wait here while I finish kneading the bread and we'll see how you are doing." Ella watched her work the dough with strong quick strokes, and admired her. She had come to love her mother-in-law and now she trusted her to guide her through this most important time of her life.

By the time the bread was kneaded and in the big wooden bowl to rise, Eleanor could see it was time all right. "Little George," she said, "you please go for your pa. He is out cutting ice. Tell him I need him at Ella's house." Obediently, George put on his jacket and went out.

They walked back up the hill to Ella's little log house. How she wished Win would get home. She felt frightened. She thought about some of the little babies who were born lifeless. What if...? But she shuddered and put the thought out of her mind.

Eleanor fixed the bed, built up the fire and put a pot of water on to heat. All the time she worked she was telling Ella what to expect. Her confident kind voice brought a measure of assurance. "Try to relax, honey," she would say. "Let nature take its course. Here, drink this red raspberry leaf tea. It will help."

Ella tried to relax, but her fear and worry made it almost impossible. Finally, the door opened. It was George.

"Well, Ella, don't you worry, now." His kind voice made her feel better. "Everything is going to be all right."

"Father Gould," she said hesitantly, "I've seen so many blessings happen when you pray. Will you pray for me?"

"I sure will," he answered. "I'm so glad you asked. I brought the consecrated oil in case." He poured a small amount of the olive oil on her hair and placing his big hands on her head addressed his Heavenly Father in a humble, pleading way for His blessing in this time of Ella's need, and for the little life about to be born. To Ella it seemed as if all her fears and worries were gone when his hands were lifted from her head. A feeling of peace settled over her and strength for the task ahead was hers. "Thank you," she whispered and managed a little smile.

"I'll stay, George," said Eleanor, "but you run along. Please check the bread dough and punch it down if it has risen."

It was nearly dark when Winfield came home and snow was falling. "I'm home, Ella," he called as he stamped the snow from his boots. "How are you?"

"She's fine, and she has a surprise for you.

"Ma! What...?" He reached the bed in one bound.

"You have a son, Winfield," said Ella proudly. "See?" and she lifted the blanket to show him his little red-faced baby boy.

"Oh, Ella! How wonderful! But I'm so sorry I wasn't here to help."

"That's all right," answered Ma. "We really didn't need you pacing the floor."

"She was wonderful, Win," said Ella, "and your pa prayed for me and I got along fine."

Winfield took down the ledger where he kept track of important things and wrote the name they had chosen: "Leon Arthur Gould, born April 7, 1876."

CHAPTER 17

Grasshoppers

Leon was a toddler when his little brother was born. Another entry was made in the journal: Winfield William Gould, born June 10, 1877. Ella had insisted he should have his father's name. Her heart was full of happiness. No matter that there was always hard work to do. She was strong and Win was well. Even the fact of their differences in religion seemed to matter less, now. He never coaxed her to join his church. They prayed together, took turns going to each others services and love was strong between them. The summer was good, plenty of rain and sunshine. The garden was doing fine and the green beans were ready. She took Leon and the baby out and sat them on a blanket, and while she picked the beans, she sang happy little songs.

Suddenly the sky darkened and something began falling on her. She looked quickly at the babies wondering if it was hail. "Grasshoppers," she cried, "they're everywhere!" Picking up both babies, she ran into the house and closed the door and windows. Back she ran for the beans and the blanket, shaking grasshoppers out of the blanket as she ran and knocking them from her hair.

As she watched from the window, she saw them falling like rain from the great cloud overhead. They were eating the flowers in the little bed she had fixed by the path and they covered the lilac bush. Would they devour their precious garden plants? and the wheat? Soon she saw Win coming from the field. He leaned his hoe against the house, his broad shoulders drooping.

"Is it very bad, Winfield?" she asked gently as he dropped into a chair.

"They will destroy the crops, Ella. There is nothing we can do. The wheat was the best we have had. And our dream of stocking our cellar with plenty of vegetables is gone. We may have to leave the farm."

The baby cried and Ella took him from the cradle and sat in her little rocker to nurse him. Leon, hearing his daddy's voice, hurried to him on short unsteady legs. Winfield picked him up and held him close as he looked over at Ella. She met his gaze and smiled. "We'll manage, some way, won't we? After all, we still have each other and our faith."

"Bless you, Ella. Yes, we will find a way. God will help."

All the members of Zion's Hope Branch gathered at George's house for Wednesday evening prayer service. It was a dejected group. True to form, the grasshoppers were leaving nothing green.

"They even ate my onion tops," moaned Orris, Roseltha's husband. "I could smell their breath when I came by the garden."

"Do you think the potatoes have developed enough to keep?" queried William Oaks.

George cleared his throat. "Time will tell," he said. "The outlook for the winter is not encouraging. But I think the best way is to go ahead with our work, trusting in the same Power for the harvest that has provided for us in the past. Remember," he counseled, "the Lord has told us He will have a tried people. So let us trust Him and be faithful, as well in adversity as in prosperity." He took his Bible and turned to Romans 8 and read verses 35, 37, 38, 39, "Who shall separate us from the love of Christ? shall tribulation, or distress, or persecution, or famine or nakedness, or peril, or sword?...Nay, in all these things we are more than conquerors through him that loved us. For I am persuaded, that neither death, nor life, nor angels, nor principalities, nor powers, nor things present, nor things to come, nor height, nor depth, nor any other creature, shall be able to separate us from the love of God, which is in Christ Jesus."

Then George, elder, father to most of the ones there, prayed for a blessing on these dear discouraged ones. Other humble prayers followed, petitions for forgiveness and for God's providence for the coming days. At last, a blessed spirit of calm assurance permeated their hearts and they were able to sing the closing song with enthusiasm.

"Praise Him, praise Him! Jesus our blessed Redeemer!
Sing, O Earth, his wonderful love proclaim!
Hail him, hail him! highest archangels in glory!
Strength and honor give to his holy name!
Like a shepherd, Jesus will guard his children,
In his arms he carries them all day long.
"Praise Him, praise Him! Tell of His excellent greatness
Praise Him, praise Him! Ever in joyful song."

It came almost to be a game with the women to see who could think up ways to use the meager greens they found, either left behind by the grasshoppers, or springing anew from the roots. Aunt Net made a pie with sheep sorrel, and Eleanor showed Ella how to use the red root leaves as greens. One day, after most of the harvest was over, the Goulds all went to visit Uncle Lute and Aunt Net.

"Did you have much wheat left, Winfield?" asked Uncle Lute.

"I got exactly eighteen bushels," he answered, "out of all those beautiful acres. I'll need most of that for seed."

"It may not be any better next year. Those hoppers have laid their eggs everywhere. Some of the settlers are leaving the area. Old Dan skipped out one night, leaving debts at every shop."

"We'll stick it out," said George. "There's bound to be a better day."

"We can learn from the Indians," ventured Aunt Net. "The squaw who helps me sometimes, said they use the red root seeds in bread and soups, and the bark of the root for tea for sore throats. She also said, Ella, 'White flour no good for papoose.' They grind their corn and wheat with stones. 'Makes papoose strong,' she said."

"That makes sense," said Ella. "There is no waste. I often wondered about separating the flour. Shall we take some of the wheat to the grist mill over by Ottertail, Win?"

"We can try it if you like," he answered skeptically.

By late summer, the lilac bushes had put out new leaves as though to say, "See, there is still hope." When everything was gathered in, they counted stock. Many of the root vegetables had survived, if not in the best condition. There was enough corn and hay for feed. The wheat for seed was safely put away, and Winfield had taken a load to the grist mill to be ground into flour, as Ella had requested. They found hazelnuts left by the grasshoppers, which helped their meager food supply. But there had been almost nothing to sell. Winfield and George planned to hunt game for food and trap for furs to sell, so there would be some money for the staples. Thanksgiving that year was a humble affair; however, all were grateful for whatever they had. Ella cooked the coarse flour into a mush for the children, and made a dark, delicious bread using the flour and some of the red root seeds. Sometimes with their scanty supply of white flour, she made one biscuit for herself and two for Win, being sure nothing went to waste.

CHAPTER 18

The Storm

Winfield had made another entry in his journal. "Lenna Maude born June 13, 1879." Their little girl had grown and was just now learning to walk. She was a happy, healthy child.

"We love our little boys, but it is wonderful to have a little girl," said Winfield fondly, as he picked her up and lifted her high above his head. "She looks like you, Ella. We must help her grow to be as fine a person as her mother."

"You flatter me, Win," she returned, a serious look on her face. "Sometimes I feel far from fine. Yesterday I was even cross with Leon when he teased Winnie. It is difficult to learn how to be always patient, but I keep trying."

"You have had so much responsibility since I have been driving the stage," Winfield responded. "But we need the extra money now that we have a family of three. I'll ask Ma to come and help you, she will be glad to. You are doing a fine job, though, and you are a very fine young lady." With that, he gathered her in his arms and smothered her with kisses.

Ella felt the warm glow of his love and she determined to be all he wanted her to be. She knew he still hoped she would join his church. Sometimes when Father George talked to her about the Lord and the church, she was almost persuaded. But the sight of her mother's sad face when she learned Winfield was baptized, caused her to put the thought aside. Win still took her to her church often and she went with him. They studied the scriptures together and had prayer. Little Leon was even learning to say his prayer, and Winnie would say, "Wuv Zesus, amen." How she loved the little ones and prayed often for guidance from above in caring for them.

Winfield had taken the job of driving the stage from Clitherall to Perham once a week—one day up and one day back, so that he was away two days and one night. Sometimes he hauled supplies for some of the settlers, or hauled a sack of grain to the mill to be ground into flour for a neighbor. Whatever freight he hauled meant extra money, sometimes doubling his wage. Other days, in the summer, he was busy in his fields or helping his pa. But always on Sunday, he hitched Molly to the buggy and took Ella and the three little ones to church.

"Where shall we go today, Ella?" asked Winfield. "Over to Girard or down to Clitherall?"

"Norie invited us to dinner after church today," responded Ella. "I think Ma and Pa will be there, too. Is it all right if we go to the Cutlerite service?"

Yes," he answered, soberly, "I'll get the buggy ready while you bundle up the children."

The children were restless in the meeting. Leon let it be known in a stage whisper that he needed to go potty, so Winfield took him out. The other two kept Ella so busy she really didn't hear much of the sermon, and was finally relieved when the service was over.

Aunt Net and Uncle Lute joined their daughters and their husbands for dinner. Cordie and Lester who were eleven and six respectively, were with them. Aunt Net was slim and prim in her long fitted black dress and black straw bonnet. Uncle Lute, though a little stooped, was still tall, an imposing figure with his white beard. Norie's baby was a dear, all agreed, and Grandpa thought Ella's two little boys were very special. Ella laid Winnie and Maude on the bed after lunch for their naps. Cousins Leon and Lester went outdoors to play. When the little ones were sleeping, the grownups talked of many things.

"Hiram's daughter, Emily, is keeping company with that young Abner Tucker," said Aunt Net. "He seems like a nice young man. His mother, Mrs. Abigail Tucker, lives with Mrs. Corliss, who is Abigail's daughter."

"That's good for Emily," answered Norie. "She has seemed a little lonesome. I hope they stay together."

"We were sorry to learn that Clayton and Dee's baby daughter had died," said Uncle Lute. "It must be very hard for them."

"Yes," answered Winfield, "they have decided to sell their homestead. I think they will take over the hotel in Battle Lake. Orris Albertson is planning to buy lots there, if the railroad goes through as planned. They anticipate the tracks will be laid by 1881. That's just next year."

"Have you seen the new schoolhouse?" asked Norie. "They built it up near where they think the tracks will be. We're beginning to call that 'New Clitherall.'"

"Yes," returned Ella. "It is a nice frame building. It should be more comfortable for the children, and the teacher. I remember how cold it used to be in the old log school."

Winfield, turning to Ella, said quietly, "There is a Josephite meeting in town this afternoon. I plan to go. Would you like to go with me?"

Before Ella could answer, her mother quickly intervened. "No, Winfield, she doesn't want to go!" she snapped. "You can go if you want to."

Ella glanced quickly at her husband. She saw the hurt in his eyes and was sorry, but she said nothing. Winfield stood a moment, opened his mouth as though to speak, but turned and walked out of the house without a word. Tension was strong in the room after he was gone, broken at last by little Winnie calling "Mama," as he woke from his nap. Ella handed little Maude, who had awakened earlier, to her mother. "Grandma will rock you, Maudie," she said, and went to Winnie.

Jannette's face softened as she cradled her little grandchild in her arms. Softly, she sang a gentle lullaby. Maudie smiled up at her and made sounds as though to join in the song.

"Ella," she began, as Ella returned with a sleepy little boy. "I, I'm sorry I spoke so harshly to Winfield. He is a good man. He loves you and the children. It's just that I know he wants you to join that other church. Your father and I can't see how it can be right and it hurts us to see our family making a mistake. But I suppose you must be able to choose for yourself. I will try not to intervene any more, but please be very sure before you make a commitment."

"I understand, Ma," said Ella quietly. "And I feel sure Win will, too. He is so kind and patient, Ma. He never pressures me about the church, but we study the same books and pray together."

As they rode home through the twilight, Winfield was quiet. Ella busied herself with the little ones. It was one of those rare summer evenings when all nature was at its best. The cloudless sky seemed to reach forever. The prairie grass waved gracefully in the gentle breeze and the lake reflected the beauty of trees and sky. As they topped the hill overlooking their home and Silver Lake, a high thin cloud caught the last rays of the sun and turned the western sky to a wonderful brilliance.

"Look Pa," exclaimed Leon from the back seat, "God painted the sky pretty!"

"Yes, son," answered Winfield, "He knows how to make us happy, doesn't He?"

Ella reached out and touched Win's hand that was holding the reins. He pulled the horse to a stop, took her hand in his as they both soaked up the beauty of the scene. Peace flowed like a river into each heart, and praise rose silently to their Creator. He gave Ella's hand a squeeze and a look of love passed between them. There was no need for words. Both knew that same wonderful Artist would help make things right for them.

It had been a big day for all of them. While Winfield did the chores, Ella fed the little ones and put them to bed, Leon and Winnie in the loft and Maudie in the trundle bed beside the big bed.

"There's a strange feel in the air," said Winfield as he came in with the pail of milk, "and a cloud bank in the northwest. We might have some rain tonight. I shut your hens in the barn."

Ella fixed them each a bowl of fresh warm milk and bread, adding a little maple syrup. As they ate, it became suddenly dark and they heard the whine of the wind in the oak trees.

"It's good we got home when we did," Win said, as he went to shut the windows. "These Minnesota storms come up so fast." The wind increased, pushing against the cabin and finding its way through the cracks. Outside, they could see the great trees bending low with its force. Thunder cracked loudly nearby.

"Let's bring the boys down with us, Win," cried Ella excitedly, "the storm will frighten them."

She tucked the two sleepy children in the big bed. The two of them knelt beside the bed for their evening prayers, each thanking God for His love and asking His protection and guidance. Suddenly, the whine of the wind became a roar. There was a cracking, rending noise and rain poured down through a gaping hole in the roof! Instinctively, Ella gathered Maudie in her blanket and headed for the cellar, followed by Winfield carrying both boys. It was only a short distance to the safety of the cellar, but the force of the wind made every step a struggle. Winfield kicked open the door and, pushing Ella ahead of him, deposited the boys on the cellar floor.

"You'll be safe here, Ella. I will run to get Orris to help me fix the roof, before all our things are ruined. Be brave, dear," and with that he was gone, closing the door after him.

Ella was beside herself, trying to comfort three crying children and calm her own fears. There had been no time to think of a candle. Were there spiders hiding in the darkness? What trouble is ahead for Win? she wondered. But the children were demanding her immediate attention. She felt around and found one of the big kraut crocks to sit on and pulled the boys close to her.

"We're safe in here, children," she said, trying to make her voice sound sure. "Your pa has gone for Uncle Orris to help patch the hole the wind made in the roof. Let's sing some songs, that will make us feel better." And so they sang "Jesus Loves Me," and "Yankee Doodle." Spreading the blanket on the floor, she coaxed the boys to lie down and go back to sleep.

"But sing some more, Ma," coaxed Leon.

"Very well," she answered, tucking the blanket around them and holding Maudie close. "You lie still and I will sing."

So she sang all the songs she knew, hymns, love songs, ditties and finally, "Home Sweet Home."

> "Mid pleasures and palaces though we may roam,
> Be it ever so humble, there's no place like home!
> A charm from the skies seems to hallow us there,
> Which seek through the world, is ne'er met with else-
> where.
>
> "Home, home! Sweet, sweet home!
> There's no place like home! There's no place like home!"

The children were finally quiet, and strangely, her own fears were stilled. She thought about their little home and how truly sweet it had been, for it was filled with love—their love for each other and God's love for them. She leaned back against the stones of the wall, relaxing, knowing that Winfield would somehow be able to fix the roof. The noise of the storm was abating and at last she dozed.

How long she had been there in the dark she could not tell, but she heard someone call her name. "Ella, it's George. I've come to take you to my house."

"Oh, that's wonderful, Father George, although we have been sleeping. Is the storm over?"

"Yes," answered George, "the stars are even shining. I'll carry the boys if you can carry the baby and the lantern. Winfield and Orris are trying to fasten a tent over the hole until morning."

They made their way carefully, having to walk around many tree limbs broken off by the storm. The quarter of a mile seemed extra long but at last they came to the welcome light and warmth of George and Eleanor's comfy home. Eleanor put the children in her big bed, and they snuggled down happy to know they were in Grandma's house.

It took several days to repair the roof and dry the bedding, clothing and rugs. Eleanor watched the children while Ella filled the clothesline, day after day, with their soaked belongings, while the long summer days and the light dry air did their work

One evening, George came to the house with his arms full of muskmelons from his garden. "These are the first of the crop. Let's have a feast," he suggested. "Remember, Winfield, how we used to build a smudge to keep away the mosquitoes while we ate Ma's dishpan full of melon? Now we are so fancy we have screens. The Lord has been good to us. Look at my grandchildren here," and he reached over and patted Winnie on the back.

"I do feel blessed with these three little ones," agreed Ella, "as well as a wonderful husband, and you folks have been a blessing to us. But I have been thinking about Clayton and Dee and their loss of little Nora Etta. It has been so hard for them. Tell me, Father Gould, what the church believes about little babies that die before they are baptized.

George cleared his throat and a kind look came over his face. "Ella," he said, and there was tenderness and conviction mingled in his voice, "their little spirits go straight to Jesus' arms in Paradise. Do you remember what He told his disciples when they tried to send away the mothers with their little children?"

"Yes," answered Ella, "He told them to let them come to him for 'of such is the kingdom of heaven.'"

"You have a good memory," added George. "And He went on to say that whoever did not receive the kingdom as a little child could not enter therein. This implies that the children were ready for the kingdom. However, there is a more detailed answer in the Book of Mormon." He stood up and reached for the book on the shelf. "This is Mormon writing to his son, Moroni. 'And the word of the Lord came to me by the power of the Holy Ghost, saying, Listen to the words of Christ, your Redeemer, your Lord, and your God.

"'Behold, I came into the world not to call the righteous, but sinners, to repentance; the whole need no physician, but they that are sick; wherefore little children are whole, for they are not capable of committing sin; wherefore the curse of Adam is taken from them in me...Behold, I say to you that this shall you teach: repentance and baptism to those who are accountable and capable of committing sin; teach parents that they must repent and be baptized, and humble themselves as their little children, and they shall be saved with their little children; and their little children need no repentance, neither baptism.'"[25]

Winfield spoke up then. "So at what age do you think a child becomes 'accountable and capable of committing sin?' Leon, here, is four. Once in awhile," and he stopped to reach over and tweak that little boy's ear, "once in a while he does something he shouldn't."

Grandpa grinned at Leon. "It takes more than four years for a child to learn discipline. People who have made a study of children say that most understand right from wrong by the time they are eight. This is supported by the Lord's counsel in the Doctrine and Covenants. However, if they have never been taught, it may take many more years. That is where the parents' responsibility comes in. I know you and Ella are teaching these little ones, but let's read Section 68:4. Eleanor, will you please hand me the book?"

He turned to the place and read: "'And again, inasmuch as parents have children in Zion, or in any of her stakes which are organized, that teach them not to understand the doctrine of repentance; faith in Christ the Son of the living God; and of baptism and the gift of the Holy Ghost by the laying on of the hands when eight years old, the sin be upon the head of the parents.'[26] So you see, the children are still protected. Does that answer your question, Ella?"

"Oh, yes it does. I feel much better. I still have questions about life after death, though, which I would like you to explain some time. But now I had better put these little cherubs into bed."

The family knelt for prayer, each one taking their turn, even little Winnie added his "Me wuv Jesus." While Eleanor and Ella put the children to bed, George got out his flute and played softly one hymn after another. No children ever heard sweeter lullabies.

CHAPTER 19

The Family Grows

The roof of the house was soon repaired and the contents dry, so the summer work proceeded. Winfield worked from dawn to dark in the field on the days he was not driving the stage and helped his pa on his new frame house as he could. Ella and Eleanor worked together tending the gardens, gathering, drying and canning berries, green beans and corn. They salted down many jars of sauerkraut and pickles. The boys were five and six now, that adventurous age, and Maude had turned three. Even though Ella was clumsy with yet another life growing within her, they took a picnic lunch and went to pick red raspberries near the clay bank.

Ella put Maudie on the blanket for her nap while she picked, letting the boys play nearby. She was thinking while she worked about how faithful Winfield was to keep the commandments. He fasted often and prayed so sincerely. He always kept track of his expenses and paid tithing every year, one tenth of the increase. He hadn't told her, but her mother said that Hiram didn't have money for the stage fare when he had to go to the hospital, so Winfield had paid it for him. He was always doing something for somebody. When she asked him how he could afford to help others so much, he had replied, "I can't afford not to. Look what the Lord has given me. It is only mine to use for His Kingdom's sake." The Lord seems so close to him, she mused wistfully.

Suddenly, her reverie was broken by Leon crying, "Ma, Winnie rolled down the bank!"

Panic mounted as she lifted her skirts and ran to see. There at the foot of the bank sat her little boy, calmly brushing the brown dirt from his hands. Luckily he had missed the few bushes that grew sparsely on the steep bank of clay.

"Mother Gould," she called to Eleanor who was a little distance away. "Please watch Maudie while I go and fetch Winnie." She took the empty lunch pail and going around to the side where the bank wasn't so steep, climbed down and went to him. "How did you like that slide, Winnie?" she asked as she picked him up. "Did it frighten you?"

"I just wanted to catch that pretty butterfly, but he went too fast."

"Well, after this," cautioned his mother, "better watch where you are putting your feet. You must thank Jesus that you didn't get hurt. Now, let's gather some of this dirt in the bucket and when we get it soaked up, I'll help you make something with it." With that she struggled back up the slope, Winnie tagging along behind.

"I'm concerned about you," said Eleanor, "are you all right? We had better get you home to rest." Ella agreed and they gathered up their berries and headed home.

By evening, Ella knew it was time to prepare for the birth of their new child. "Win," she said when he came home from the field, "please take the children to your folks and ask your mother if she can come. I guess I exercised a little too much today," and she told him of their berry picking and Winnie's episode.

The next morning, Winfield wrote yet another event in his ledger. "Hallie Mae Gould, born July 18, 1882." "What a fine family we have, two boys and two girls. But you must have some help."

"Oh, Win," she countered, "can we afford to pay help? Maybe I can manage."

"Now Ella, this time, you are the one I want to help. Don't you argue with me."

One day, when he was to have a short run, Winfield took

Leon with him on the stage. When they returned, that little boy was full of the adventure.

"Tell me what you saw, today, Son," asked his mother.

"Well, Pa sent me to the store for some shoe-nails. There was an Indian there with a fish as long as that," and he stretched his arms as far as he could. "He wanted to trade it to the store man for a pair of shoes. I had to wait while they talked about it. The fish smelled bad," and he pinched his nose closed and made a horrid face.

"Well, did you get the nails?"

"Yes, but then he asked me whose boy I was. When I told him he took the package back and put another big handful of nails in and tied it up again."

Ella looked at Win with pride showing all over her face. He only shrugged and said, "I think he was taken with Leon's red hair." But he tousled the red hair and returned the look of pride, with a smile, to Ella. Then in a down to earth tone, he asked, "Do you think this boy is ready for school this fall?"

"I think he is ready to learn," she answered, "but I wondered if we could wait and send both boys together next year. They would be company for each other."

"Maybe that would be good. Besides he is big enough to help some with the chores, aren't you, Leon?"

"Sure, Pa, I can fill the wood box and feed the chickens and get the eggs."

"I can help, too, Pa," piped up Winnie. "Let me get the eggs!"

"All right, we have two good helpers," said Pa. "Now, let's see how many Bible questions you can answer. Winnie, what was the name of the first man?"

"Adam!" was the quick answer.

"And Leon, who built the city of Zion?"

"Enoch!" was just as quick an answer. He loved this game.

"Maudie, what baby was born in a barn?"

155

"Baby Jesus, and the shepherds came to see." Maudie's smile was almost heaven to see.

"You all did fine. Now, I have a surprise for you," and he pulled an orange out of the sack for each of them. "Your Uncle Orris sent them to you."

"That was so good of him," said Ella, "we don't often see them up here."

And so ended a typical day in the Gould household. Love was the binding that held them together, their love for God and for each other.

—————————

The first day of school finally came. Leon had been counting the days. Ella made sure they were clean and combed.

"What a fine day you have to go to school," she said cheerily. "See how blue the sky is. I love you boys. Here is your lunch pail. You can take turns carrying it. Do be good and listen to the teacher and come straight home when school is out."

"Do we have to go?" asked Winnie. "It's a long way to the school."

"You will be fine, Winnie," assured his ma, "remember, we walked together to the school last week, so you know the way. Bye, bye, now," and she gave them each a hug.

She watched them start off around the house toward the road. Seven-year-old Leon, with his shock of red hair and Winnie, just one year younger, still showing a little baby fat. Her heart yearned to shield them, but she knew it was time to begin to turn loose just a little. They turned and waved and she went back in the house to tend to Maude and baby Hallie. Hallie had toddled over by the cook stove and was reaching for the shiny knob that controlled the draft.

"No, no! Hallie," cried Ella and quickly grabbed her up. "That is hot! hot!" But Hallie cried loudly, still reaching for that shiny object.

"Ma, I'm hungry," said Maude, "can we have breakfast now?"

"Yes, Maude, just as soon as Hallie settles down. Would you like to feed her?"

"No, I want my mush," she answered and stamped her foot.

"You forgot to ask nicely, Maude. Try again."

Maude looked sober for a minute. Then she looked up at Ma, smiling her sweetest, and said, "Mrs. Gould, may I please have some mush with cream?"

A happy laugh from their mother caused Hallie to stop her crying. Quickly, Ella tied her in the high chair and dipped up two bowls of wheat meal from the pot on the back of the stove. "Here you are, Miss Maudie," said Ma, with a gracious bow. "I do hope you like it." So while Maudie ate hers, Ma fed Hallie, all the while telling nursery rhymes.

"Now, girls," said Ma, when the bowls were both empty, "we need to go out and feed the hens. They will think we have forgotten them." She put their sweaters on and out they went into the bright sunshine. As they went past the corner of the house, there, sitting on the bank, were Leon and Winnie, calmly eating their lunch!

"Leon! Winnie!" she called in astonishment, "why didn't you go to school?"

"Well, Ma," answered Leon, "Winnie didn't want to go and I didn't want to go and leave him, so we decided to have a picnic out here in the sunshine."

Ella didn't know whether to laugh or scold. Such forthright honesty in Leon she had to admire. "All right boys, tell you what we will do. You go feed the hens. Then I will leave the girls with Grandma Gould. Tomorrow, you must go by yourselves."

The boys soon grew accustomed to going to school. Leon was a quick and eager student. Winnie learned, but he would much rather run and play in the woods. He loved to watch the chipmunks and see them come for the hazel nuts he put out for them. He was apt to dawdle on the way home, hunting pretty rocks and chasing after grasshoppers. Leon, young as he was, assumed a sense of responsibility for his brother, making sure he reached home safely.

Ella was hanging out the clothes one mild day in February, when she smelled smoke. Looking toward the southeast, she saw the source. It was far away, but a great column of black smoke billowed into the sky. It is too high and too black for a prairie fire, she thought. Quickly she ran over the hill where Win was cutting wood.

"Win," she called loudly, "there is a big fire down toward Battle Lake! Come up where you can see." She ran just as quickly back to the house to check on her two sleeping girls. Finding all quiet, she went out again to find Win hitching Mike to the sleigh.

"Looks, bad," he shouted. "Has to be a building. I must go and see if I can help. Orris owns several of the buildings in Battle Lake. Sure hope he isn't in trouble."

"Do be careful." Ella called after him as he sprang into the buggy and was gone.

She waited with a sense of uneasiness as she went about her work. When the girls woke up, she carried Hallie and with Maude hanging to her skirt she went over the hill to Grandpa Gould's house.

"Have you folks seen the smoke?" she asked anxiously. "Win went to see if he could help. He was afraid it was Orris' store."

"Yes," answered Father George, "it is a good thing there is snow on the ground or we would be in for a prairie fire."

The smoke continued to billow out most of the day. Ella bundled the little girls and walked to meet Leon and Winnie on their way home from school. "Teacher said he thinks all of Battle Lake town is burning up," said Leon, his eyes big with excitement.

Ella's uneasiness increased as the day wore on. She sent the boys to gather the eggs and feed the hens. Then she left them in charge of the girls and went to milk the cow. Just as twilight was merging into night, she saw Win coming. She hardly recognized him as he came to the door. He was quite black from head to toe, and his shoulders sagged with weariness. She poured warm water in the basin so he could wash.

"It was Orris' General Store, all right," began Winfield when his face and hands were clean. "And several others, burned, also. It is a big blow when they were just getting started. But Orris seemed determined to rebuild. He is sure an industrious fellow. We worked all day trying to save other buildings from burning. Even Roseltha and some of the other women helped to carry water, but we could not save the ones it took hold on."

"It does seem," said Ella, "there is no end to the hardships experienced here by the pioneers. But it is like most of them to shrug it off and begin again."

CHAPTER 20

Alma Talks of Zion

Winfield was home from another stage run. His pockets were bulging with treats for the children and they gathered around him, two on his lap and one at his knee. They searched his pockets, finding a big red apple, an orange, some pieces of maple sugar. The treats were wonderful to them, but best of all was to be held on his lap and feel his love for them.

"Ella," he said, when he could shift his attention from the children, "I saw Alma today. I invited him and his family up to the service for Sunday and thought we could have them here for lunch. Is that all right with you?"

"Surely," she answered enthusiastically, "I do enjoy them, and the children all have a good time together. I will fix some food on Saturday, so we can have time to visit."

Sunday morning found the little schoolhouse near Silver Lake nearly full of worshipers. Sure enough Alma and Ann Sherman and their children were all there. "Hope of Zion Branch" was the name given to the Silver Lake organization. And it was a fitting name, for all believed in the dream of Zion one day becoming a reality, where they would all be of one heart and one mind, living in righteousness, with no poor among them.

Father Gould welcomed them and led out, in his strong sweet voice, the opening hymn from Emma Smith's little book of hymns: Hymn 70. C.M.

> "Great is the Lord; 'tis good to praise
> His high and holy name.
> Well may the saints in latter days
> His wondrous love proclaim.

"The Comforter is sent again,
　　His power the church attends,
And with the faithful will remain
　　Till Jesus Christ descends.

"Praise Him, the time, the chosen time,
　　To favor Zion's come
And all the saints from every clime
　　Will soon be gathered home."

After prayer, George invited Alma to tell some of his experiences in the gospel and offer his testimony of the truth of the Reorganized Church of Jesus Christ of Latter Day Saints.

"The Lord has been confirming the word with signs following, as He promised," began Alma. "I feel such humble gratitude for being a tool in His hands. Many times the sick have been healed instantly. The Spirit has spoken to the young people, encouraging them to study and prepare for service. My faith is secure that truly this is Jesus Christ's church restored in these last days, to call all of us sinners to repentance in preparation for His return.

"We don't know how long it will take to preach this gospel of the Kingdom to all nations, tongues and people. We know Noah preached one hundred and twenty years before the Lord gave up and sent the flood. But we must work diligently to share the wonderful message. He has told us, that he who has been warned must warn his neighbor. For judgment is coming on those who refuse to hear him and repent. The following message came through the prophet Joseph, so it is for our day. You know, he says in one place, 'It is called today, until the coming of the Lord.'

"'Wherefore the voice of the Lord is unto the ends of the earth, that all that will hear may hear; prepare ye, prepare ye for that which is to come, for the Lord is nigh; and the anger of the Lord is kindled, and his sword is bathed in heaven, and it shall fall upon the inhabitants of the earth; and the arm of the Lord shall be revealed; and the day cometh that they who will not hear the voice of the Lord, neither the voice of his servants, neither give heed to the words of the prophets and apostles, shall be cut off from among the people;

"'For they have strayed from mine ordinances, and have broken mine everlasting covenant; they seek not the Lord to establish his righteousness, but every man walketh in his own way, and after the image of his own god, whose image is in the likeness of the world, and whose substance is that of an idol, which waxeth old and shall perish in Babylon, even Babylon the great, which shall fall.'[27]

"Jesus taught the people to pray, 'thy kingdom come, thy will be done.' Isaiah paints such a wonderful picture of that day, when there will be no more enmity between man and the animals and the 'earth shall be full of the knowledge of the Lord, as the waters cover the sea.'

"I recently received a copy of Joseph's New Translation. You know his wife Emma took care of the manuscript which Joseph had worked on, correcting and supplying some missing parts by Divine inspiration. God has restored the missing story of Enoch. All we have in the King James Bible is a teaser, saying, 'Enoch walked with God: and he was not; for God took him.'[28] However, I had always wondered, because back in Jude it talks about a prophecy which Enoch, 'the seventh from Adam,' had made, which is not in the King James Bible.

"Now we know, Enoch was such a righteous man and great leader, that he and his followers established a city. Quoting now, from the New Translation: 'And from that time forth, there were wars, and bloodshed among them; but the Lord came and dwelt with his people, and they dwelt in righteousness...And the Lord blessed the land, and they were blessed upon the mountains, and upon the high places, and did flourish. And the Lord called his people, Zion, because they were of one heart and of one mind, and dwelt in righteousness; and there were no poor among them...And it came to pass in his days, that he built a city that was called the City of Holiness, even Zion...And all the days of Zion in the days of Enoch, were three hundred and sixty-five years. And Enoch and all his people walked with God, and he dwelt in the midst of Zion. And it came to pass, that Zion was not, for God received it up into his own bosom; and from thence went forth the saying, Zion is fled.'[29]

"There is also the account of the vision Enoch received from God, in which he saw far down the stream of time. He saw the flood, the day of the coming of the Son of Man in the flesh, His death and resurrection, the tribulations of the last days before the return of Christ, and the wonder of His return.

"'And righteousness and truth will I cause to sweep the earth as with a flood, to gather out mine own elect from the four quarters of the earth, unto a place which I shall prepare; an holy city, that my people may gird up their loins, and be looking forth for the time of my coming; for there shall be my tabernacle, and it shall be called Zion; a new Jerusalem.... Then shalt thou[speaking to Enoch] and all thy city meet them there; and we will receive them into our bosom; and they shall see us, and we will fall upon their necks, and they shall fall upon our necks, and we will kiss each other; And there shall be mine abode, and it shall be Zion, which shall come forth out of all the creations which I have made; and for the space of a thousand years shall the earth rest.'[30]

"Isaiah, prophesying of the last days, wrote, 'And he shall set up an ensign for the nations, and shall assemble the outcasts of Israel, and gather together the dispersed of Judah from the four corners of the earth.'[31] Also in Isaiah we are told Zion will be that ensign for the nations. 'And it shall come to pass in the last days, that the mountain of the Lord's house shall be established in the top of the mountains, and shall be exalted above the hills; and all nations shall flow unto it; And many people shall go and say, Come ye, and let us go up to the mountain of the Lord, to the house of the God of Jacob; and he will teach us of his ways, and we will walk in his paths: for out of Zion shall go forth the law, and the word of the Lord from Jerusalem.'[32]

"In the ancient American scripture, the prophet Ether wrote these words, '...after the waters had receded off the face of this land, it became a choice land above all other lands, a chosen land of the Lord; wherefore the Lord would have that all men should serve him, who dwell upon the face thereof; and that it was the place of the New Jerusalem, which should come down out of heaven, and the holy sanctuary of the Lord.'[33]

"Joseph Smith received this message concerning the Kingdom: 'Pray unto the Lord; call upon his holy name; make known his wonderful works among the people, call upon the Lord that his kingdom may go forth upon the earth; that the inhabitants thereof may receive it, and be prepared for the days to come, in the which the Son of man shall come down in heaven, clothed in the brightness of his glory, to meet the kingdom of God which is set up on the earth.'[34]

"Last of all, we have the everlasting covenant God made with Enoch, saying, 'And this is mine everlasting covenant, that when thy posterity shall embrace the truth, and look upward, then shall Zion look downward, and all the heavens shall shake with gladness, and the earth shall tremble with joy.'[35]

"When the Kingdom of God is functioning as it was intended to do, with Jesus as the 'Chief Corner Stone' and His various officers—apostles, prophets, elders, bishops, priests, etc.—each working according to the guidance of the Holy Spirit, then many people will be drawn into the kingdom.

"So you see," continued Alma, "the great responsibility which has been placed within our care. The Lord is depending on us, with His guidance and power, to prepare a place of righteousness which can become an ensign to call the nations to learn of His ways. We need to get the message of the Book of Mormon to this great nation for it is a message of warning. '...that it is a land of promise, and whatsoever nation shall possess it, shall serve God, or they shall be swept off when the fullness of his wrath shall come upon them.

"'And the fullness of his wrath cometh upon them when they are ripened in iniquity...whatsoever nation shall possess it, shall be free from bondage, and from captivity, and from all other nations under heaven, if they will but serve the God of the land who is Jesus Christ who hath been manifested by the things which we have written.'[36]

"It has been a privilege to share with you, today," concluded Alma, "and a greater privilege for all of us to be part of this great work. May the Lord bless you all as you endeavor to serve our Lord and Master, Jesus Christ."

Lunch was a happy affair. The day was warm for October, so Ella spread a blanket out on the grass for the children. Effie stayed with the little ones to help out. Leon and Plinnie had fun teasing the girls, Maudie and Lucy. Winnie divided his attention between his food and a chipmunk he was tossing crumbs to.

Inside, the grown-ups caught up on the news of each other's families. Ann had two more children, and Ella introduced Hallie who was now fifteen months old. Winfield told them of his stage driving experiences, and George showed off some of his crop of squash, giving Ann and Alma one of the biggest ones.

"We came through Fergus Falls on the way back from Becker County," said Alma. "That town has surely grown since the railroad went through. The river has been dammed up in several places, providing power for mills."

"Yes," answered Winfield, "the last time I had flour ground, I took it to Fergus Falls. It sure is a heap closer than when Pa used to take it to St. Cloud."

When the conversation turned to religion, as it always did among the believers, Ella asked, rather timidly, "Do you think Zion can ever begin in Missouri as first thought?"

"The scriptures say God's word cannot go back to Him void," answered Alma. "He said in a revelation through Joseph Smith in 1831, '...In this land which is the land of Missouri, which is the land which I have appointed and consecrated for the gathering of the Saints: wherefore this is the land of promise, and the place for the city of Zion.'"[37]

"When Zion is a reality," ventured Ella once more, "do you expect the people to have all things common?"

"She means, I think," spoke up George, "as the Cutlerites practice it, with all turning their property over to the church."

"I see," said Alma thoughtfully. "Let's check again with the prophets. Micah, speaking of the day when the law shall go forth out of Zion, said: 'they shall sit every man under his vine and under his fig tree...'[38] We believe that each man will be made steward over his own property, or business, that which he has the talent or ability to do. But that which he earns above his needs, his increase accumulated from his wise use of his stewardship, will be turned into a common fund, or storehouse. This fund, or property, or whatever the commodity may be, can be drawn on from time to time by those in need. They in turn, when their circumstances are better, will begin to contribute to the storehouse. For the Lord has said 'he that is idle shall not eat the bread nor wear the garments of the laborer.'[39]

"He also said, 'there is enough and to spare; yea, I prepared all things, and have given unto the children of men to be agents unto themselves. Therefore, if any man shall take of the abundance which I have made, and impart not his portion, according to the law of my gospel, unto the poor, and the needy, he shall with the wicked, lift up his eyes in hell, being in torment.'[40] It must be a voluntary offering, done out of our love for God and our fellowmen."

Alma turned to Ella. "How is it with you, Ella?" he asked kindly. "Have you not received your testimony of the Reorganization?"

Ella studied her hands for a long moment. "No, Alma," she said at last, "not sufficiently at least to warrant wounding my mother and father another time. Granted, your church seems to receive the greater blessings, but the evidence for Father Cutler seems so strong. I must know for sure."

"Well, continue to pray with an open mind," advised Alma, "and the Lord will grant your blessing."

Ella thanked him and then feeling she must escape, went to see about the children. How she wished she could feel like she was one of them. They seemed so happy and sure. She was torn between pleasing Winfield and remaining loyal to her parents. But she realized that neither reason was valid. She really did need a testimony from the Lord, as Alma had said. She decided to spend more time in prayer. Perhaps she would fast once a week for that special purpose.

The next morning, Leon and Winnie kissed their mother good-bye and started down the little sandy road toward school. In a few minutes, however, they came running back. "Ma," shouted Winnie, "come and see!"

"What is it, Winnie?" asked Ma, "why have you not gone on to school. You may be late."

"It's the geese, Ma," said Leon, "there's millions of them on the wheat field and all of them talking at once!"

Ma picked up Hallie and taking Maude by the hand, followed the boys. Outside, she could hear the noise of their conversation. Sure enough, as they topped the hill, she could see the wheat field almost completely covered by wild geese, their necks outstretched and mouths open honking loudly to each other. While they watched, another flock, snow geese, came from the north, but instead of landing, they remained in the air, circling, diving and seemingly doing aerial acrobatics, their pure white feathers reflecting the morning sun. For several minutes they hung there, suspended in mid air, and then one lone goose rose from the field, followed by several others. As they rose, the group of snow geese, joined them, falling into formation. At last all of the geese rose from the field, their calling almost deafening, and several great V formations filled the sky heading to the south. Ma and the children watched until they were nearly lost from sight.

Ma bent down and hugged the boys. "I'm so glad you came back to tell us about the geese, boys. That was a wonderful sight. They have been feeding on the grain left in the field. The ones in the air were just waiting for the ones on the ground, and they were all talking about the long trip they were about to take. They will fly many, many miles before they reach their warm winter home in the south. You know, Jesus talked about the birds to his disciples. He said, 'Behold the fowls of the air, for they sow not, neither do they reap, nor gather into barns; yet their heavenly Father feedeth them.' So he told them not to worry about their own food and clothing, because God loved them even more than the birds."

As Ella walked back to the house amid the bright beauty of the fall colors, she thought about the example of the birds and remembered the years of the grasshoppers, when in spite of the fact that there was hardly any harvest, they had been provided for. A wonderful feeling of gratitude to the Heavenly Father filled her being and she renewed her decision to pray and fast about the Lord's will in her life.

The geese had been a harbinger of the winter days to come, for in less than a week, a blizzard nearly hid the little log cabin from sight. The bitter cold came in, then, and it was as if the Gould household were the only one on earth, isolated by the snow and cold. But though it was cold outside, there was warmth and love inside the little cabin. Winfield piled a large supply of wood inside and kept the fire roaring. Ella kept a tub of snow on the stove to melt for water to use. She cooked up big kettles of stew and porridge and huge pans of cornbread to eat with maple syrup.

CHAPTER 21

Ella's Decision, 1884

There was no school for the boys during the deep winter months. Christmas came and went, with little outside activity, aside from the chores. The days were short and the dark nights seemed endless, for their candles and tallow lamps gave feeble light.

One day when the morning work was done, Ella settled down to knitting wool socks and mittens. Winfield gathered the children around him and told them stories from the Bible and the Book of Mormon.

"Tell us the story of Nephi," said Winnie, "when he broke his bow."

"Very well," answered Pa, "do you remember where they were when he broke his bow?"

"In the wilberness," was Winnie's quick reply.

"It's wi*lder*ness, Winnie," corrected Leon.

"What is the wilderness?" questioned Maude.

"That is a good question, Maudie," said Pa. "A wilderness is a place where there are no people living, no cities or farms, no stores to buy food from. When your Grandpa George and I first came here to Silver Lake, this was a wilderness. There were only trees and prairie, bears and deer and other wild creatures. Sometimes Indians came through on hunting trips, but they had no village here. The wilderness where Nephi and his family were may have been a desert, where there is only sand and cactus, we're not sure.

"But Lehi and his family and Ishmael and his family had stopped to rest in this wilderness, and get food. They were hungry. They didn't have any vegetables or fruit and had to depend on killing wild animals for food. So Nephi and his brothers went out to hunt, but first thing, Nephi's good steel bow broke. Laman and Lemuel were angry with Nephi for breaking his bow, because it was the only good bow left. They had only slings, with stones, like I made for you boys, with a forked stick, remember?

"The whole group was suffering from hunger and even Father Lehi began to complain to the Lord. But Nephi made a bow out of wood and whittled some strong straight sticks for arrows. He went to his father and asked him to ask the Lord where he should go to hunt for food, because Nephi had faith in God. The Lord caused writing to come on the ball or compass which He had given them at the beginning of their trip. The Lord scolded them for complaining instead of having faith, and told Nephi to go up the mountain to look for food.

"He went by himself, believing what the Lord had written on the ball. And sure enough he was able to kill some animals that would do for food. We don't know what they were, it just calls them beasts, so maybe one was a deer and another a big bear. When he went back to the camp with his catch, everyone was happy and joyful, and they thanked the Lord over and over and told Him they were sorry they had complained. It was another lesson for the people to have faith and trust in God. He will take care of us, too, if we trust Him."

That evening, as they sat by the fire, Ella was knitting and Win was enjoying scraping a big juicy turnip. The children were all asleep. Ella looked up from her work and said to Win, "You are doing a good job teaching the children. What will you tell them about the church?"

He looked at her with a quizzical grin on his face. "I'm waiting for that until we think alike."

"Oh, Win," she said with a sigh, "I have prayed and prayed and I don't seem to receive an answer."

"Suppose we talk about our beliefs," he suggested. "Maybe that will help."

"All right," she answered, "where shall we start?"

Win thought for a few minutes. "I'm sure we both believe in God as the Supreme Power, and in Jesus Christ as His only begotten Son." Ella nodded. "We believe Jesus established His church while He was on earth, but that because of apostasy, the Holy Spirit was withdrawn and the authority to administer the ordinances was taken away."

"That was why," interposed Ella, "there had to be a restoration. Even though there were many people who believed in Jesus, His church was not visible on the earth. He had placed apostles, prophets, bishops, elders, etc., as officers of His kingdom, each fulfilling specific tasks and performing specific ordinances. But 'without the ordinances thereof, and the authority of the priesthood, the power of godliness is not manifest unto men in the flesh.'"[41]

Win smiled at her. "You see," he continued, "we are very close in our beliefs, my dear. Then we agree, also, that as was prophesied in Revelations 14:6,7, the angel came to bring the everlasting gospel back to earth. It was done through the human vessel of Joseph Smith, who sought earnestly to know concerning Jesus' church, and others whom the Lord called to help. John the Baptist was sent to ordain Joseph and his friend Oliver to the Aaronic priesthood.

"The same gifts and blessings of the Holy Spirit," continued Winfield, "were manifest among the Latter Day Saints, that were found among the early ones, as long as they continued obedient. The time came when false precepts were being introduced by some of the influential people, although denounced by Joseph and Hiram. Joseph came to realize he would sacrifice his life, and appointed his son, Joseph, to take his place."

"That is the point on which we differ," said Ella. "Joseph appointed seven men to take charge of the church. Alpheus Cutler was the last of the seven and he reorganized the church. I just can't see how it can be any different, Win, I'm sorry."

"However, that was never recorded," countered Win, "and there are several witnesses to the fact that Young Joseph was set aside."

They were both quiet for a long time. Finally, Win said, "Jesus said 'Ye shall know them by their fruits.' Keep that in mind, dear."

One cold day, George came to the house. As he stamped the snow from his feet, he said gently, "Buckley Anderson received a letter from a friend in Lamoni, Iowa. In it is a testimony I thought might interest you. I will leave it with you to read, and pick it up before next Sunday. He wants it back."

"Thanks," returned Ella, "I will read it when the children take their naps."

She fixed lunch for the children, but refrained from eating as she had been fasting from lunch for some time. She felt she had her answer since the day she and Win had talked of their beliefs, but she still prayed for a special answer from the Lord that perhaps she might persuade Win. At last, all was quiet and she sat in her rocker to read the letter. There was news of the many new people who had been led to the Reorganized Church of Jesus Christ of Latter Day Saints, as it was called. There was a quote from a man who had been a scribe or secretary to Joseph while he was alive. This man, James Whitehead, had written thus:

"I recollect a meeting that was held in the winter of 1843, at Nauvoo, Illinois, prior to Joseph Smith's death, at which the appointment was made by him, Joseph Smith, of his successor. Joseph Smith did the talking. There were present Joseph and Hyrum Smith, John Taylor, and some others who also spoke on the subject; there were twenty-five, I suppose, at the meeting. At that meeting, Joseph Smith was selected by his father as his successor. He was ordained and appointed at that meeting. Hyrum Smith, the Patriarch anointed him, and Joseph, his father, blessed him and ordained him and Newell K. Whitney poured the oil on his head, and he was set apart to be his father's successor in office, holding all the powers that his Father held. I cannot tell all the persons that were present, there was a good many there. John Taylor and Willard Richards, they were two of the twelve, Ebenezer Robinson was present and George J. Adams, Alpheus Cutler and Reynolds Cahoon. I cannot tell them all; I was there too."[42] The friend of Buckley's added that he had heard Brother Whitehead tell this many times, and he would hold up his hands to heaven before God, and say, "This is the truth, for it is a positive fact."

As Ella read those words, there came to her the warm rush of the Holy Spirit. Tears streamed from her eyes and she knelt there praising God, and into her mind came the words of Jesus, "When he, the Spirit of truth, is come, he will guide you into all truth." It was the first time she had known such an outpouring of the Holy Spirit. Never, in the Cutlerite meetings had she sensed it so. No doubt was left in her mind. She knew it had come as confirmation to the testimony of that man, in answer to her prayer for guidance.

Several days went by. She could not bring herself to tell Win what she had experienced, nor did she show him the letter. It was still too sacred and personal. Secretly she knew that she was ready to be baptized. Was it pride, she wondered, that kept her from telling Win. How long had it been since his experience of being told "his companion would one day be one with him?" She counted up. It had been in the fall of 1875. This is already 1884. Over eight years. How patient he had been, she thought. He had known she would one day see the light. Tears of joy came once again. How good the Lord had been to give her such a wonderful husband. She remembered how angry she had been when he told her he was going to be baptized. He had tried to explain the wonderful experience he had received. She could understand now. She felt her pride melting away and she knew she must tell Win soon. Then and there, she begged forgiveness of her heavenly Father and covenanted with Him to be obedient to His commandments.

—————➤•◦•◄—————

"My throat hurts, Ma," complained Maude. "I don't feel good."

Ella felt her forehead. "You have a fever, dear," she said. "Climb up in my bed and I'll fix you some tea. Remember Aunt Norie telling us about the Indian plant, yellow root, she uses? I found some of the plants in the woods last fall and dug them up so we could use them if we got sick. Here is your rag dolly to keep you company."

Ella cut the dried root in small pieces and set them to boil on the stove. She stirred the coals and laid dry bark on them for a quick fire. While the root simmered, she sang some of the little songs the children loved. Winnie listened and began to sing along with her. Leon, the studious one, was busy reading in the Wilson Reader. Hallie was asleep still in the trundle bed.

When the tea was ready, Ella fed Maude a spoonful. "It tastes awful, Ma, I don't like it!"

"Just think about it making you better, Maudie," said Ma. "Take just a little more, now." Obediently, she opened her mouth, but such a grimace as came on her little face! Ella put cold cloths on her forehead to lower the fever, but nothing seemed to help.

"Tell me a story, Ma, Please?" Maude asked in a tired little voice.

Ella dipped the cloths again in cool water and placed them carefully on her head. "Very well, dear," she began, "I'll tell you an Indian story. This story happened when I was a little girl, just about your size. Ma had just brought in some vegetables from the garden. She asked Lu and Em to wash them for her. They had picked up all but a great big rutabaga, when an Indian squaw walked in the door. She was carrying her papoose in the cradle board on her back. I was kind of scared of her so I hid behind a chair. The Indian lady kept standing there looking at that big rutabaga. Finally, she motioned to Ma that she wanted it.

"'What will you trade me for it?' Ma asked her. 'Will you give me your Papoose?'

"She shook her head, but kept standing there. After a long time, she took the cradle board off her back, handed it baby and all to Ma, picked up the baga and away she went. We were all so surprised! Ma fixed a pan of warm water and bathed that cute little baby. She didn't have any clothes on. She was just padded all over with the fuzz from the cattails. We dressed her in some of May's little clothes. Ma let each of us take turns holding her, it was such fun. When she went to sleep, we laid her in the little cradle. Ma went outside to get a bucket of water. While she was gone, we saw that squaw slip back in the house. She went straight to the cradle, picked up her baby and slipped back out into the shadows.

"Ma just laughed when she came back. She said 'I thought she would be back when the baga was eaten, but we had the fun of having that sweet little thing for a few hours."

Just then Win came in. Ella told him about Maude's trouble. "The fever is worse, Win. I don't know what else to do. Her throat is so red. Do you suppose it is diphtheria?"

Winfield's face was grave at the thought of that deadly disease. "It is simply too cold to take her out to the doctor and I doubt if he could get here through the drifts. Suppose I go get Pa and ask him to administer to her. Is that all right?"

"Oh, yes," answered Ella, "please do. Of course, it is cold for him to get out, too."

"But he never lets anything stand in the way, when he is called to do the Lord's work," assured Win. "The path is broken between our houses, so it won't take long. I'll go right away."

Wrapping Maude in her blanket, Ella picked her up and sat with her in the rocking chair by the fire. "Grandpa is coming to pray for you, Maude," she said comfortingly. "Jesus will help you to feel better."

The door soon opened and the two men entered along with a whoosh of cold air. They hung their coats on the pegs by the door and came to the fire to warm their hands. Leon left his book and ran to welcome his grandpa, who gave him a hug. "You'll soon be big enough to come down and help me with my chores, Leon," he said, as he tickled his ribs. "Before I go back home, I want to hear you read."

"I like to read, Grandpa," answered Leon. "Books are wonderful. I can even read some of the Bible."

"That's a good book to read, Leon, the best. The Bible tells about Jesus laying His hands on people and making them well. It tells us in James 5:13,14, 'Is any sick among you? let him call for the elders of the church; and let them pray over him, anointing him with oil in the name of the Lord; and the prayer of faith shall save the sick, and the Lord shall raise him up.' Do you believe that?"

"Yes, Grandpa, are you an elder?"

"The Holy Spirit spoke to apostle T.W. Smith and told him to ordain me to the office of elder, the same day I was baptized. So I have authority to use the ordinance of the laying on of the hands to administer to the sick in Jesus' name. That is what we will do now for little Maudie." Leon's eyes were big with wonder, and Winnie, who had heard every word, came close.

Father George, his hands now warm from the fire, poured a small amount of oil on Maudie's head and held it gently between his hands, as he prayed humbly and earnestly to the Heavenly Father. He admitted that he, himself, had sins, but asked forgiveness and that his faith and that of the others would be recognized by the Lord. He asked Him to remove the trouble from her body, that she might be well, and that He would continue to bless her that she might grow in strength and understanding. When he had finished, he bent down and kissed Maudie's cheek, and she looked up at him with a sweet little smile.

"Thank you, so much, Father George," said Ella. "You always bring such comfort." She put Maudie back in the bed, tucking her in, giving her a kiss. "You rest now and when you wake up, you will feel better."

"But Ma," she said, "I feel better now. I'm hungry."

Ella felt her head with her own cheek. The fever was down. She looked at Winfield. As their eyes met she felt such a power of love as to nearly overpower her. "Let her eat," was all he said.

While Maudie ate her soup, Winnie sat on Grandpa's knee and Leon read from his Reader. Then it was Winnie's turn. Grandpa coaxed him to read and helped him with the words he didn't know. "Learn all you can, boys," said Grandpa George, "it is much easier to get along if you can read and understand about God's world. When the weather warms and you go back to school, I want you to come to my house to study your lessons. I would be happy to help you practice your spelling and learn your numbers." They both agreed it would be fun to do that.

Maudie continued to feel better. Her fever did not come back. Her throat was still a little sore. So Ella continued to give her small doses of yellow root tea. She remembered reading something in the Doctrine and Covenants about herbs.

She asked Win to look it up.

"Here it is," he said, "in section 42:12. 'And whosoever among you are sick, and have not faith to be healed, but believe, shall be nourished with all tenderness with herbs and mild food, and that not by the hand of an enemy.' The Lord has provided the herbs and plants for our benefit. I believe Maudie would be well anyway, but perhaps this herb with help to strengthen her system to help her stay well."

That evening, their prayers were full of gratitude for the blessing of the day. Maude was sleeping peacefully and so were the others. Ella had picked up her knitting and Win was reading the scriptures. Suddenly, he lay down his book and turned to Ella. "Ella," he began carefully, "suppose you knew that tomorrow you would die, and you believed your eternal salvation depended on belonging either to the Josephite or the Cutlerite church, which one would you rather belong to?"

Ella knew the moment had come. She took her time putting her knitting down and then she turned to him. Emotion nearly choked her speech, but she managed to say, "I would rather belong to the Josephite Church! And I have promised God I will be baptized at the first opportunity."

Instantly, she found herself enveloped in his strong embrace and she clung to him. The moment was too full for words, but the happy tears flowed freely down both of their faces. Wrapped up in that moment, were his many prayers, the prophecy by Brother Smith, her prayers and fears, his patience with her. It was as if those eight years had melted away. Later, she told him of the letter Father George had brought, and of the wonderful Spirit of confirmation the Lord had given her. "I knew then," she told him, "but I had to overcome my pride. Today put the final touch on that. I remembered what Alma said that day, that 'the Lord was confirming the work with signs following.'" Winfield was still too full of emotion to respond.

The weather was cold and two feet of snow on the ground, but the little schoolhouse was full every night. Brother Thomas Nutt was preaching a series of missionary sermons. Ella felt he was answering any remaining questions she might have had. Ella's sister May and her husband Freeman Anderson were attending, also.

"What do you think, Ella?" asked May, the first evening.

"Well, May, I had already promised God I would be baptized at the first opportunity. He gave me a wonderful confirmation. I can no longer hesitate. I am sorry our parents feel so sad about it, but I feel I must obey God."

"It is because of Mother that I have hesitated," answered May. "But I truly believe this is Jesus' church and I want to be a part of it. If you are going to be baptized, I am too."

"Em and Ed plan to be baptized down in Battle Lake the next day," reminded Ella. "That will be a big blow to the folks, but at least it will be over all at once. It does seem strange that they cannot see how clearly the scripture is concerning the succession (forgetting for the moment that it had taken her eight years to see it clearly). I wish Cordie and Lester could be baptized, too."

By the last night of the series there were seven ready for baptism. Winfield, Freem and Jedidiah Anderson with Brother Nutt worked almost all day March 4, 1984, shoveling the two feet of snow from frozen Silver Lake, and then cutting through two feet of ice to make room for the baptisms.

Ella was first to enter the icy water. Win lowered her gently down into the water. Brother Nunn spoke briefly to her before he raised his hand to heaven, saying in a firm clear voice, "Ella Gould, having been commissioned of Jesus Christ, I baptize you in the name of the Father and of the Son and of the Holy Ghost, Amen." She gasped as she was raised out of the cold, watery grave, but she looked up and smiled at her waiting husband, feeling that, indeed, her old rebellious self had been buried, and she was a new creature in Christ.

Win drew her out again, immediately wrapping her tightly in a woolen blanket and carrying her to the sleigh. "I love you, Ella," he said as he quickly kissed her and then went back to help with her sister, May. When May and Amanda Anderson were also tucked snugly in, Win drove the sleigh to his house and helped the girls inside so they could change. The others would be taken to George's house.

When all the candidates were thoroughly dry and warm, the people gathered at George and Eleanor's home in the spirit of celebration. The Andersons were so glad to have their family united in the church. And Ella and Win felt the Lord had indeed blessed them. George led the group in singing some hymns. Brother Nutt offered prayer and then one by one, Elder George and Elder Nutt laid their hands on the heads of the baptized members, confirming their covenants and bestowing the gift of the Holy Ghost. The sweet influence of the Holy Spirit moved among them creating the tie that binds.

CHAPTER 22

Reconciliation

A bright blue sky arched beautifully over the "Land between two shining lakes," as Winfield and his family rode past Old Town, on into new Clitherall and out around the east end of Battle Lake. The feel of spring was in the air and even though there was still some ice on the lakes, the promise was there. This was their first trip to see Ella's parents since her baptism. Both wondered in their hearts whether they would be welcomed. No worries bothered the four children, however.

The buggy rattled over the outlet bridge. "That's Uncle Vet's house, Winnie," said Leon. "And there is the schoolhouse. We're almost there!"

Maude and Winnie stretched their necks trying to be the first to see Grandma Whiting's house. "Is that it?" asked Maude, pointing to the little house on the right.

"That's Aunt May's house," chimed in Winnie, proud to give some information, "but there, see Maude, that's Grandma's house, it's bigger."

Winfield looped the reins around the hitching post, lifted Hallie from Ella's arms and then gave her his hand to help her down. "I'm so frightened, Win" she murmured. "I do hope Ma will not be rude to you again."

"Don't worry, Ella," he replied, "your people are true Christians. They are hurt, but we must show them we love them and I am sure they feel the same way."

"Hello, Uncle Lute," said Winfield as he reached to shake hands. "We brought our little tribe for a visit if you are not too busy."

"No, come on in."

Grandma came to take their coats and busied herself a minute in the bedroom. When she came back, her hair was smoothed back, her apron changed, but her eyes were red. An awkward silence filled the room until Lester showed the children the cat and kittens in a basket in the kitchen.

"Oh, Grandma," Maude coaxed, "can I hold one, please?"

"Yes, dear," she answered, "just be careful."

So all the children, even Hallie went to see the kittens. Ella went to her mother and put her arms around her. She detected a few more lines in her forehead, but she was still the pretty lovable mother she had always been. The return embrace was warm and strong and Ella knew she was welcome. They visited about the weather, the family, the children.

"I am expecting another baby in September, Ma," said Ella.

"Oh, my dear! and you went into that icy cold water in March? How could you?"

"I could not do otherwise, Mother." She paused. "The Lord has blessed me so much. The baby is beginning to move, so it is fine. I am so sorry if my sisters and I have made you feel bad. We love you so much and respect your feelings. We wished you were with us. We have had some wonderful experiences." She had a sudden desire to explain how the Lord had answered her prayers, but sensed a slight withdrawal in her mother's gestures and stifled the urge.

Meanwhile, Winfield and Uncle Lute talked about the good syrup crop and the possibility of getting into the fields in the next two weeks. Winfield studied the man he had come to love almost as his own father. Although he was a little stooped and his hair was streaked with gray. his stern features showed the honesty and integrity of his character.

"Uncle Lute," he said finally, and there was tenderness and feeling in his voice. "Please don't feel you have lost your daughter, or that she has rejected you. She loves you more than ever. No one coerced her; she made her own decision after an experience with the Holy Spirit. And she could hardly wait to obey."

"I'm trying not to blame you, Winfield. There have been so many bitter words, I will not add to them. Though I am concerned for my children's welfare, they must live their own lives. My hope is the Lord will have mercy because of their desire to serve him." He was quiet for a time, then the slightest smile crossed his face. "Family ties are very important," he said, "and I would not think of breaking them. You come and bring my grandchildren here as often as you can."

Late in the year, the Minnesota District conference of the Reorganized Church of Jesus Christ of Latter Day Saints, or "Josephite" church as many people called it, met in Girard, at the home of Buckley Anderson. The main business was the decision to build a church in that area. A committee was chosen to carry out the plans. The committee included three of the Anderson men, Buckley, William and J.R. Also chosen were Clayton Gould, and Henry Way, who had recently moved to Girard from Oak Lake.

Clayton was enthusiastic. "Pa," he said, "we need to get this going and have it ready for the next conference. How many hours can you donate a week? You, too Winfield?"

"My work on the stage is over, so I will have more time," answered Winfield. "I'll divide my time between helping Pa on his house and volunteering for the church."

"Now that my house is roughed in," said Pa, "I can spare time to help. Will you get the lumber from Rueben Oaks saw mill?"

"Yes, we will, except for the inside sealing lumber. If we can get plenty of work donated, it shouldn't cost too much."

The work progressed on the church as the weather made it possible, with many of the men of the church donating their time. By the conference held in June, 1885, it was ready, though not completely finished inside. All the saints from Silver Lake, Oak Lake and Girard, met rejoicing. This was the first church building erected in Minnesota by the Reorganized Church of Jesus Christ of Latter Day Saints.

CHAPTER 23

A Trial of Faith

The new baby Ella had told her mother she was expecting was born September, 9. She was named Ethel Jeanette. By the time she was a year old she was walking and beginning to talk. Leon was now eight, Winnie seven, Maude five and Hallie three. Effie Sherman spent a great deal of time at the Gould household, helping Ella with the work and caring for the little ones. When weather and time permitted, the Goulds and Shermans visited each other. They now had the church in common and many were the conversations they enjoyed, discussing different aspects of the gospel. Often, when the weather was cool, the children played on the floor hearing and learning, while their parents talked religion. Effie, young and interested in the children, helped guide their play.

"You have a new horse, Alma," said Winfield one day as the Sherman wagon drove up to the door. "Looks like a spirited young fellow."

"That he is," rejoined Alma. "But I think he has good possibilities, if I can train him right."

"Come on in, Ann," called Ella. "Stew is just about ready. I thought it would taste good this cold day."

"I can smell it clear out here," answered Ann. "I brought some pumpkin pies to go with it."

Ella sent Leon, Winnie and Plinnie to gather the eggs. Lucie and Mattie hurried in with their treasures of paper dolls, to play with Maude and Hallie. Effie took charge of the younger ones, singing songs and telling them stories.

Over the dinner table, the talk turned to the hard times. "The drought just about ruined us," began Alma. "I have been cutting wood to sell to make ends meet. We are thankful, though, for many blessings. The children have been well and we have hope for the future. How wonderful are the promises of the Lord. I believe the hardships of this life help to shape us for the life to come."

"We felt the drought here, too," returned Winfield. "Wheat was poor. However, we were able to put away plenty of vegetables."

"Yes," chimed in Ella, "our crop of rutabagas was especially good. They took advantage of the late rains. We have plenty to share." She looked at Win. "Can't we send some home with them?"

"We sure can. Come on, Alma, let's go get them, and some fresh air in the mean time."

The afternoon passed too quickly. Winfield and Ella promised to return the visit soon and the wagon load of Shermans headed back to Clitherall, thankful for the gift of rutabagas.

———————

Winfield opened the door, letting in the cold November wind. He seemed not to notice the little girls waiting to be picked up as usual. His heart was heavy with the tragic news he had learned in the village. He lowered his tired body down onto the chair by the door.

"Win!" she said, trembling, "what has happened?"

"I have bad news, Ella," he began, and shook his head, trying to rid his mind of the trauma. "It's Alma. That skittish horse. He never should have tried to use it."

Ella went to him, laying her hand on his shoulder, waiting for his sobbing to subside.

He looked up at her, tears in his eyes. "He's dead. He was hauling a load of wood into Clitherall. The train whistled...the horse bolted and ran...he fell...somehow between the wagon and the train and the wood."

"Poor Ann," sobbed Ella, "what will she do? They were having it hard already."

The children stood wide-eyed. "Plinnie's Pa?" asked Leon.

"Yes, Leon, your friend's Pa," he answered, suddenly aware of the children's worried faces. "It is hard for such a thing to happen. Our consolation is that he was a friend of Jesus, and I feel sure that is who he is with now. It is Ann and the children we must pray for and try to help." He took out his kerchief to wipe his tears. "I can't understand why the Lord allowed it to happen. He was doing such a good work."

The Cutlerite's log church was packed and some people stood outside. Everyone had known and respected Alma Sherman. The preacher, Elder Hiram Holt, a Josephite, took his place behind the pulpit and the quiet whispering became hushed.

"Cutler Alma Sherman," began the minister, "was born Dec. 6, 1848, at Silver Creek, Iowa. He was the son of Almon Sherman and Lois Cutler Sherman and grandson of Alpheus and Lois Cutler. The Sherman's homestead was near Battle Lake, but they later moved to Oak Lake in Becker County. Alma married Ann Whiting. Just last year they returned from Oak Lake and settled near Old Town.

"Alma was an elder in the Reorganized Church of Jesus Christ of Latter Day Saints, and was known widely and respected for his faith in Jesus Christ, and the many healings the Lord performed under his hands. He was a man of God. I am sure that when he stood before our Lord for that first judgment, he was ushered into Paradise and welcomed there. Remember, Jesus said to the repentant thief on the cross, 'Today shalt thou be with me in paradise.'

"There is a partial judgment at the time the spirit leaves the body and goes to God and the body to the grave. The spirits of the righteous go to Paradise; that is, those who have had opportunity to learn of Jesus and have believed. There they will have opportunity to continue learning, and may have the privilege of ministry from Jesus and others who have achieved a high level of spirituality.

"This partial judgment also sends those who were not willing to believe or conform their will to Jesus' teachings, to hell, or the prison house. But evidently, according to Peter, even there they may obtain ministry. How wonderful to think that possibly Alma is preaching to some of those disobedient souls. He was certainly qualified. Truly the opportunities of life and service are gone beyond recovery, but there is still hope for them in the star glories if they respond, repent and confess that Jesus is indeed the Christ. We are told that even the glory of the telestial, or star glory, 'surpasses all understanding.'

"Our God is a just God, and wills that all people might obtain eternal life. When Jesus gave his life on the cross, and was resurrected, he overcame death and obtained the 'keys of hell and of death.'[43] Those souls who have chosen evil are sent to the prison house. John quotes Jesus as saying, 'The hour is coming and now is, when the dead shall hear the voice of the Son of God; and they who hear shall live.'[44] And after Jesus had ascended to heaven, Peter wrote: 'For Christ once suffered for sins, the just for the unjust, being put to death in the flesh, but quickened by the Spirit, that He might bring us to God. For which cause He went and preached to the spirits in prison, some of whom were disobedient in the days of Noah....that they might be judged according to men in the flesh, but live in the spirit according to the will of God.'[45]

"At the return of Christ, the righteous dead will be resurrected, spirit and body reunited, and live and reign with Him on earth for a thousand years. 'And the graves of the saints shall be opened, and they shall come forth and stand on the right hand of the Lamb, when he shall stand upon Mount Zion, and upon the holy city, the New Jerusalem, and they shall sing the song of the Lamb day and night for ever and ever.'[46] Also, those who died without having had an opportunity to know about Christ, will at this time, it seems, have that opportunity. It is at the end of the millennial reign that Satan will again be loosed to test those who have been born during those years. But the forces of evil will be destroyed and death and hell shall give up their dead. Then will take place the resurrection of the unjust, for as Paul said, 'there shall be a resurrection of the dead, both of the just and unjust.'[47]

"'And I saw the dead, small and great, stand before God; and the books were opened, and another book was opened, which is the book of life; and the dead were judged out of those things which were written in the books according to their works.'[48] Then shall each one be sent to their final destiny. Each soul will be awarded that place which he has been willing to fit himself for. And only those who continue to be rebellious, after all Christ can do, will go away into the second death, or the lake of fire and brimstone.

"'And this is the gospel, the glad tidings which the voice out of the heavens bore record unto us, that he came into the world, even Jesus to be crucified for the world, and to bear the sins of the world, and to sanctify the world, and to cleanse it from all unrighteousness; that through him all might be saved, whom the Father had put into his power, and made by him; who glorifies the Father, and saves all the works of his hands, except those sons of perdition, who deny the Son after the Father has revealed him.'"[49]

The sad procession of wagons and buggies wound its way slowly up the road from the log church to the top of the hill where the bodies of many of the pioneers lay waiting the day of resurrection. There, Ann and their children said their last farewell to husband and father. Winfield and Ella took their turn comforting them, assuring Ann they would help her all they could.

As Winfield stood there in the cold winter sunshine, he remembered the first time he had stood on that same hill, looking out over the land between the two shining lakes. Today the lakes lay frozen and still, symbolic of the body of his friend. But, now, within his heart burned clear and strong the faith that one day, Alma's righteous spirit would be reunited with an incorruptible body, vibrant and full of life, just as he knew that after the long cold winter, the lakes would again be shining, full of life and movement. Crowding out the sorrow, was a great feeling of wonder and awe at the marvelous love of God and Christ who had made that possible.

CHAPTER 24

Changing Times, 1888

Twenty years had passed since the Gould family first began to plow the prairie, build their home and put down their roots. The wild and lonely wilderness had developed into a progressive, industrious countryside. Minneapolis was the flour capital of the world. Nearly one thousand roller mills were operating in the state, powered by the rivers which coursed their way between the lakes. Ottertail County was the largest flour producing area west of Minneapolis. In 1887, a man by the name of William E. Thomas, bought land in a picturesque spot on the Ottertail River in the Maine Township. The river was swift, deep and dependable. He visioned a booming flour mill on the spot, and began building a dam.

The railroad companies continued to increase the network of rails out to small towns, making the transportation of wheat and flour much easier than in previous years. The telegraph and at last the telephone helped the pioneers keep in touch with the rest of the nation. Fergus Falls, now the County Seat, was producing a newspaper.

The Indian people, who had moved from place to place to follow the seasons' yield, were being pushed, gradually, but surely, onto the reservations. White Earth Reservation was established in 1867. However, those living in Ottertail County were slow to give up their woodland life for the new and difficult one of farming. As the population of white farmers increased, game became less plentiful and the wild berry patches were on private property. The pioneers were tapping the maple trees. The inevitable was finally taking place. To be able to survive, they had to go to the reservation and try to learn the white man's ways.

Both George Gould and his son, Winfield, were known as successful farmers. They were sought after for advice, as well as for positions in the county and township. Both were active workers for the Republican party, especially in national elections. Winfield held a position as treasurer on the school board in Everts Township. He was supervisor and assessor for a time. The principles of honesty and integrity, coupled with an interest in people, attracted his neighbors and friends to him. He believed he was to be a good steward over those resources which came to his hand, knowing that all things belong to God.

That principle of good stewardship carried over to his family. He felt deeply his responsibility to teach the children those things which would encourage them to strive to become good citizens, both of the nation and of the Kingdom of God. The family continued to grow. Another daughter was born, February 16, 1888. They named her Nina Belle. She, too, was born in the log cabin, with only the prayer of her Grandfather Gould, and the wise care of Grandma, to bring her safely through. Effie Sherman was there, too, to carry on the work and take care of the needs of the children.

The evening after Nina was born, the family gathered around Ella's bed. Each child said a prayer of thanks for the new baby, kissed their ma and pa, and Effie helped them prepare for bed.

"My, what a household we have," said Winfield. "We have sure been blessed. But you know, there is hardly room in the loft for all of them to stretch out! What would you think if I began to plan for a bigger house for us?"

Ella smiled. "I've been dreaming of that for some time. It would be really wonderful, if you think we can afford it, and you have time. As they grow, they will need even more room than now. We could start saving for that purpose and maybe have enough to start it by the next spring."

"We'll do it!" Winfield was excited. "My job as assessor brings in extra money. I'll try to put it all aside. By the way, at that last county meeting I met Abner Tucker. He is road supervisor. We talked quite a bit. He and Emily have two children, Frank who is six and Orison who is two. They are Cutlerites."

In a few days, a letter came from Clayton and Dee. It had been nearly a year since they had loaded their covered wagons and headed for Independence, Missouri. Their immediate purpose in going was to get Dee to a milder climate for her health. But the dream of going to the place which had been designated as Zion had been in their hearts all along. Ed and Em Anderson had gone with them.

Winfield recalled with a shudder the incidents just prior to their departure. Only a few days before they were to start, their son, Orlow, who was only five years old, had died in a tragic accident. Now, however, they wrote that life was brighter. They had purchased a house on the corner of Lexington and River streets which had "five rooms, two closets, a pantry and two porches, a good barn, a cistern and an outside toilet." They also wrote of attending the laying of the corner stone for the Stone Church. Clayton had a job hauling stone for the church with his teams, son George helping. "To be involved in that work, and to meet with many other saints, including Brother Joseph, is really a taste of Zion," they wrote.

For a long moment, Winfield held the letter in his hand. He let his mind go back to the dream he had, soon after he was baptized. He had seen himself with a multitude of people on the way to Zion. Part of the dream came true, he thought. Ella is walking with me in the cause of Zion. We will yet realize the rest, I'm sure.

Ella, watching him, said gently, "Would you go, Win, if it were not for the children and myself?"

"It is because of you and the children that we must keep

the dream alive," he returned, "and well planted in their hearts. The Cause of Zion is the task the Lord Jesus has given us. I go often to the words God spoke to Oliver Cowdry through Joseph. 'I say unto you, Keep my commandments, and seek to bring forth and establish the cause of Zion: Seek not for riches, but for wisdom; and, behold, the mysteries of God shall be unfolded unto you.'[50] But just going to the Center Place doesn't make it Zion. We must learn to be obedient to the commandments, and become pure in heart. We can have a little bit of Zion right here if we do this. Then, if and when we go, we will take it with us."

CHAPTER 25

The New House

The little "Hope of Zion Branch" of the church at Silver Lake had dwindled in number. Em and Ed, Clayton and Dee were gone. Many of the Saints at Girard had moved away. Most of the members were now living close to Clitherall. George and Winfield talked with Charlie Pierce and Will Barnhard about the situation. It was decided to hold a meeting of all the members to plan what to do. The meeting was called for February 16, 1890. After much discussion, they voted to organize a branch in Clitherall combining Silver Lake, Girard and Clitherall groups into one and calling it "Union Branch."

The officers of the branch were voted as follows: William Barnhard, President; George Gould, Teacher; Charles Pierce, Priest; W.W. Gould, Clerk and Mrs. Rhoda Hunter, Treasurer.

Two years of careful planning, saving and hard work made Ella's dream come true. The new frame house was nearly ready. They had decided to build up on the next hill, just a little farther from Grandpa Gould's house. Many hands had helped with the building, including those of Leon and Winnie, who were anxious to help when they were not in school. Work had progressed through the summer, when field work permitted, in hopes it could be ready for the next baby to be the first one born it. However, little Iva Roseltha was born in the log cabin on August 19, 1890.

"The house is ready, Ella" announced Winfield one evening, soon after Iva was born. "Ma will help me arrange things and get ready, if you want, and..."

"No, Win," she answered, "I have waited this long, I can wait another week or two. Your mother has done so much and I will be glad for her help. But I do want to see to the arrangement and be a part of this important event of our lives. Thank you so much for all your hard work and thoughtfulness. It will be good to spread out a little with our brood of seven children."

One early morning, two weeks later, with the wagon loaded with the trundle bed, some chairs, and Ella sitting in the rocking chair holding baby Iva, the first load was taken to the new house. The children carried their own precious belongings and scurried over the hill to watch the proceedings.

"Leon," said Winfield, "you come help me load, while Little George and Winnie put things where your Ma wants them."

Grandpa and Grandma Gould came to help, and by late afternoon everything was moved. Effie Sherman helped Maude and Hallie make the beds in the two bedrooms upstairs, while Grandma and Ella put the finishing touches on the nice big living room and bedroom down stairs. Ethel and Nina watched baby Iva.

"Cooking is going to be fun in this nice roomy kitchen," said Ella to Grandma, as they filled the shelves in the pantry with the summer's canned and dried food. "The pantry will be such a help, and there is plenty of room for the big table. You and Father George please stay and eat with us. We need to celebrate the new house."

"I baked some pies yesterday," said Eleanor. "I'll send Maude and Hallie down to get them. I agree, we should celebrate."

When they were all assembled around the table in that big spacious kitchen for supper, Winfield asked his pa to return thanks. His prayer was a humble one of thanks for the years the Lord had watched over them; for the wonderful family He had given them; for the new home; for the gospel that was such a binding force holding them together and for the harvest that made possible the abundance of food on their table.

Looking around at the happy faces, Winfield's mind went back in time to the night he slept in Henry Way's sugar camp, when he, Pa and Clayton were on the way to Silver Lake. He remembered how he imagined himself with a good farm, and how he would build a house for a beautiful young lady. He had planned, too, to have the best home possible. In all my dreams, though, he thought, there was nothing as wonderful as what I see here tonight: two young men sons, and five beautiful daughters, and Ella, precious Ella, who has made it all possible.

"Ahem," said George, clearing his throat, "I just happened to bring my flute up with me. We have enough voices for a full choir. Soon as we finish eating, let's have a good sing."

"Let's do," chimed in Winnie, "and the first song should be 'Home Sweet Home.'"

"That brings back some memories to me," Ella remembered, "the night the children and I spent in the dark cellar when the storm took the roof off the cabin. I was so scared, but to calm the little ones, I sang to them. 'Home Sweet Home' was one that calmed me. I thought what a really wonderful home Winfield had made for me, humble though the cabin was, it was full of true love," and as she smiled at him, her eyes glistened with happy tears.

While Maude helped Ma pick up the dishes and put the food away, George began to play "Home Sweet Home." The others gathered around, blending their voices in the words of the song. The children's bedtime came and went as the singing continued. Little Nina climbed up on her ma's bed and went to sleep. Ella held Iva and nursed her, while she continued to sing. At last, it was time. They held hands in a circle and prayed their thanks to the Heavenly Father for each other and His wonderful watch care.

The harvest work was put on hold for the fall conference. Saints from Clitherall, Girard and other areas came to Silver

Lake schoolhouse. Brother I.N. Roberts and Swen Swenson preached, and Winfield was glad to have room to offer them for sleeping. On such nights, the whole family would sit up late, listening to the preachers tell experiences of healings and testimonies of how the Lord was blessing so many by confirming the truth that Jesus is truly the Christ, the Savior, and how the Book of Mormon is another witness to that fact.

CHAPTER 26

A Near Tragedy

A light rain was falling, sending showers of yellow leaves, heavy with moisture, from the basswood trees. A flock of blackbirds swooped gracefully from the sky and lit, chattering loudly, in a big oak. There was a chill in the air, bringing the knowledge that summer was definitely over.

It was the first day of the fall term of school. Leon, Winnie, Maude, Hallie and Ethel were dressed for the weather. The girls wore their capes, the boys their wool sweaters. The girls held their skirts up as they walked through the tall wet grass.

Winfield and Ella stood watching them out of sight. "This is Ethel's first year and it will be Leon's last year in our little school," mused Winfield. "He has about learned everything they can teach him. It makes me wonder where he will go in life. I hope we have given him enough training in the gospel, so he can always remain faithful."

"You have done a wonderful job teaching all of them," said Ella. "Your questions and answers on the Bible and the other books have made it fun for them to learn. Besides, you have set such a good example of living by Jesus' counsel. I suppose Leon will want to go to Battle Lake to high school next term. I'm not sure about Winnie. He is more interested in helping with the farming and in hunting and fishing."

"You are right, Ella, but he is quick to see how to improve methods and is a wonderful help to me on the farm even at his young age of thirteen. He will likely be a better farmer than I am." Winfield had a special spot in is heart for Winnie. "Well," he concluded, as he bent to give Ella a good-bye kiss, "the clouds seem to be breaking. I must get that load of wheat out to Vining. They tell me the price is good right now.

Unless there is a very long waiting line, I should be back before dark. If not, tell the boys to start the chores."

He hitched the team to the loaded wagon, securing the tarpaulin tight against the possibility of more rain. The horses pulled the load from the shelter of the barn and headed down the familiar road. He passed the schoolhouse just as the teacher rang the bell. Reining in the horses, he alighted and walked up to speak to him.

"Good morning, Mr. Hall," he said, reaching to shake hands, "it's good to have you back. Let me know if you need anything. Make sure my boys don't give you any trouble."

"If all the boys were as well behaved as yours, Mr. Gould, teaching would be a dream. They are fine. Do I see a new little girl?"

"Yes," answered Winfield, "that is Ethel. She will be six the ninth of this month. Her grandfather has taught her the alphabet and numbers. I think she will pick it up quickly." As he turned to leave, he called back to the teacher, "You will be boarding with us next month, see you then."

The sun was breaking through when Winfield reached Vining. There were several wagons waiting to be unloaded into the flathouses, most of them drawn by oxen. Winfield tied the reins to a hitching post and walked up the line. Some of the farmers recognized him and greeted him cheerfully.

"Hi, Uncle Winfield," called a young fellow from the group.

"Oh, it's you, Plinnie Sherman," came the answer, "do you have a load of wheat here today, sir?"

"Naw," he answered grinning, "I came along with Alva Murdock. I've been helping him some."

"That's fine, Plinnie, how is your ma?"

"She's doing better since she remarried," answered Plinnie thoughtfully. "She doesn't have to work quite so hard."

"Give her my best regards, Plinnie, and if you need work, just come up to Silver Lake."

"Thanks, Uncle Winfield, I may take you up on that." As Plinnie walked away, Winfield thought how tall he had grown, and how responsibility was making a man of him before his time, since the death of his father, Alma.

He went on past the waiting wagons to the office of the Andrew Grain Co. Mr. Lund greeted him cordially. "How are you, Mr. Gould. I hope your harvest was good this year. Reports are good from most places."

"Yes," answered Winfield, "my wheat made thirty bushel and it's good quality. What seems to be the going price?"

"Seventy cents for good quality," answered Mr. Lund. "By the way, you might be interested in storing some. The almanac is predicting a severe drought for 1891."

"So I heard," returned Winfield. "We had better be wise and prepare, like Joseph had the Egyptians do. Hopefully, though," he added rather jokingly, "this drought won't last seven years."

Heading back to his wagon he met Alva. "Howdy there, brother," he remarked. Ever since Alva had married Ella's sister Lu, Winfield had called him brother, their one time rivalry long forgotten. "I met your helper a while ago," he continued. "I hope he is a good one."

"Sure is, Winfield," answered Alva enthusiastically. "He is the best help I ever had."

"Ella and I have been talking about having you and Lu come up while the weather is good," said Winfield, "Orison and Cordie, too. Let's try for Saturday. Bring all the children and stay all day. I'll stop by Orison's on the way home and tell them. Think you can?"

"Sure, sounds great," returned Alva. "I'll have Lu fix up some apple pies. Is your cow still fresh? How about some whipped cream?"

"I'm sure we can manage that. We'll have a great time. Don't forget!"

With his wheat finally unloaded, Winfield headed for home as the afternoon sun dipped low in the west. He would make more trips down with wheat, he knew, but he decided to enlarge his wheat bin in the barn. Then, if there should be a shortage next year, they would have bread for themselves and to share.

———⇒►-0-◄⇐———

Such an air of festivity pervaded the new frame house on the hill. Pa and the boys were out early doing the chores. As soon as breakfast was over, Ma gave each of the girls a job.

"Maude, you make the beds and straighten up the house," she instructed. "Hallie and Ethel, I'll fix the water so you can wash the dishes. Nina, do you want to help?"

"Yes, Ma," answered that little girl, "I want to help get ready for Aunt Cordie."

"That's fine, little one," and she stooped down to give her a hug. "Your job is to keep watch of Baby Iva. If she wakes up, you talk to her and keep her happy."

When the house was shiny clean, Ma had Hallie and Maude help her with the cooking, and soon wonderful aromas began to fill the house.

"Here they come, Ma!" shouted Ethel. "I see their fancy buggy. It's Aunt Cordie and Uncle Orison."

Ma took her lovely white apron from its hook and put it on over her work apron. She smoothed her hair. Win had seen the buggy and went to meet them. Ma and all the children gathered around.

"Lu and Alva are close behind us," said Orison as he stepped off the buggy and went around to help Cordie. "We appreciate you inviting us, and it is such a nice day."

"We ordered it just for you," said Leon, laughing. Then seriously, he asked, "Is Plinnie coming with Uncle Alva?"

"Yes," returned Cordie, "he was with them. Oh, there they come now!"

Ella welcomed her sisters and proudly took them in to show off her new house. Maude, Hallie and Ethel invited Ralph and Lucie May to go to picnic rock. Win took the men and boys out to the barn.

"The boys have been good help in the field this summer," explained Winfield. "They did most of the cultivating. Leon is studying short hand. He would take his book to the field and study while the horse rested.

"The wheat did so well this year," he told them, "that I enlarged the wheat bin. I thought it especially important to save plenty, since the Almanac is predicting next summer will be a dry one." He ran his hand through the wheat, letting the grains run slowly through his fingers. "So if the Almanac is correct and you have a need for bread, remember this bin of wheat. It will be here to share. I'll soon be taking a load to the mill on Ottertail River at Phelps, for flour. That mill can put out sixty to seventy-five barrels a day."

"I was talking with Thomas, over at the mill," said Orison. "He is finally doing a booming business. He was telling me what a time they had building a dam that would hold. But the building proceeded much better. He hired a man named Royal Powers to oversee the building. He built the entire four story building with no construction sketch, but he did such a remarkable job that not a single stick of lumber was scratched or marked in any way."

Alva lifted the scythe from its hook above his head and examined the blade. "You keep the tools of your trade in good shape, Win," he commented. "I could shave with that blade!"

"They are developing a machine, now," said Orison, "that will make that scythe obsolete. It will cut and bind the sheaves."

"Seeing is believing," said Alva, as he stood the scythe down beside the bin. "You can't always count on these new-fangled ideas."

"Let's walk over to Pa and Ma's house," invited Winfield. "Pa is so proud of his flowers, and many of them are still blooming. I need to tell them to come up for dinner. Pa isn't as strong lately, but he can still keep wonderful gardens, both of flowers and vegetables. The boys and I farm his land along with ours."

Dinner was a joyful affair and when Lu's apple pie and Bossie's whipped cream had been devoured, the adults sat around the table talking of old times. Leon and Winnie, Maude and Plinnie went for a walk down to the lake. The children had gone outside to play. Suddenly there was a piercing scream, followed by cries of "Help! Come Quick!"

Quick as a flash, Cordie and Grandma Gould, who were closest to the door, ran to the barn. They came back just as quickly, carrying Hallie, blood streaming from a foot. Winfield took her in his strong arms and held her tight. Ella quickly took off her white apron and wrapped it tightly around the foot. In moments the cloth was saturated.

Hallie controlled her sobbing long enough to say, "I want Grandpa to pray for me."

George took from his pocket the ever-ready consecrated oil, and anointing her head, gave a humble, but urgent petition to the Heavenly Father for this child. Instantly, she stopped crying. Ella removed the soaked apron, calling for a clean tea towel. However, the bleeding had stopped completely!

Grandma Gould examined the wound. "It is cut clear to the bone," she announced sadly, "but the bleeding has miraculously stopped! Bandage it with the clean towel and keep her foot up. The Lord has blessed us once again."

By now, all the children had gathered around looking so solemn. "Ralph," asked Winfield gently, "can you tell us what happened?"

"We were playing in the wheat bin," ventured Ralph, chin quivering. "Hallie jumped out and landed with one foot on the scythe," and big tears streamed down his face.

A groan came from Alva. "It's my fault! Oh, God forgive me! I left that scythe standing there."

"We're not blaming anyone," consoled Winfield. "What is important is the fact that God has been at work in our midst, as you can see."

Cordie had been very quiet, but now she spoke. "I saw the blood pouring from the wound as we carried her to the house. I saw it stop instantly during Father George's prayer. Even though I am a Cutlerite, I have to admit God heard and answered the prayer of a Josephite."

Hallie's foot healed so quickly she missed only a few days of school that fall of 1890. The scar remained, however, to remind her of the blessing she had received.

CHAPTER 27

Massacre

Even though the weather was very cold, Winfield was in Clitherall on business. It was New Year's Day of 1891. As he drove the sleigh near the depot, he saw quite a crowd gathered. Tying Molly to the hitching post he walked over to investigate the reason for this gathering. Orison and Alva saw him and hurried over to him.

"News of an Indian massacre just came over the wire," explained Alva.

"Where," asked Winfield? "I thought the Indians had given up fighting since Sitting Bull was killed."

"It wasn't whites that were massacred," said Orison, "it was a band of unarmed Indians, more women and children than men. They were trying to reach Red Cloud's camp for protection from the soldiers. They got as far as Wounded Knee Creek. Their leader, Big Foot, was sick with pneumonia. The soldiers let them camp that night, but in the morning they ordered all the weapons turned over. One young buck didn't want to give his up. The soldiers grabbed him, the gun went off and then the soldiers fired indiscriminately. They are saying there were three hundred killed out of the three hundred fifty who were there."[51]

"Some of the men were saying the soldiers did a good job," said Alva, "that the only good Indian is a dead one. How can they think it right to kill women and children?"

Winfield shook his head. "If the government keeps this up," he said sadly, "there may not be any left to take the Book of Mormon to. Perhaps it is our fault. If we had persevered in teaching them the gospel, things might have been different. Nephi's vision is surely coming true. What was it he said? 'I beheld the wrath of God that it was upon the seed of my brethren; and they were scattered before the Gentiles, and were smitten.'"[52]

The tragic news of the murdered Sioux people weighed heavily on Winfield's mind. At the family devotions that evening, he told them the news he had heard. "Certainly," he said, "the Indians have done many wrong things, but in most instances they were prompted by broken treaties and being pushed from their lands. As far back as six hundred years before Christ, God had made known to Nephi that the unbelieving Lamanites, who had been cursed with dark skins, would ultimately destroy their white brothers."

"Was that why the Spaniards found no white people among the dark natives?" asked Leon? "Why did God allow it?"

"Well Leon," answered his pa, "the Lord could let it happen only because those who had once known the blessings of God, had willfully rebelled against Him. You remember that Jesus, Himself, had ministered among the Nephite people, organized His church, and all the people, including Lamanites, were converted and became righteous for two hundred years. So all the people had a knowledge of the blessings and promises of God.

"If we search through the sacred history of those people, though," continued Winfield, "we find hope for them. It is in another of Nephi's prophecies. He told that after this record, which he was making of his people the Nephites, should come to the Gentiles, they would take it to the *remnant* of their seed. So you see, there will be some left. The Lord's promises are sure. Maude, will you read to us from Second Nephi?"

Maude took the book from his hand, quickly found the place and read: "'And then shall the remnant of our seed know concerning us, how that we came out from Jerusalem, and that they are descendants of the Jews. And the gospel of Jesus

Christ shall be declared among them; wherefore, they shall be restored to the knowledge of their fathers, and also to the knowledge of Jesus Christ, which was had among their fathers. And then shall they rejoice; for they shall know that it is a blessing unto them from the hand of God; And their scales of darkness shall begin to fall from their eyes: and many generations shall not pass away among them, save they shall be a white and a delightsome people.'"[53]

"Is there not a promise also to the Jews?" asked Ella.

"Yes. Maude, go ahead and read the next two verses, please."

"'And it shall come to pass that the Jews which are scattered, also shall begin to believe in Christ: and they shall begin to gather in upon the face of the land; And as many as shall believe in Christ, shall also become a delightsome people.'" Maude finished the reading and handed the book back to Pa.

"The title page of the book, of course, tells us the book was written for the Lamanites, but also for the Jews. There are many prophecies concerning the return of the Jews to the knowledge of their Redeemer in the last days. But let us go to Isaiah 29. Winnie, will you look that up, please? It starts off with the prediction of woe to 'Ariel, the city where David dwelt,' which we know means Jerusalem and its inhabitants, telling us that they shall be brought down low, and shall speak out of the dust. He goes ahead to tell about a sealed book, but because the people are not truly worshipping God, what does he say in verse 14, Winnie?"

Winnie found the place and proceeded to read. "'Therefore, behold, I will proceed to do a marvelous work among this people, even a marvelous work and a wonder: for the wisdom of their wise men shall perish, and the understanding of their prudent men shall be hid.' Is that all, Pa?" he asked.

"It is all interesting, but skip down to read the 18th, 22nd and 23rd."

"'And in that day shall the deaf hear the words of the book, and the eyes of the blind shall see out of obscurity, and out of darkness.'" Winnie paused. "Does that mean the sealed book, Pa?"

"That is the book he is telling about just a few words back, Son. It also refers to the City of Ariel, or the house of Israel, speaking out of the dust. What book do you think he is talking about? Was the Bible sealed or did it speak out of the dust?"

"We learned in history," spoke up Leon, "there was a while in the dark ages, the only copies of the Bibles were had by the Monks or were chained to the pulpits of the churches, but there had always been copies in existence."

Hallie had been quiet, but now she said, "Pa, maybe it is talking about the Book of Mormon. It had been buried in the ground for a long, long time and then was taken out of the dust of the earth. And besides, it tells about the people who came from Jerusalem."

"That sounds like very good reasoning, Hallie," said Pa. "Now, Winnie, read the other verses. What are the results of the words of the book and the marvelous work and a wonder?"

"'Therefore thus saith the Lord, who redeemed Abraham, concerning the house of Jacob, Jacob shall not now be ashamed, neither shall his face now wax pale. But when he seeth his children, the work of mine hands, in the midst of him, they shall sanctify my name, and sanctify the Holy One of Jacob, and shall fear the God of Israel.' Shall I read the last one?" Pa nodded, and Winnie continued: "'They also that erred in spirit shall come to understanding, and they that murmured shall learn doctrine.'"

"You see the wonderful promises of the Lord," concluded Pa, "to both the people of the house of Israel on this land, the

Jews and also to all the other tribes of the house of Israel. They will not always be living in ignorance of the Lord Jesus and be in terrible circumstances. Perhaps some of you may have an opportunity to share this good news with someone of those people. One thing we can do is to pray that the gospel will soon go to them to give them hope."

CHAPTER 28

Winter 1894–1895
Birth and Death

The burdens seemed too heavy during the fall and winter. Ella was expecting, but she was not well. Many times Winfield went for Pa to come and administer. George, however, was also ill that winter, but nothing could stop him from going to Ella's side, time after time, to intercede to the Heavenly Father for this lady who was like his own daughter. Winfield watched them, and came to see a beautiful relationship develop between them.

Effie Sherman, who had always been there to help at such times, was gone. Typhoid had claimed her young life, to the sorrow of her mother as well as the Goulds. Maude at fifteen, began to take some of the responsibility for the cooking, and Hallie and Ethel helped with the care of the younger ones, the washing and house cleaning. It was a difficult time for all, but a time of learning and growing. During the cold weather, the family seldom attended services, but they had their own little devotionals at home. Occasionally, Ella's brother Art came for a visit, bringing hope and cheer.

One afternoon in early February, after George had prayed for Ella, she seemed to be feeling much better. That cheered George so much he asked the children to read to him from their text books. "You need to keep in practice, children," he said, "so you won't be behind when the spring term starts."

Hallie read from her history book about Abraham Lincoln. As she read, George, with hands clasped behind his back, paced the floor, listening and nodding at particularly interesting parts. "He was a fine man, Hallie," he would say, "a very fine man." He would continue his pacing, stopping occasionally to reach up and take from the rafter a small piece of dried beef. Using his knife, he would slice thin pieces and hand to each of the children. Winfield, watching him, felt a yearning in his heart that this good man, his father, could live a long time, he was doing so much good. Somehow, though, he felt his days were numbered.

He was called out of his reverie when Ella quietly motioned him to her side. "It is time to prepare for the birth of this child, Win," she whispered. "Do you think your Ma is able to help?"

"Are you sure, Ella? Shall I go to Battle Lake for the doctor? How soon..."

"No need for excitement, or the doctor," she said, trying to calm him. "It will be a while. I just thought we should begin to prepare. When Father George is ready to go home, perhaps you could take him and the older children to his house and bring Mother Gould back."

Win leaned down and kissed her tenderly. "I'll do anything you say, Ella. I'll ask Pa to administer once more and then I'll take them." Restraining his excitement, Winfield spoke quietly to Pa, telling him the situation. After the administration, Grandpa invited Leon, who was home from his classes in Battle lake for a few days, Winnie, Hallie and Ethel to spend the evening with him. Maude fixed a light supper for the younger ones, and after stories and prayers, she put them to bed.

Several hours later, when the baby was safely delivered and mother and baby resting, Winfield took his ma home.

"We have another girl, Pa," announced Winfield proudly, "and both are fine."

"Praise the Lord," replied George and there were tears in his eyes. "I was so worried. If you haven't named her yet, please name her Ella."

"We will consider that, Pa, your opinion should be honored. You have surely been attendant to her."

The children were excited to return home and find the new baby. "Ma," said Leon, "could we name her Gladys, she is so pretty?"

"Grandpa asked us to name her Ella," spoke up Winfield. "We will let your ma decide."

"Suppose we call her Ella Gladys," said Ma, as she smiled a tired but happy smile.

The April sun began slowly to melt the snow. The sap ran freely in the maple trees. A few brave geese returned to their nesting ground. Farmers began to plan their summer work. But Grandpa George was too tired and sick to work in his lovely garden. He seemed to know his time had come. He refused to let them call the doctors. "Only let the elders administer to me and leave me in God's hands," he said. His body succumbed to the kidney disease which had been bothering him. With his wife, Eleanor, his son, Winfield, Ella and others of his family around him his great heart beat its last.

How do you mourn the passing of a righteous man? There is sorrow for the separation, loss for the fellowship of a dear one, but ultimately there must be celebration for a life lived the Kingdom way to the very end. There must be thanksgiving for having been a part of that life. And most of all, there is hope through the Redeemer of a glorious resurrection. All of these feelings were expressed among the family, saints and friends of this good man.

At home, the family delved deeply into the scriptures, searching out those passages which spoke of eternal life, the millennium, the inheritance of the saints. Their favorite seemed to be in the experience of Joseph Smith and Oliver Cowdry, when they were given a vision of the state of the spirits of men.

"And again, we bear record for we saw and heard, and this is the testimony of the gospel of Christ, concerning them who come forth in the resurrection of the just: They are they who received the testimony of Jesus, and believed on his name, and were baptized after the manner of his burial, being buried in the water in his name, and this according to the commandment which he has given, that by keeping the commandments, they might be washed and cleansed from all their sins, and receive the Holy Spirit by the laying on of the hands of him who is ordained and sealed unto this power; and who overcome by faith, and are sealed by that Holy Spirit of promise, which the Father sheds forth upon all those who are just and true;...these are they whom he shall bring with him, when he shall come in the clouds of heaven, to reign on the earth over his people;"[54]

One of his children wrote the following tribute to him, prefaced with these words:

In loving remembrance of George Gould,
who died April 14, 1895, Age 76

In the dear old days of childhood, before I went from
    home,
O very sweet and saintly did the Sabbath morning come,
With footsteps hushed and quiet whatever wind might
    blow.
And I'd hear father singing as he walked to and fro.

The fragment of a hymn tune in tender lilting air
Would early as the dawn-light come floating up the stair.
Now martial and triumphant, now soft and sighing low
But I'd know 'twas father singing as he walked to and
    fro.

And in the little kitchen where he had knelt to pray
And crave for us a blessing at the very break of day
I'd hear his dear voice lifted from his pure heart aglow.
And it hallowed Sabbath morning as he walked to and fro.

Long years have passed since father sang in those quiet
    hours;
He's found the happy country and the fields of fadeless
    flowers.
But still on Sabbath mornings, I wake, and soft and low,
I yet can hear him singing as he walks to and fro.

As Emma had done for Grandma Sherman, Maude, now
sixteen, went to live with Grandma Gould and care for her
and George. She had her own nice room and sometimes invited her sisters to spend the night with her. Other friends
came also. Plinnie, who now wanted to be called Plin, was
living north of Ottertail lake at Town of Maine. However, he
often made the trip to Silver Lake to visit Maude. Their simple
friendship of earlier times began to blossom into love. He
was a handsome young man, and industrious. Unable to find
sufficient employment for what he had in his mind, he turned
his back on Minnesota and took the train to Independence,
Missouri. There he found a welcome with his uncle and aunt,
Clayton and Dee Gould.

Grandma's health soon began to decline. Maude was asked
to go back home to care for the rest of the family, and Winfield
and Ella went to live with Grandma and George. Less than
three years later, Grandma's tender spirit went to join that of
her husband. Little George was taken to the new house on the
hill to live with Winfield and Ella's family. Grandma's house
was left empty, but for many years, the beautiful lilacs shed
their wonderful fragrance in the spring, in testimony of the
one who had planted and carefully tended them.

May, 1898, a letter came to Ella from Clayton and Dee. She said little Minnie was still sickly, but pure sunshine to have around. Herb had been playing hooky from school. All seemed to be well otherwise. She sent a family picture which had been taken by a photographer in Independence. The whole family treasured that picture and showed it to all who came to the house.

"We need to do the same thing," said Ella one day. "War Whiting has his studio set up in Clitherall, Win. Let's plan a day when everybody can be here. You could talk to War next time you're in town." Seeing no reaction to her words, she persevered. "Please, Win, you know Winnie is planning to go to Bemidji to work in the logging camp. And Hallie and Leon will be going off to teach. We should get a family picture sometime soon."

"Takes money," said Win, a frown deepening the wrinkles between his eyes. "Besides that, I suppose you will want all of us in our Sunday best. It will take a whole day, by the time we travel the ten miles to Clitherall, spend several hours in the studio, and get back home. It's a lot of bother."

"Pa," spoke up Hallie, "I have the money from my last month's teaching. We can use it."

"We'll help you with the work when we get back," said Ethel, "won't we Nina?"

"Sure, Pa," said Nina, "we'll do all the chores so you can work in the field."

"Looks like I'm outnumbered," griped Pa. "But don't forget all these promises! I'll speak to War next time I see him. In the meantime you girls practice looking your prettiest." He gave a quick wink at Iva and went out the door.

Arrangements were finally made, protested by both Leon and Winnie. But Ella's gentle prodding finally won and all were dressed and ready to go. The day was mild and all enjoyed the ride, even Winfield. He drove the buggy up the main street of Clitherall and stopped before the building that had a sign which read: WARREN WHITING, FAMILY PHOTOGRAPHER. Winnie jumped out, looped the reins around the hitching pole, and came back and helped the little girls out.

True to Winfield's prediction, it took several hours in the studio, before the photographer was satisfied he had the best poses. He had divided the family into two groups, the older four, Leon, Winnie, Maude and Hallie in one; Winfield, Ella, Ethel, Nina, Iva and little Gladys in the other. All breathed a sigh of relief when at last they could leave. The pictures were promised for next week.

Before leaving town, they drove on over to see the new schoolhouse. "This one has two rooms," said Leon, "and will make room for two teachers, so it will be easier to teach."

They had just moved the other frame school, built in 1880, from the lot, but left it close. "The church is going to use the old one for a meeting place. So at last we have a permanent place to meet," said Winfield.

After a few stops to visit and get some supplies, they headed home as the sun told them it was about four o'clock.

"Is it all right if I say, I told you so?" said Win with a sly grin.

"Yes, Win," replied Ella, "I will give you that satisfaction. I will also say to you, thank you for your patience through the whole time. You were wonderful." She reached over and touched his hand and he squeezed it.

CHAPTER 29
The End and the Beginning

The darkness of the Middle Ages began to be pushed back during the Reformation, although there were many very dark corners remaining in the beginning of the nineteenth century. Slavery, witchcraft, child labor, oppression of the masses by the few in power, were some of those dark places.

In 1830, though only a comparative few would see, a great light began to shine. God broke the silence of the ages and spoke to a young farm boy. Once again, the foundation was laid for the coming Kingdom of Heaven. The gifts of the Spirit were again experienced. The message was sent out that the Lord was preparing to send the good news to the scattered house of Israel; He had not forgotten them, they were still His covenant children, and would be gathered together in preparation for the coming of the Lord.

The light filtered through to the sound thinkers of the day. Men's minds began to stretch and discover how to use the resources God had given, to make life easier. The cotton gin, the harvester, the steam engine, the loom, the telegraph, telephone and electricity, gave great hope that wonderful things were in store for the country.

Some of the great literature of our country was written at that time. William Cullen Bryant, who interpreted nature so beautifully, wrote these lines taken from "A Forest Hymn."

"My heart is awed within me when I think of
    the great miracle that still goes on, in silence, round me—
      the perpetual work of Thy Creation, finished,
        yet renewed forever. Written on Thy works
          I read the lesson of Thy own eternity."

William Wordsworth, wrote these inspiring words:

> "And I have felt a presence that disturbs me with the joy
>> of elevated thought,
> a sense sublime of something far more deeply interfused,
> Whose dwelling is the light of setting suns, and the round
>> ocean
> And the blue sky, and in the mind of man;
> A motion and a spirit that impels all thinking things, all
>> objects of all thought,
>> And rolls through all things."[55]

Though neither Wordsworth nor Joseph Smith had ever heard of each other, Wordsworth's words reflect a glimpse of the light of the immortal words penned through inspiration by the nineteenth century prophet:

"This Comforter is the promise which I give unto you of Eternal life, even the glory of the celestial kingdom; which glory is that of the church of the Firstborn, even of God, the holiest of all, through Jesus Christ, his Son; he that ascended up on high, as also he descended below all things, in that he comprehended all things, that he might be in all and through all things, the light of truth, which truth shineth. This is the light of Christ.

"As also he is in the sun, and the light of the sun, and the power thereof by which it was made. As also he is in the moon, and is the light of the moon, and the power thereof by which it was made. As also the light of the stars, and the power thereof by which they were made. And the earth also, and the power thereof, even the earth upon which you stand."[56]

In many ways, the end of the nineteenth century was a time of great hope for peace and prosperity for all. Alfred Lord Tennyson wrote these lines about that time.

"For I dipt into the future, far as human eye could see,
Saw the Vision of the world, and all the wonder that
would be;
Saw the heavens fill with commerce, argosies of magic
sails,
Pilots of the purple twilight, dropping down with costly
bales;
Heard the heavens fill with shouting, and there rain'd a
ghastly dew
From the nations' airy navies grappling in the central
blue;
Far along the world-wide whisper of the south wind rush-
ing warm,
With the standards of the peoples plunging thro' the thun-
der storm;
Till the war-drum throbb'd no longer, and the battle-
flags were furl'd
In the Parliament of Man, the Federation of the World.
There the common sense of most shall hold a fretful
realm in awe,
And the kindly earth shall slumber, rapt in universal law."

As the new century began, John Morely wrote: "The oracle of today drops from his tripod on the morrow. In common lines of human thought and art, as in the business of the elements, winds shift, tides ebb and flow, the boat swings. Only let the anchor hold!"[57]

And well he might. In 1831, the Lord spoke through Joseph Smith some warning for our nation and the world. It is a message that calamity is coming on the earth, and it behooves mankind to repent and trust in God. For He says, "And again, verily I say unto you, O inhabitants of the earth, I, the Lord, am willing to make these things known unto all flesh, for I am no respecter of persons, and will that all men shall know that the day speedily cometh—the hour is not yet, but is nigh at hand—when peace shall be taken from the earth..."[58] Few heeded that warning, though some did. But the new century was to prove those words true. Only a few short years were to pass before the earth was twice bathed in blood and an economic depression would devastate the years between. The scientists would continue their fast pace of discovery and invention. However, the social and spiritual development of the nation still lagged far behind. Tennyson's vision of world peace will come, but only as the result of the Kingdom of God replacing the kingdoms of man.

CHAPTER 30

The Greatest Trial

There seems always to be something to upset the status quo of our lives. All things change excepting God, and His truth. It comes to each person in one way or another. Some are crushed and turn bitter with life. Others, whose faith is anchored in God, are able to take the humbling circumstances, remembering the Lord's promise to "be with you always." The struggle to overcome brings stronger faith and growth of spirit.

Winfield and Ella had reached that low point the winter of 1900. We find them in the frame house on the hill that Winfield had built five years before. He is seated at the table, his ledger before him, pen in hand. In his deep set eyes is a look of dejection, matching the sagging of his broad shoulders.

"There won't be much tithing to pay this year," he muttered half to himself.

"What did you say?" asked Ella.

He laid aside the ledger and turned to face her. "Our losses," he said sadly, "are greater than our gains." He was quiet a while and then resumed. "There was the late frost that killed the strawberry blooms and damaged the wheat. The hot winds of July dried up much of the corn. But that was only the beginning, the minor blows.

"Our children," here his voice became choked with emotion. "Leon and Alice were married in June and he is halfway around the world."

"I know," returned Ella, "I miss them too. But remember, he is doing the Lord's work, being a secretary to Alexander Smith, out there in Australia. He is using the shorthand he taught himself while he helped with the farming."

"I'm trying, Ella, but the fact remains, he isn't here. And of course..." but the pain was still too deep and fresh to mention Winnie's name. Winnie, the one he had depended on, the one interested in the farm, was gone forever. Silently, his thoughts went back to that October night when he and Ella had returned from conference to find him with a raging fever. The doctors had pronounced it typhoid, contacted from an old well he drank from as he worked on a neighbor's field. The elders came with the Laying on of Hands. Bertha Hunter came to help care for him; she who was to have become his bride in December.

"Why, oh, why wasn't he healed? If Pa had been here..." but his voice gave way.

Tears dimmed Ella's eyes, also. But she searched for words to comfort Win, as well as herself. She rose from her chair and picked up the Doctrine and Covenants on the shelf. Opening it to Section 42, verse 12, she read aloud: "'And the elders of the church, two or more, shall be called, and shall pray for, and lay their hands upon them in my name; and if they die, they shall die unto me, and if they live, they shall live unto me.

"'Thou shalt live together in love, insomuch that thou shalt weep for the loss of them that die, and more especially for those that have not hope of a glorious resurrection.

"'And it shall come to pass that those that die in me shall not taste of death, for it shall be sweet unto them...'"

Both were quiet while the essence of those words permeated their souls. A picture came quietly into Win's mind. It was the peaceful, almost smiling look on Winnie's face as he gave his last breath. Had he seen the Lord, perhaps? or his Grandpa?

"Ella," he said at last, "what a comfort there is in those words. It's just that I want him here, a selfish feeling, I'm sure."

"It has been a hard year," said Ella, finally. "Now we have sent Maude off to be married. Three of our children gone in so short a time."

"I felt as if I were carrying out her casket when I put her trunk on the train and sent her off to Independence," he returned. "And that isn't fair, either. Plin is a good boy and he loves her. He has much of his father, Alma, in him. I look for him to do a good work for the Lord."

Ethel, who had been studying in the kitchen, came and sat by the fire. "I had a dream the other night," she said hesitantly. "I didn't understand it so I didn't tell you. But it seemed I was standing by Winnie's sick bed upstairs, looking out the window. It was night, but I saw a very black cloud. It was small, but an odd shape and very black. Then a large hand came out through the cloud and a voice said, 'Out of the cloud will I thrust my hand and pour blessings on my children.'"[59]

"Bless you, daughter," said Winfield, with a feeling of awe, "that was a spiritual dream, given you from God. The black cloud represents the troubles of this year, especially Winnie's death. If we can be faithful through this and whatever may come in the future, the gracious Lord can bless us. He has told us that after the trials come the blessings. That is truly comforting and we must thank Him for this blessing. There are other blessings I have overlooked. There was the miraculous healing of Cordie and Orison's little Jannette, remember, when she drank kerosene, and Brother I.N. White administered to her. And as a result of that, Cordie and Orison were baptized into Christ's Church. Leon was ordained a priest in June, just after his wedding. Our girls are well, intelligent and obedient." He paused, realizing there were many things to be thankful for, food, clothing, warm home.

"Yes." he said finally, " I am so thankful for these blessings, and especially for the knowledge of God's love. I'm sorry there is no increase to tithe. I will send an account to the Bishop and tell him I hope to be a better steward next year."

"Tell me Pa," spoke up Ethel, "how to figure tithing."

"Remember, when you were baptized, we figured the cost of the things that were your own?"

"Yes, and it didn't come up to very much," she answered.

"Well, we are expected to pay a tenth of our net worth as a consecration when we begin to keep the law. That is what we did for you soon after you were baptized. After that we are to pay a tenth of our increase—that which we have left after our needs and just wants are met. That is why I try to keep a record of all of our income and expenses. It says here in the Doctrine and Covenants, '...for it is expedient that I, the Lord, should make every man accountable, as stewards over earthly blessings, which I have made and prepared for my creatures.'[60] Also in Deuteronomy 14:22, it says, 'Thou shalt truly tithe all the increase of thy seed, that the field bringeth forth year by year.' You see, Ethel, everything belongs to God. We are only stewards, or caretakers, over what He has blessed us with. If we work hard to earn a living, using the talents we have been given, and use our money wisely, we will have an increase, or enough to share for the Lord's work. That way, those who can't work, the widows, and other unfortunate people, will be taken care of. Does that help?"

"Yes, Pa," answered Ethel as she gave him a hug. "I don't have much money, but I am well and strong. I can tithe my time by helping you and Ma until I am older."

Later, when all was quiet in the house, Win moved his chair close to Ella's. He didn't know how to speak the thought on his mind, but he needed to try.

"It's going to be lonesome around here now," he began. "Pa and Ma are gone, Will Oaks and Em have moved away. Our Scandinavian neighbors are kind, but none of our church folks are left but us."

"Yes, Win," said Ella, quietly waiting.

"All we have is the house and land and our girls."

"But you have the land which you have worked hard to develop, and made a good and prosperous farm of it. We can hire some help if needed. The house is comfortable. All the memories of our married lives are tied up here by Silver Lake. All of our children were born here. These things mean a lot." Ella watched him with a worried look.

"All you say is true," remarked Win after a while, "but there is something we lack. We need the companionship of others of like faith. Our girls need the opportunity to be with the young people of the church, as well as the ability to attend meetings regularly." Both were quiet for a long time. Finally Win said "Perhaps it is time for us to make the move to Zion. Suppose I go to Independence to check on land there. We have as many relatives there now, almost as we do in this area." The decision was made and he took the trip on the train. However, land was so much more expensive, he decided against buying there.

The dead of winter was upon them, short days and long nights with the cold so intense it made outside work very difficult. Winfield was restless as a caged bird. The decision about a possible move weighed heavily on his mind. It seemed as if his prayers bounced back at him from the ceiling. But he dared not do anything until he felt some guidance from the Lord.

Ella had written to her sister, Lu, about their possible move. Lu had taken a claim out in North Dakota after Alva died. She had to live there six months of the year in order to keep it. "I'll be leaving the first of March," she wrote. "I hate to leave my house empty all that time. I wondered if possibly you and Win might want to move into it until I get back. You would be doing me a favor."

Reluctantly, Ella handed the letter to Win, watching him carefully as he read. He raised his eyes to hers, finally, and in them was the first glimpse of interest she had seen in a while.

"Well?" he asked. He knew he must move carefully, but he believed this was the sign he had been praying for.

Ella was thoughtful for a time. "It has been a good home," she mused, "for twenty-two years, from the log cabin days until now. I am not happy at the thought of leaving, but if you feel like starting over on new land, I will help you all I can."

He reached over, taking her hands in his. "It has been a good home, my dear, because you have made it that way. I built the structures, you made them home."

"No, Win, it took all of us working, playing, and worshipping together, inviting the Holy Spirit in our midst. And now I begin to see; it is our togetherness that has made it home. We can take that with us, perhaps, wherever we go." She smiled at him. "It's going to be all right."

CHAPTER 31

Moving Day, March, 1901

The house was already humming with activity, by the first faint light of dawn. Moving day had arrived! Hallie was getting breakfast while Ma began packing dishes and food from the pantry. Each of the girls were responsible for their own things, doing up bundles of clothing, and what few belongings they had, in their blankets.

"We can't take everything this first trip, girls," reminded Ma. "So sort out the most important things. We won't need summer clothes for a while. Discard anything you can. Your Aunt Lu's house isn't very big, you know."

"Can I take my paper dolls?" asked Gladys.

"You can make more paper dollies, dear," said Ma kindly. "That will give you something to do until school starts."

"Where will we go to school, Ma?" asked Iva.

"You will be going to the new school in Clitherall, girls. You will be making many new friends."

"Will Ellis be there?" asked Gladys.

"Yes, I am sure your cousin will be there," answered Ma. "Now don't you two get into mischief!"

Before noon, the wagon and sleigh were loaded, all were bundled against the cold and ready to go. "We're on a new adventure, girls," said Winfield. "We are not sure what the future holds, but because the Lord has been with us this far, we can trust Him to guide us. Saying good-bye to our old home isn't easy, but who knows but what there are far greater blessings and opportunities waiting for us. So we will be thankful for the years we have had here at Silver Lake, but look forward now." Seeing a tear in Ella's eye, he slipped an arm around her. "Drive carefully," was all he said.

And so with Ma driving the sleigh and Pa the heavily loaded wagon with George on the seat beside him, they set out. Their way led across the frozen surface of the three Silver Lakes, shortening the distance to Battle Lake.

"Can we stop at Aunt Rosie's, Ma?" asked Nina, as they came in sight of Battle Lake Village. "I'm cold."

"Yes, child, we will stop in a few minutes," answered Ma. "I'm sure she will be glad to let us warm up." She pulled Molly to a stop and called to tell Winfield, who had been following the sleigh with the wagon. "The children are cold, Win. We are going in to Roseltha's to warm."

"That's fine," he called back, "but George and I will go on and begin to unload. You come on when you can."

"Girls," cautioned Ma, "be sure to clean the snow from your shoes before you step on Aunt Rosie's carpet."

Aunt Rosie's house was one of the nicest in Battle Lake, with carpeted floors and fine furniture and even an organ in the parlor. So it was always a special treat to the girls just to step inside and look around.

Winfield coaxed the horses to work a little harder, telling them they were nearly to the journey's end. They came at last to the little road that turned south by Clitherall Lake, and to the little house that had been Lu and Alva's, at the foot of Cemetery Hill. With the wagon close to the door, he unhitched the horses and led them to the barn, where he forked some hay into the manger for them. He filled a bucket with corn-cobs from a pile in the barn to use as kindling, and went into the house and built a fire. He did want the house to seem cozy when Ella came.

He and George had most of the things in the wagon un-packed and in the house by the time Ella and the girls arrived, but of course they were simply piled inside the door.

"Oh, my," said Ella, "where do we begin?"

"You tell us where you want things, Ma," said Hallie, "and

we will carry them. Then each of us will take a room, to clean and arrange. It won't take long."

"I'll carry the beds and heavy things," said Pa. "Then I need to put Molly in the barn and get up some more wood."

Ethel worked in the living room and before evening had it neatly arranged, with the lamp lit and placed on the little table Pa had made. She put Ma's newest rag rug by the door. The others had barely finished their rooms, when there was a knock on the door.

Pa opened it and welcomed in Emily Tucker and her son, Frank.

"How nice of you to call on your new neighbors, Mrs. Tucker," he said.

Ella hurried to take her hand and offer to take her coat. "It is going to be so nice to have near neighbors," she said warmly. "It is so sweet of you to come. I think you have met George. Do you and Frank know all our girls? In order of height and age we have Hallie, Ethel, Nina, Iva, and Gladys, our least one." Each nodded as her name was mentioned and Gladys did a tiny curtsey.

"We are just as glad as you to have neighbors moving in," said Emily. "We are pleased to be living on the Murdock place. My folks are both gone now, so we are buying the home place. Abner would be glad to visit with you, Winfield. He was busy this evening. Here," she said as she handed Ella a dish wrapped in a towel, "I brought a pot of stew. Thought you might be too busy to fix a hot supper. We'll not stay, but please feel free to visit any time."

"Thank you both so much for coming, and the stew is a wonderful gift," said Winfield. "Do come again soon."

When they were gone, Win and Ella looked at each other. "What do you think, dear?" he asked.

"It's going to be all right, like I said," and there was a light in her eyes that was good to see.

231

"Girls, you were wonderful," exclaimed Ma. "Now, with the house arranged and warmed by the good fire you built, Win, we can sit down and enjoy this delicious-smelling stew. Come on George and everyone so we can enjoy the first meal in our new surroundings."

While they ate, Winfield told them of a piece of ground he was thinking of buying. "It belongs to Albert Fletcher. It runs clear through from Battle Lake to Clitherall Lake, part of the 'Land Between Two Shining Lakes.' There are some nice fields on the Battle Lake side, plenty of timber and certainly access to water for the cattle and horses."

"Where is it?" asked Ella. "Could we ride out to see it?"

"Yes, let's go tomorrow," chimed in Nina.

"Tomorrow is the Lord's Day, Nina," said Pa. "And here is one of our first blessings of living close to Clitherall; we have only a little way to go, so we can all attend the meeting."

"Oh, goodie," cried Gladys, clapping her hands, "can I go, too?"

"Yes, Little Half Pint of Cider Half Drunk Up, you can go, too," assured Pa, using the pet name he had given her.

Morning came and with it a light snow falling, However, they each dressed in their winter best, squeezed into the big sleigh and rode the mile into Clitherall to the little church. They happily, but quietly, greeted relatives and friends: Ella's brother Art with Lois, his wife, and children; the young man Birch Whiting; Cordie and Orison Murdock, Winfield's cousin, Rhoda Sherman Hunter, who had married Hugh Hunter, the man who was now blind. There were some of the Kimbers from Girard, and a few others they did not know. The feeling of love was intense, as they shared in prayer, testimony and song.

After the service there was much visiting and many congratulations to the Goulds because of their move to Clitherall.

"Norie and Ret," said Winfield, "It is so good to see you here."

"Yes," said Ret, "We are taking turns going to the Josephite's and the Cutlerite's services. By the way, Win, Norie prefers to be called Eleanor since she is, ahem, mature."

"Well, I'm not sure I can break a life long habit, but for her sake I'll try," and Win gave her a playful pat on the back.

Ella hugged Norie. "Please, 'Eleanor,' do come over and spend the day sometime. I am just beginning to see how nice it is to live close to people."

Ret called Win aside. "I need to talk to you," he said. "Eleanor and I are trying to decide about joining the church. We both are sorry to disappoint my parents, who cling to the Cutlerite faith. But we are leaning toward the Reorganization. Could you come over sometime and answer some of our questions?"

"I'll be glad to, Ret, but maybe you need a priesthood man."

"If you want to bring Art with you, that's fine, but I think you are as righteous a man as there is in these parts."

"There is none good but God, remember," said Win, "but I am glad you are investigating. I'll be there."

"Ma, why do we always have soup for Sunday dinner?" asked Iva, as they ate the bean soup Ma had left simmering on the stove while they were gone.

"You tell her, Win," suggested Ella.

"That's because," began Pa, "the Lord has asked us to prepare our food with singleness of heart on the Sabbath Day. The Lord's Day is for rest, worship and study of His word. The less time we take preparing food, the more time we have for the important things. Since you brought up the subject, I'll read what the Doctrine and Covenants has to say about the Sabbath."

He arose and took the little book from the little table by the door, where Ella had carefully placed their Three Standard Books. Opening it, he began to read, "'And on this day thou shalt do none other thing, only let thy food be prepared with singleness of heart, that thy fasting may be perfect; or in other words, that thy joy may be full. Verily this is fasting and prayer; or, in other words, rejoicing and prayer.'

"Then he gives a promise, that '...inasmuch as ye do these things, with thanksgiving, with cheerful hearts, and countenances; not with much laughter, for this is sin, but with a glad heart and a cheerful countenance;

"'verily I say, that inasmuch as ye do this the fullness of the earth is yours: the beasts of the fields, and the fowls of the air, and that which climbeth upon the trees, and walketh upon the earth;

"'yea, and the herb, and the good things which come of the earth, whether for food or for raiment, or for houses or for barns, or for orchards, or for gardens, or for vineyards; yea, all things which come of the earth, in the season thereof, are made for the benefit and the use of man, both to please the eye, and to gladden the heart; yea, for food and for raiment, for taste and for smell, to strengthen the body, and to enliven the soul. And it pleaseth God that he hath given all these things unto man...'"[61]

"I like that," said Nina. "It makes me want to keep the Sabbath and makes me love God, too." Turning to Iva, she said, "Does it make you feel that way?"

"Yes," answered Iva. "I felt all tingly inside while Pa read that."

A few days later, Winfield took Ella and the younger children in the sleigh to see the land he thought of buying. It was not very far, only back out to the main road, east a little way to a little road that turned off to the north. They followed it until they came to the edge of Battle Lake. He pointed to the area which seemed the best spot for a house, back just a ways from the lake.

"It is nice," said Ella. "There are enough trees on the north for a good windbreak. And it is still close to the neighbors and to Clitherall. I think it will be fine, if you think so."

The deal was soon completed, and as soon as the weather permitted, they would begin to build. Hallie went back to her teaching job and the girls started school.

"Ma," said Gladys excitedly, "Ellis was there! and Genevieve! and lots of other kids."

"Some of the kids came to school on their skis today," said Nina. "Sometime I would like to have a pair. It's different with so many in school, but I made a friend today."

"Teacher said I only needed to take Civics," said Ethel, "since I already passed the eighth grade. She said I could take the teacher's examination in the spring and be ready to teach school."

CHAPTER 32

Ret and Eleanor Make Their Covenant

"Ret and Norie, oh, oh, I mean Eleanor," began Winfield one Sunday after church, "want to ask some questions about the church. I told them I would try to be over this afternoon. Art is going to be there, too. I'll be back by chore time." Turning to George, he said gently, "Will you please bring in some wood for the fire?" George nodded and took his coat from its peg. He may only bring in one stick, thought Winfield, but it will do him good to go out a little.

Art was there ahead of him, and when the four of them were seated around the table, Winfield asked, "what is your main concern, the thing you need help understanding?"

"It's the organization," replied Ret, "how important is it to have apostles and prophets and all the other offices that were in the original church? Of course, there are no apostles in the Cutlerite church."

Winfield opened the Bible. "All I know to do is go to the scriptures. Ephesians 4 is a wonderful chapter, but for your question I'll read verses 11 through 15."

"'And he gave some, apostles; and some, prophets; and some, evangelists; and some, pastors and teachers;' and he gives the reason, 'For the perfecting of the saints, for the work of the ministry, for the edifying of the body of Christ; Till we, in the unity of the faith, all come to the knowledge of the Son of God, unto a perfect man, unto the measure of the stature of the fullness of Christ; That we henceforth be no more children, tossed to and fro, and carried about with every wind of doctrine, by the sleight of men, and cunning craftiness, whereby they lie in wait to deceive; but speaking the truth in love, may grow up into him in all things, which is the head, even Christ;'"

"You see," spoke up Art, "God's plan is always perfect. Each priesthood has its own function. Because of this, all the needs of the people can be met. The apostles are to go out taking the gospel to new places, just as Apostle T.W. Smith came up here, teaching the good news that Jesus' Church was again organized and functioning. It is part of their responsibility to receive knowledge from the Lord concerning those who are called to other offices. You know, I guess, that all those called into the priesthood are called by God through revelation to an elder or apostle who is in charge of the area. As the Bible says, 'And no man taketh this honor unto himself, but he that is called of God, as was Aaron.'[62]

"The evangelists are fathers to the church, admonishing the people in spiritual things, and have the gift of laying on hands for the patriarchal blessing. The elders are to take charge of meetings," continued Art, "and have the power of the laying on of the hands for healing the sick, for ordination, for confirmation and bestowal of the Holy Ghost, and blessing children. These three offices are of the Melchisedec priesthood, which was given to Adam after his repentance, and was handed down from father to son through the righteous line of Seth until the flood, and continued through the line of Shem, son of Noah. This priesthood, was called in the beginning, 'the holy priesthood after the order of Son of God.'[63] In respect for the name of the divine Being, the name was changed to the priesthood of Melchisedic, after that righteous man. That priesthood was taken away when Moses died. After it was restored by Jesus, it continued until the church went into apostasy in the middle ages. Thus, it was again restored by angels, through Joseph Smith, for this last dispensation."

Winfield turned again to the Doctrine and Covenants. "Concerning the Aaronic priesthood, Section 104, paragraph 10 says, 'The power and authority of the lesser, or Aaronic, priesthood is, to hold the keys of the ministering of angels, and to administer in outward ordinances—the letter of the gospel— the baptism of repentance for the remission of sins, agreeably to the covenants and commandments.' They, as well as the deacons, take ministry to the homes, teaching the people, helping them with their problems."

"And if the church is to be guided by it's great head, Jesus Christ," resumed Art, "there must be someone to receive His messages for the church. Thus, the Lord appointed Joseph Smith to be prophet, seer and revelator. He was told that office should continue through his progenitors. And so it was that Joseph anointed and ordained his son, Joseph, some time before he was killed, to be his successor as prophet."

"Of course, that is a matter of opinion," said Eleanor. "Alpheus Cutler said he was given that power."

"The Lord has always used two or three witnesses to substantiate His truth. Think about the scriptures of the Bible, how many witnesses are in the New Testament about the life and ministry of Jesus? And now the Book of Mormon is a wonderful added witness for Christ. But Cutler had no other witnesses. History records at least two times when Joseph the third was blessed and ordained before witnesses, as successor. One occurred when Joseph and some others were in Liberty jail and Emma went to see her husband, taking young Joseph along. Lyman Wight, who was also a prisoner with Joseph, testified that Joseph asked him to assist him in laying hands on young Joseph, and saying to him, 'You are my successor when I depart.'"[64]

"The other strong testimony is from James Whitehead, who was a scribe for Joseph at the time"[65] interrupted Winfield. "That is the one that caused Ella to know that the Reorganization was right. You might go and ask her to tell you her experience, Norie. Oh, I'm sorry, Eleanor, but you are still my little sister and I love you. I want so much for you to experience the blessings that the saints are enjoying."

Eleanor gave him a smile and patted his hand. "I also have desired to see the blessings that I hear are happening among the Josephites. There is a fellowship among the Cutlerites that is good, but the gifts of the Spirit are not manifested openly."[66]

"Remember," said Art, "Jesus said tell them to ask and it shall be given to them.

"You have the privilege of asking Him where the truth is. If you are sincere, He will let you know."

"Thanks," said Ret, "We will make it a matter of prayer. If we need you, we will ask more questions, but this has helped."

The next Sunday Ret and Eleanor attended the Reorganized Church of Jesus Christ of Latter Day Saints, and the next and the next. And one spring afternoon, they were baptized in the crystal clear water of Clitherall Lake.

CHAPTER 33

The New House and Life in Clitherall

As the ground began to thaw, Winfield fenced pasture for his cattle and horses on the new land. When the ground was ready, he planted spring wheat and plowed more land ready for corn. Ella wanted her garden spot ready as early as possible, so by the first of May, she and the girls began planting potatoes, cabbage, peas and onions. It was only a short walk to the new place from Aunt Lu's house. And each time they went, they discovered more had been done to the new house. Pa had to hire some help with the building, since he was so busy with the field work. Little George spent much time roaming the woods around the new place, and walking the beach. He often brought home some treasure he had found. When the choke cherries ripened in the little trees along the edge of the woods, he would spend hours picking the little dark berries and bring home to Ella a bucketful, asking her to make him some jelly.

They visited as a family with the Tuckers. Eleanor and Ret came often, and always brought their daughter Genevieve, who was close to Gladys' age. They were not only cousins, but became the best of friends. Orison and Cordie always welcomed them, and there again, Gladys found a best friend in her cousin, Ellis. All of their visiting, however, did not diminish their enjoyment as a family in their own home. No matter how much fun the girls might be having, to reach home again, with Pa and Ma, was as close to heaven as they cared to be.

Just before it was time for Aunt Lu to return from North Dakota in the fall, the new house was finished. What a magnificent structure it was, even nicer than the new one at Silver Lake. There were two full stories and an L-shape for the parlor, with a nice porch. They moved their things in and the girls had great fun arranging the rooms. When all was finished, they went back to clean every inch of Aunt Lu's house to have it ready for her return.

A few days later, Gladys called excitedly, "Ma, it's Grandpa and Grandma Whiting! They're here!"

"How nice," said Ma as she hurried to the door to greet them. "Come in, Pa and Ma. I'm so glad you came. It isn't nearly so far between us now, is it?" She hugged her ma and reached her hand to Pa, but he pulled her to him for a hug.

"We just had to see your new house," said Grandma, as she hugged Gladys, "but, of course, we wanted to see you and the rest of the family, too."

"Come here, Gladys," said Grandpa, "I have something for you." Reaching in his pocket he pulled out a little sack. She came over to him, smiling, took the sack, peeked in and said, "Thank you, Grandpa, I love peanuts."

"Winfield should be coming soon," said Ella, "and the girls will be coming in from school. Gladys didn't feel well this morning, so I kept her home, but she is fine now. Come on and we will show you the house. We even have an extra bed for guests, can you spend the night?"

"Since Lester is home again from Iowa," said Grandpa, "I suppose he will do the chores. Would you like to stay, Jannette?"

"It is so kind of you to invite us, Ella. Yes, I would like to stay."

The rest of the family was soon home, the chores done, and Ella, with Grandma's help, put supper on the table. Grandpa asked the girls about their school work, and Winfield about his harvest.

"How did Lester feel about his work in Iowa?" asked Ella.

"He thoroughly enjoyed his stay," returned Grandma. "He

visited some of the people we knew when we lived there so long ago. He cleaned up the ground around my father's grave and even built a little fence around it. That made me feel good."

"He and Effie Kimber are planning to be married next year," said Grandpa, "if she can be spared from the care of her mother. You know, of course, he is taking over my farm. He expects to have all of you heirs paid for your share before long."

"What do you hear from Em and Ed?" asked Winfield.

"They are planning to move on up to Canada. I suppose," said Grandpa, with a shake of his head, "it has something to do with a group of folks of your church."

There was an awkward silence until Iva piped up with a question for her grandma. "Is Aunt Cordie's little girl, Jannette, named after you, Grandma? She is so cute."

"Well, yes, Cordie did ask if she could give her my name. She is a precious little one. We are so thankful God healed her when she drank that kerosene."

Another silence. All knew that she was healed after Brother I.N. White, a Josephite elder, had anointed her with oil and prayed for her. Winfield wondered how long before these good people would realize the greater light and blessings of the Reorganization.

"We have some news," said Ella with a smile. "Maud is coming for a visit soon. She is bringing her little girl, Winifred Alma, with her. I will be so glad to see my little granddaughter."

The rest of the evening was pleasant. Winfield read some scripture for their devotions, and invited Grandpa to pray with them. In his prayer, Lewis Whiting, father, grandfather, to this family, invited the Holy Spirit to bless this home and hold each one in His safe-keeping.

The girls counted the days until it was time for Maud to come. At last the day arrived.

"Maud is coming on the train, today," announced Ma to the girls. "If we hurry, you can help me get the house cleaned and the spare bed made up for her and little Winifred Alma, before you go to school. We want her to feel at home with us in our new home."

"Can I stay home and help till she comes?" asked Iva.

"The train comes in about four o'clock," said Pa. "You can be home by the time I bring her from the train. Better go on to school." Winfield gave her a hug, and she obediently resigned herself to doing as she was told.

When it was time, Winfield and Ella went in the buggy to meet the train in Clitherall. "I felt so bad when I sent her off on the train," remembered Winfield, as they waited. "But how much better I feel now, to welcome her back."

The train had barely pulled to a stop, before the conductor was offering Maude his hand to help her down the steps. She was carrying her beautiful little daughter, while the conductor tended her luggage.

Ella was first to reach her, hugging both daughter and granddaughter. "Oh, it is so good to see you, and little Winifred is so pretty. What blue eyes she has. The girls are so anxious to see you."

"Welcome home, Maude," said Winfield, as he gave her a hug. "We've been looking forward to this. I'll get your luggage in the buggy and we will get you home so you can relax and rest."

There was a happy family reunion that evening. Little Winifred Alma was doted over by her aunts, until she finally wearied and went to sleep in Grandma's arms. Maude told them of life in Independence, of going to the Stone Church and hearing Brother Joseph preach once, when he had come down from Lamoni. She told of visiting with Clayton and Dee and their family. She said that Plin worked hard in the furniture business, but was so good to her. They were glad for the news that his mother and step-father, Ann and William Barnhard, had planned to sell their Minnesota home and move to Independence soon.

"The gathering does seem to be going forward," said Winfield, rather wistfully. "When the time is right, Maude, we will also take our journey that way." That time came, but there were many things to transpire in the meantime.

The visit ended too soon. The whole family went to the depot to see them off. All the girls had to hug little Winifred Alma and kiss her good-bye. How they loved both Maude and her little one. Winifred Alma seems too beautiful and sweet, thought her grandpa, I wonder if she is long for this world.

<hr />

The town of Battle Lake was thriving. There were several businesses. Winfield listened to the people talking about the town and an idea formed in his mind. During the winter months, he could run a butcher shop, something the town lacked. He raised his own fine beef, as well as some hogs. Ella had chickens, hens and eggs. Others would be glad for a market for their products.

The shop was built next to the Post Office on Main street. It became a place not only for the sale of meat, but a place for a friendly gathering. Many afternoons there might be found a dozen citizens discussing world affairs, or when the next blizzard was expected.

"I'll tell you, seems like this year of 1903 was a peak year for happenings," said Charley Pierce. "Did you hear somebody made a trip in an automobile, clear across the country, from San Francisco to New York? It only took him from May 23 to August 1!"

"Well," said Ed Fletcher, "what do you think will come of what the Wright Brothers are doing? They each got their flying machine off the ground. One of them stayed up for 59 seconds."

"For my part," said another, "I'll trust my mule to get me where I want to go, and keep my feet on the ground."

Winfield thought about the new inventions, the speed of the train taking the place of the ox teams, the telegraph and telephone, and now the possibility of electricity coming to Battle Lake soon. "The scriptures tell us" he said, "that if we keep the commandments of the Lord, we will prosper in the land. I believe He wants to bless us, and that more new things to make life better will yet be discovered. But we need to keep in mind that if we let these things make us proud and we forget to be thankful to God for the blessings and to worship Him, we will be in danger. The ancient American prophets left a warning that the Gentiles must worship the Lord, Jesus Christ, or be swept away out of the land, remember, when they are fully ripe in iniquity. It is simply a matter of realizing that all good things come from God, and that man is allowed to discover them and use them for the good of society."

With these sobering thoughts, the conversation ended, and one by one the men left the shop. Winfield began preparations to close the shop and write the day's sales in the ledger.

CHAPTER 34

Blessings and Trials

The Church people had planned a reunion to be held in Clitherall that summer. Brother Alexander Smith, who was the Presiding Patriarch, was to be there. When Winfield and Ella learned that Leon would also attend as secretary to Brother Smith, they were so glad. Ella wrote to Leon and Alice and invited them to bring their little daughter, Alice Leona, and stay with them, instead of in a tent. All the girls looked forward to having another little niece to pamper for a while.

One evening after they arrived, Leon invited Birch Whiting and his wife, Abbie, over. Hallie joined the group as they began to talk of the things they hoped to happen at reunion. Winfield and Ella kept in the background, thoroughly enjoying listening to the young people.

"My work with Brother Alex is so interesting," said Leon. "It is inspiring to sit and write his words as they come from the Lord to the people. I would like to take down the blessings of all my relatives while I'm here."

"Ma and Pa had their blessings in 1898," said Hallie, "but I haven't even thought about it before."

"What about you, Birch, you surely would like your blessing wouldn't you?" asked Leon.

"Who, Me?" returned Birch. "I certainly don't think I'm worthy."

"It seems to me," said Leon thoughtfully, "if a person feels worthy to partake of the Lord's supper, he should be worthy to ask the Lord for His blessing."

"Well, explain it to us," said Abbie. "What is the purpose of it."

"It gives a person a guide for his life," returned Leon, "and let's him know God recognizes him. All the patriarchs of Old Testament times blessed their sons. Remember Jacob blessed his twelve sons, saying, 'that I may tell you what shall befall you in the last days.' God inspires the patriarch what to tell the person."

"I still feel afraid," said Birch.

"Why don't you just go with me tomorrow and sit and listen? It may help you feel differently."

Birch thought about it a while. Finally he said, "Abbie, if you and Hallie will go, I will."

"Brother Alex usually asks them to go praying and fasting," explained Leon. "He will be glad to see you there."

The following evening Winfield asked Leon how Birch and the girls felt about listening to the patriarch.

"Well, Pa," said Leon, "Brother Alex was only well started on the first blessing when the tears were running down Birch's face. All three of them asked for and received their blessings. It was a wonderful experience. I must transcribe them tonight and be ready to give them to Brother Alex tomorrow."

"Yes, Pa," said Hallie, who had just come in, "it was too wonderful to talk about just yet."

Late that night as Winfield and Ella knelt by their bed for prayer, he said to her, "Ella, remember Ethel's dream about the hand out of the black cloud? We just realized another great blessing from the hand of God. Leon is busy in the work for the Lord, fulfilling his office as priest. Through his urging, Hallie was so blessed by the Holy Spirit she couldn't talk about it. And Birch Whiting has received more evidence of the Lord calling him. How can we ever thank Him enough?"

"Only by continuing to serve Him, humbly," she answered, "in the very best way we can. Remember, these blessings have come to us after we endured the trials. This should help us to be faithful, no matter what dark cloud of trouble should come in the future, knowing God's promise is true, that after the trials come the blessings."

—————⇒►-0-◄⇐—————

It was March of 1905, and winter was still king. Snow drifts were up to the windows of the house by Battle Lake. Wagons and sleighs had made roadways on the ice across the lake, and ice fishermen had to cut through two feet of the stuff to get to the water. Horses and cattle were all housed in their barns, where the farmers pitched hay to their mangers from the loft above, and must carry bucket after bucket of water to them to satisfy their thirst. Life, however, was not all hard work. The warmth of the home fire at the end of the day was a pleasure to look forward to. And the powerful aroma of country cooking, of roast venison, baked squash, bean soup or dried apple pie, was enough to make any man thankful to be alive.

Winfield was thinking these thoughts as he and Ethel finished up the chores. He knew Ella was preparing a good hot supper for him and the family, and he was anxious to join her and the girls for another evening of togetherness. These days, however, they didn't need such a big table. Ella needed to set only six places. Hallie was away teaching in Battle Lake and was only home weekends. Nina was teaching her first term, in Girard, and staying with her Grandpa and Grandma Whiting. Leon and family were living in Lamoni, Iowa, the headquarters of the church. He had recently been called by the Lord and ordained an elder. George, though, was still with them and would always be, he thought. He was beginning to show some gray hair around his temples, but was still the same sweet childlike person they had all loved. Ethel had finished her schooling, but had decided against teaching. Instead, she was a big help to both Pa and Ma.

"Ethel," he said, "if you will take the milk in, I will fill the wood box and we will be through. Thanks so much for your help."

"You're welcome, Pa. I enjoy the outdoors. Besides, we girls promised to help, remember?"

"Yes, daughter, and you have all fulfilled your promises."

Supper was only well begun when someone knocked at the door. Gladys quickly went to open it. "It's Uncle Art, Pa," she announced, so glad to see him she forgot to pull the door clear open for him.

Art stamped his feet to get the snow from his boots, took off his hat and thanked Gladys for letting him in.

"Come on in, Art, and have some supper with us," said Ella. "We have plenty."

"Thanks, Ella, but Lois is expecting me. I stopped by the depot." He was holding a yellow paper in his hand. "I'm sorry to be the bearer of bad news, but a telegram had just come for you, and I told the depot agent I would deliver it." He handed the paper to Winfield.

Winfield read silently, closed his eyes briefly, quietly asking God for strength for his family to bear yet another burden. Handing the paper to Ella, he said simply, "It's little Winifred Alma."

"Oh, no," Ella cried, "surely not. How can one stand so much. Maude has had more than her share of losses. I can not bear this."

The wonderful supper was forgotten. Iva ran to her room to cry, and Gladys stood by Ma, consternation in her face. "That beautiful little blue-eyed girl that Maude brought to see us, Ma, she's dead?" Ella pulled her to her lap and they cried together.

Finally Art, feeling a prompting to help, spoke gently. "You know, it takes most of us at least three score years and ten to learn life's lessons and become fit for Paradise. This little one was so perfect she learned enough in her four years to fit her for the kingdom of God. Don't weep for her. She is likely cradled in the Savior's arms, the most wonderful place in the universe to be. For those who loved her so much, the awful blow will pass at last, and only the memory of her tender sweetness and beauty will remain."

"Thanks, Art, you have helped to soften the blow," said Winfield as he rose to see Art to the door. "You might remember Maude and Plin in your prayers. I'm sure they will need all the strength the Lord can give."

The following day, Winfield took Iva with him in the sleigh to pick up Hallie at her school and share the news with her. Together they went out to Girard to Nina's school. Hallie and Iva went in, serious faced, to wait until she dismissed school, and then told her their little niece had gone to heaven. It was a sober group that rode back to their snowbound home by Battle Lake.

There was one bright spot in this trauma. Just a few days before the accident that took Winifred's life, a new baby came to the Sherman home, a baby girl they called Joy. She was a joy and helped her family overcome their grief, and grew up to be a joy to all who knew her.

CHAPTER 35
Weddings

Ethel and Nina were enjoying being part of the group of young people in the area. The Murdocks, their Uncle Orison and Aunt Cordie, often invited the young people to their home for parties. Frank Tucker began to ask Ethel to be his partner at those affairs, and often walked her home afterwards. Nina attended the parties sometimes, but she also enjoyed being home with Iva and Gladys on her weekends. She didn't want to grow up. One afternoon, though, she was with Ethel and a group of young people gathered at Tucker's house. They skated on the smooth ice and, in the house later, played a game with question and answer cards. She was seated opposite Orison Tucker, so his questions were asked of her. He read from his card, looking her in the eyes, "Would you allow me to offer you a plain gold ring?" The answer on her next card read "Sometime." Gradually, with gentle persistence, Orison won her over. Often he was allowed to take her back to her school, or go in Pa's place on Friday night to get her.

Winfield watched his girls dating these two brothers. Always he noticed they were perfect gentlemen. When Orison visited Nina on Friday evenings, they would sit in the kitchen by the wood cook stove. They would pop corn, crack walnuts or sometimes play anagrams. On summer nights, he took her for a boat ride in the moonlight.

"Well Nina," said Pa one cold snowy Friday evening, "Orison surely won't come out in this storm."

Nina just looked at him and smiled. A moment later, they heard his feet stamping the snow at the door. Winfield welcomed him in and went to stir up the fire in the kitchen range, while Nina took his coat and hat and hung them on the peg by the door. After their time together he said good night to the family, held Nina's hand and thanked her for a lovely evening, and went out into the stormy night.

"Nina," said Pa, as he looked into her face, "he must love you a lot to come out to see you on a night like this. How do you feel about him?"

She studied her hands a few moments. "I think he is really nice, Pa," she began. "I really enjoy his company. He is always kind and thoughtful. But you know, I also enjoy being a girl at home with you and Ma and Gladys and Iva. I'm not sure I want to grow up."

"That is a wonderful compliment, Nina, to know you feel that way about your home. Your ma and I are pleased, wouldn't you say, Ella?"

Ella laid aside her knitting. "Bless you, Nina," she said as she put her arms around her. "That is all a mother could ask. However, you are eighteen and the years will come and go, and you will grow and so will your sisters. Each of you must decide what you want to do with your lives. Pray for guidance, dear. The Lord knows the right partner for you and He will let you know when the time comes."

It was in December of 1906. Orison brought Nina home from her school on Friday night. She was happy to be home and spent the evening telling the family her experiences of the week. Later, Ma went upstairs to tell the girls good night. When she came down, she took Win by the hand. "Orison has asked Nina to be his wife," she said. "She told him she would have to think about it. We must pray for the Lord to help her with her decision."

Not quite two years later, Nina planned a trip to Lamoni and Independence. She wanted to visit Leon and Alice in Lamoni and see Joseph Smith III and hear him preach. From there, she would go on to Independence to visit Maude. She wanted to enjoy the big city. She had been gone only about two weeks, when Orison came over to see Winfield.

"How do I rate a visit, Orison?" asked Winfield. "Are you as lonesome for Nina as we are?"

"I sure am," returned Orison, "and she may be gone several more weeks! We are keeping the post office busy with our letters, that helps."

Winfield sensed the purpose for Orison's visit. His mind went back thirty-one years. Once again he stood before Uncle Lute, shaking in his boots for fear of the answer he might receive. Remembering the concern and wisdom of that good man, he began to shape his answer, but also tried to put this young man at ease.

"We had a letter from her," said Winfield. "She seems to be having a good time there in Lamoni."

"Yes, she even wrote that she might try to get a job in Independence. I secretly hope she has poor luck," said Orison. "You see," and he hesitated, "I truly love your daughter, Mr. Gould, and I have asked her to be my wife."

"What has been her reply, Orison? Is she willing?"

"Yes Sir, and now I have come to ask your permission."

Winfield studied his face, finding there absolute sincerity and a hopeful expectancy. "I know you are industrious, and believe you are capable of making a good living. You have a reputation in the community to be proud of. As you have visited in the home, we have found you to be a perfect gentleman. There is only one thing which I see that could cause conflict between you and Nina. You are each loyal to your separate churches."

Orison nodded. "That is true," he responded, "But..."

"Let me tell you," interrupted Winfield, "how it was with Ella and me. After we had been married a few months, I had a remarkable conversion experience that caused me to ask for baptism into the Josephite church. Ella, being a good member of the Cutlerite church, was heart broken. But we took turns going to each other's services, we studied the books together. We even prayed together and continued to love each other. Eight years later, she had her experience and was baptized in the dead of winter through two feet of ice. From that moment on, our joy was doubled. We were one in love of the Savior and in our attempts to teach our children about Him and His gospel. If you and Nina will do the same, studying and praying together, you going with her and she with you to services, respecting each other, then I believe everything will turn out all right."

Orison looked at him with a half smile. "If you had said no because of our differences, I would have walked away downhearted. I never could join her church just to get your consent. But I will accept your kind counsel. I can see what unity of faith has done for you and your family. The attributes I admire in Nina are a result of your careful teaching and good example. You know, Sir, you have a reputation in the community respected by all." He paused, then rose to go. They stood facing each other. Winfield realized that Orison's eyes were level with his own, he stood straight and tall and handsome.

"Does that mean permission, then?" asked Orison solemnly.

"Yes, Orison, go with my blessing," and he reached for his hand, but put the other arm around his shoulders. "I will welcome you as a son."

⚒

The lake shore was gorgeous with the flaming colors of frost tinted tree leaves. The yellow of the basswood merged with the red and orange of the maples, and the brown of the oaks. The still water of the lake reflected all the glory, doubling the beauty. Winfield watched as a family of snow geese swam sedately from shore toward the setting sun, the young nearly as big as their parents. "The heavens declare the glory of God, and the firmament showeth His handiwork," he repeated aloud.

He had come out to the edge of the lake to pray for the event that would take place tomorrow. Nina had set September 30, 1909, as the day for her wedding. He thought about life and death. They were so intertwined. We just buried Uncle Lute a few days ago, he thought. Now this joyful event; a new family begins. He thought of his own joy when he and Ella exchanged their vows, in spite of the uncertainty of how long he might be able to enjoy her because of his health. He thought how much he missed Winnie, but realized the quality of life is more important than the length of it. What matters is that we become prepared for eternal life while here. "Lord, please bless the marriage of Nina and Orison," he prayed "May they always seek your Spirit to be in their home, and ask your guidance in all things."

Inside, he found the beauty of the woods transported to form a lovely arched altar in the living room.

"Do you like it, Pa?" asked Gladys, when she saw him looking at it.

"Yes, Gladys, it is very pretty. I was just outside admiring God's beautiful handiwork. Did you help with this?"

"All of us girls helped gather the branches,and Nina told us how she wanted it arranged. I was so glad to help."

"I cut the feathery asparagus tops to lend some green," offered Iva.

At the supper table, everyone enjoyed hearing Brother Swen Swenson's Swedish brogue. "I always tot you and Orison woulda marry," he said to Nina, "but I never tot you woulda ask me. I was surpevised, Nina, yessah, I was supevised. I used to tell Orison, if we can't have you as a brudder, we will have you as a half brudder." They had all come to love him, and he was Orison's favorite Josephite preacher.

The wedding day dawned bright and beautiful, a perfect Indian Summer day. Though there were mundane chores to be taken care of, most of the activity was in preparing for the festivities of the afternoon. Ma, Ethel, Hallie and a friend of hers, spent hours preparing the wedding feast, just as Nina had planned it. She had saved enough money from her teaching to buy several pieces of furniture, buy the material for Ma to make her dress, and pay for the meal.

At last the moment had come. The handsome bridegroom ascended the stairway to escort the waiting bride. Win and Ella held hands as they watched their daughter, beautiful in her high pompadour, the long princess style white silk gown with linen lace overlay, high lacy collar and long lace trimmed sleeves. Part of her beauty, thought Winfield, is the righteousness within that shines through.

It was all over in so short a time. Orison's sister, Nettie, played the organ while the girls sang "All Hail the Power of Jesus' Name," and "I Would Be True." There was the prayer and a few words by Brother Swenson, they repeated their vows and then the kiss. It was the first time she had allowed him to kiss her in public, but she was happy this time for it to be so.

There were the congratulations from the close relatives and friends who had been invited, and the gifts to open. After the lovely three course meal, it was time to say good-bye. Nina hugged all of her sisters. She was on the verge of tears as she went to Pa and Ma. "There's no way to tell you how much I appreciate all you have done for me. I love you so much. Thank you, thank you."

They left then to go to the new house Orison had built for them on part of his father's land, by Clitherall Lake. He had been able to finish it just in time, by working late nights after long days laboring in the fields. Together they had hung the curtains, laid the rug and put the finishing touches on it. It was the product of their own hands and they were proud and happy.

It was a very weary Ella who climbed at last into her bed that night. "Win," she said as she put her head on his shoulder, "we've had our ups and downs, but today was a high to remember. She planned so well and it was all so beautiful. Surely they have God's blessing."

"If they are as blessed as we have been, Ella, it will be wonderful. We can't know what the future holds, but I believe they will be united in their faith before long. Two of our girls are married now, and Ethel planning her wedding in February. I hope they are all prepared to keep their faith in God through whatever comes."

"I was thinking," replied Ella, "of what Brother Swen told me through inspiration in prayer service one night, long ago. I was so concerned about bringing our children up to be devoted and have a desire to serve God. He told me, if I were faithful, the day would come when my children would be working with the ministry. We had Leon and Winnie at the time and two of the girls. I sometimes wonder, since four more girls came to us, how that prophecy may be fulfilled."

"The Lord doesn't make mistakes, my dear, we must continue to be faithful and trust Him."

—————⇒•○•⇐—————

February arrived with minus forty degree weather, and plenty of snow. It was not the best time for a picturesque wedding. Frank and Ethel decided to write to Elder Houghton, who lived close to Fargo, to meet them in Fergus Falls and marry them. On the sixth of the month, accompanied by Hallie, they rode the freight train to Fergus. They rented rooms in the Hotel and waited for Brother Houghton. There in the Hotel Lobby, with Hallie and the hotel keeper as witnesses, they exchanged their wedding vows. They stayed there that night, but in the morning they took the freight train back to Clitherall. Ella had invited friends and relatives and had a wedding supper ready for them. In a few days, they went to the town of Syre, Minnesota, where Frank had a position as telegrapher.

CHAPTER 36

Maturing Years

Time and tide wait for no man. It was so with Winfield and Ella. The years were beginning to show in their faces, although their lives were busy. Win had his farm work and his butcher shop. He managed well, kept excellent records and at the end of the year, there always seemed to be some gain. The tithing was faithfully figured and promptly paid.

The year 1911 was full of varied experiences. "Little" George died in March after a week of severe illness. Maude, Ethel and Nina were in their own homes. Hallie and Iva were away most of the time teaching school, and Gladys was the only one left in the nest. She felt the emptiness, and expressed her feelings in her poems.

THE LITTLE BLACK ROCKER

The little black rocker is empty now,
But it sits in the same old place,
In front of the cheerful blazing fire
That once lit up his face.
And worn and wrinkled though it might be,
Its absence brings sorrowful tears to me.

Never again will he roam the fields,
The meadow, woods or shore,
While his treasures lie moldering in the dust,
For he'll visit them no more.
But all my treasures would be gladly given
If I, like him, might be sure of Heaven.

G.G., March 21, 1911

IN MEMORY OF MY SISTERS

I sit in the desolate chamber alone,
And gaze at the empty beds,
That once were filled with flesh and bone,
Black, brown and curly heads.

And I think of the time so long ago,
When in blissful childhood days,
Six sisters lay here in a row,
To be waked by the sun's soft rays.

My eldest sister so good and kind,
With gentle manners and stature small
Far had gone, greater bliss to find
With her children three and husband tall.

The second sister tall and smart,
Filled with dignity, wisdom and lore,
Has gone with a brave and cheerful heart,
To teach the school she taught before.

My third sister so gentle and sweet,
With pretty face and wavy hair,
Has gone to make a home so neat,
For her busy husband waiting there.

Old Steven Post my dearest fourth,
With sunburned face and loving heart,
To cheer another's lonely hearth,
This happy home she did depart.

My sister fifth so timid and mild,
With a better soul than the rest can boast,

Has bravely set forth in the world so wild
To do her best where she can work most.

And so with thoughts that are tender and sad.
I am left in the chamber alone tonight,
While only my precious Mother and Dad
Are left, for the rest have taken flight.

Gladys Gould

In May, Nina's husband,Orison, and Ella's brother, Lester
Whiting and his wife Effie, were all baptized. It was a time
for rejoicing, of course, for the folks in the little white
church. But for Grandma Whiting, Lester's baptism meant
all of her children had joined the Josephite church. When
asked her feelings, she said, "It may be right, but I want to
go where Lewis is." She, however, had an added sorrow,
for she was in Bemidji with her daughter May, who was
dying of cancer.

Abner and Emily Tucker were even more distraught, and
their tears and displeasure made it hard for Orison. Winfield
counseled Orison. "The Holy Spirit cannot dwell in a heart
where the bitter spirit dwells," he told him. "We will all pray
for your father, that the Lord will release him from that burden, which could destroy him."

Iva and Gladys attended the reunion that summer, in Frazee.
They ate at the same table with Brother Frederick M. Smith.
On the last day, he carried their suit cases to the train for
them, shook both their hands, saying "Good-bye, girls." Neither of them knew that the day would come when each of
those girls would work for him, as President of the church, in
his office in the Auditorium.

Before 1911 had ended, another milestone was passed.
Uncle Ret and Aunt Eleanor had a telephone put in on December 14! Two weeks later, there was one installed in the

Gould home! My, what fun it was to be able to converse with their friends without even leaving home!

Gladys passed her exams and received her certificate to teach in the summer of 1912. In October, she taught her first school, living away from home with a Norwegian family. She spent many lonely evenings, and weekends, pining for Pa, Ma and home. But she was successful and made friends.

In 1914, word came to the Union Branch at Clitherall, that Brother Joseph had passed away, and that his son, Frederick Madison Smith had been set aside by him to take his place as president and prophet for the church. All mourned for Young Joseph, as he had been called, to distinguish him from Joseph the martyr. But he had served faithfully fifty-four years, and was loved and respected by all who knew him. A letter from Clayton contained a clipping from the Kansas City Journal for December 12, 1914. It was a tribute to Brother Joseph from the public.

"He was the Prophet, but first of all he was the Christian gentlemen, and the good citizen. As such he lived; as such he died; and as such he will be remembered by all outside the household of his faith. His followers themselves can have no legacy of remembrance more honorable than this appraisement of the people among whom he lived and labored so many years.

"Kindly, cheerful, loyal to his own creed, tolerant of those of others, standing for modesty, simplicity, good citizenship, embodying in his private and public life all the virtues which adorn a character worthy of emulation—such is the revelation which Joseph Smith leaves to the world, as the real interpretation of an ecclesiastical message translated into terms of human character."

Ella's sister, Cordie, was left a widow in 1915. Orison Murdock died unexpectedly, which was a shock to all. They had been the favorite aunt and uncle of Gladys and her sisters.

More grandchildren were being added to Winfield and Ella. Wayne was born to Nina and Orison on Aug. 5, 1912. Elon was born to Ethel and Frank on Dec. 30, 1914. July 30 of the next year, Keith was born to Nina and Orison. Frank, Jr. was born November 15, 1916, and Joyce to Nina and Orison on January 29, 1917.

These were wonderful blessings, but there was a cloud moving onto the horizon. Orison began to have trouble. It was finally diagnosed as chronic Bright's disease. He was administered to. He went to the Sanitarium in Independence for most of one winter and seemed a little better. One night he suffered pain in his head, and though he was administered to, he seemed to hardly know who was there. Abner and Emily were called. He kept trying to say something, but could hardly get the words out. "I want my folks—I want my folks," was all he could say. Finally, Emily broke down, crying, and said, "I will, Orison, I will."

When he was unable to care for his farm work, his father, Abner, came to help Nina with the chores. Helping began to bring healing from the bitter feeling he had suffered after Orison was baptized. One Sunday, Orison looked out the window from his bed and saw his father dressed in Sunday best, going into town to the Josephite church. "Nina," he asked, "please pray with me that nothing will be said there today to hurt my father." And so they did. On a bright October day, Abner and Emily Tucker were baptized in the shining blue waters of Clitherall Lake.

The last summer, Orison was able to go out and work a little in his garden. One day, as he worked, he said the thought came into his mind, "I will go to the house, the phone will ring and I will be called to the Melchisedec Priesthood." He went to the house, the phone rang. It was Hallie calling from the reunion in Frazee. She asked him if he could stand the trip up there for the day. He and Nina left the children with

Winfield and Ella while they went. Apostles Gillen and Aylor administered to him. Brother Gillen told Delbert Whiting he was given evidence of Orison's call to the Melchisedec Priesthood, when he saw him enter the tent.

That fall, Delbert, who was District President, came to ordain Orison. He was ordained an elder by Delbert and Lester, as he sat up in his bed. He was never able to function in his office, and he passed away March 4, 1918. Nina could not be reconciled as to why the Lord had called him if he could not function in this life. She wrote to brother Delbert of her dilemma. He said, "I carried her letter for a week and fasted and prayed for light to answer that letter.

"Then I was given a vision and I was permitted to see Orison seated on a low bench with the Bible and the Book of Mormon laying open on the bench beside him, and in his hands he held the Doctrine and Covenants. Seated before him in a kind of half-circle was row after row of people. They were all leaning forward eagerly listening to him explain the revelations, and I was given to know he was making clear to them the call of Young Joseph as the legal successor to his father."

As Delbert listened he was able to recognize some of the people of the Clitherall community, who had not joined the Josephite church. He was impressed by the joy in their faces. Then a voice spoke to him saying, "He is sent, clothed with the authority of the Melchisedec Priesthood, to bring truth to those who have been deceived."[67] This testimony was a comfort to Nina.

CHAPTER 37

Good-bye

It was a quiet New Year's Day celebration. The house by Battle Lake, which had seen so many happy times, stood silent amid the stark leafless trees. The walls, used to the sounds of laughter and thanksgiving, shuddered slightly. Was it the north wind that howled and pushed at them, or was it a chill of foreboding that there were lonely days ahead? The words they were hearing, caused them to tremble slightly.

The meal was over, the children at play, but Frank and Ethel, Nina and Gladys, still sat at the table with Winfield and Ella.

"Are you satisfied with the decision you have made, Winfield?" asked Frank.

"You know, Frank," returned Winfield, "for all these years, I have hoped and planned to one day go to Zion. Now that the day is close to realization, my feelings are so mixed. I truly believe the Lord has guided our decision, and has gone before me to make it possible. But my feet are so planted on the soil of this land, they are holding me back. It will be hard to leave this beautiful place, but, yes, I am satisfied it is the Lord's will that we gather to the 'Promised Land.' And since the church headquarters will be moved to Independence this year, people will begin moving in faster."

"It is easier for me," spoke up Ella, "since so many of our folks are there before us."

"Ma," asked Nina, "What was it Brother Swen Swenson told you about your children a long time ago?"

Ella smiled in reminiscence. "We had two boys and two girls at the time, but four girls followed. How, I wondered, can that promise come true that my children could all be working with the priesthood? But, the Lord is wiser than we. Here is Maude, a wonderful helpmate to Plin who is pastor of their branch and she is teaching classes. Hallie will be proof-reading for the editors of Herald House, and if the church headquarters is moved, they will probably move the publishing house soon, too. Gladys is looking forward to attending Graceland College this fall, and Iva is secretary to President Fred M. Smith, something we never dreamed possible."

"And don't forget, "interrupted Frank, "Ethel helped me see the light. She is a true handmaiden for the Lord," and he reached over to squeeze her hand.

Winfield noticed big tears in Nina's eyes. "Nina," he began, "we don't know what lies ahead for you, but it was your willing cooperation with Orison, which helped him find his way, and perhaps that was your most important work, since we know he is doing the Lord's work in the spiritual world."

"That is my only consolation," replied Nina, struggling to control her emotions. "If I can teach our children how to be Zion builders, perhaps I will be worthy to join Orison in that other world, one day."

It was only a few days later, when Win was in Battle Lake visiting Roseltha and Orris, that Orris told him of a man who was looking for farm land. "It's Isaac Whiting," said Orris, "and some others of their church." Together they went to see Isaac. Winfield knew Isaac had taken charge of the Cutlerite church after Uncle Lute had died. He remembered the day of Clayton's house raising so many years ago. Ike had been the life of the gang that day, teasing Clayton but doing his share of the work. The years had taken their toll. Isaac was now blind in one eye, old and stooped, but he met them with a friendly grin and handshake.

"Glad to see you, Winfield," said Ike. "I hear you are planning to move to Missouri. I was telling Orris, here, the church could use your good farm. If you haven't sold, we'd like to make a deal with you."

"Well, I am ready to sell, all right," replied Winfield "We have made up our minds to go south. If we can agree on terms, I think it will be fine for your church to have the place. It has been good land. Let me know when I can meet with your group and I will be there."

The deal was finally made to the satisfaction of all concerned.

<hr />

"There is one more wagon load to haul," said Winfield wearily. It had been a long day. All of their household goods that hadn't been sold, he had hauled to Nina's house. The horses were sold, except for Jack and Curly. He still needed them to complete the moving. The cattle, pigs and hens had already been sold, along with most of the farm machinery. This last trip was more to say good-bye the last time, than for the few things left.

"I'd like to go with you, Pa," spoke up Gladys, "that is if you don't care."

"I'll be glad for your company. You can check the house while I clean out the barn. Bundle up, it's cold out there."

It was only a little over a mile between the houses, but to Winfield, it seemed like the end of one long journey and the beginning of another. Surely, he thought, I will soon feel the excitement of preparing to go to Independence.

In the dark recesses of the barn, he gathered up the few things he felt he could use in the truck garden he planned for their new home. He patted the solid walls that he had built nearly twenty years ago. He thought about the fine cattle it had housed through the long winters. There was the grain bin his fertile fields had always kept filled. It has been a good time, he thought. I have tried to be a good steward over the land, and the Lord Jesus has blessed my efforts. Aside from the satisfaction of having been a successful farmer, the money from the sale is plenty to give us a new start in Missouri. Gently, a transition began to work in his mind—a wonderful feeling of gratitude for the past, and the promise of hope for the future. The Lord knows where we are going, he thought, He will still be with us there.

He found Gladys gathering a few items from the kitchen. "Is that a tear I see on your cheek, Gladys?" he asked. "Be careful it might freeze there. I understand, though," he said in a gentle tone, "I've been saying good-bye, also. But you know, the future may be even better than the past."

"I know, Pa," answered Gladys. "But it is hard to say good-bye to all the happy memories we had in this house. You and Ma gave us a wonderful life and I will be forever grateful."

There was a catch in his throat and he turned away so she didn't see a tear or two in his own eyes. "We better go," he said, "Little Half Pint of Cider, Half Drunk Up."

At the sound of the pet nick name he used to call her, she threw both arms around him and cried on his shoulder like she used to do when she was that "Little Half Pint of Cider."

⟶•◦•⟵

Nina made room for Ma and Pa, Hallie and Gladys in her nice home by the shore of Clitherall Lake. After Gladys' term of teaching Old Town school ended in the spring, she played with the children, Wayne, now eight years old, Keith who was five, and Joyce, three. Often, also, their cousins Elon and "Junior" came to play. Winfield took care of Nina's garden, her cow and chickens, while Ella helped Nina with the house work and canning.

Compared to previous years, this summer was almost a leisurely time, preparing for their move in the fall. Nina decided to make the move with them. Ella and Winfield sold most of their furniture, but Nina planned to send hers on the train.

Wayne and Keith ran up the little sandy road often to Grandpa Tucker's house. Abner loved the boys, especially Wayne, and wanted to spend as much time with them as possible before they went away. Eleanor and Ret were frequent visitors. They, too, were planing to move to Zion. They would all travel together, before school started.

As the day approached, Ella began to have some misgivings. "Win," she said one day, "we are hearing some things about the church which bother me. Are you sure it is right for us to go? Do you really think Zion will be?"

Winfield was quiet a while. "The Lord has always had to use mortal men who make mistakes," he said finally. "It is the cause of Zion we are working toward. It is not likely we will see the perfection of Zion in our lifetime. But, yes, Ella, I am sure it is right for us to go. Jesus must have a righteous people to come to. I feel we are helping lay the foundation. If our children are faithful to keep the commandments and keep the hope of Zion alive in their hearts and the hearts of their children, as well as others, in time there will be a faithful nucleus in the center place, ready and capable to be that ensign to the nations.

"When there are enough families living and working together for the good of each other, doing all things with an 'eye single to the Glory of God,' so that the place where they live will shine as Zion, then the Kingdom of Heaven will come to meet the Kingdom of God that is set up on the earth."

Slipping into his mind came memories of the stirrings of the Holy Spirit. He remembered the time he had been so angry at Clayton, and God had soothed his spirit through the sunset and the humble thankfulness of the horses. There was that cold night in which he had felt impelled to wrap his blanket around him and go outside to pray. How the Holy Spirit had flooded his being! He had known God loved him that night. How gently he led me, he thought, carefully guiding my study of the scriptures, confirming their truths. And when the gracious Lord saw fit to speak directly to me through Sister Smith, all doubt was erased.

"Ella," he said at last, "do you remember how sure I was that night I was baptized?"

"Oh, Win," she replied, humbly, "how could I ever forget. I have repented of my fear and anger so many times."

"I wanted to tell you," he continued, "that sometimes 'in the still of the night, or while riding the sulky plow across the old home farm, sometimes feeling blue and discouraged over some things that have happened in the church; some of those testimonies that had come to me in the past will pass through my mind, and I will again feel the blessed assurance of the truth of this Latter Day Work that had come to me while receiving those testimonies; and I will often find the tears running down my cheeks and will make up my mind that I will stick to this work if every other one goes back on it.'"[68]

He stood up and looked out over the shimmering blue and silver of Clitherall Lake. "I had a dream, Ella, soon after my baptism. I couldn't tell you then, but I need to share it now." He seated himself beside her again. "I dreamed I was on the way to Zion. I was out on a great big plain. I could see way ahead of me. I wasn't alone, there were thousands; the whole earth covered with people, some way ahead, some behind, and way off to each side I could see people coming down out of the mountains and they would go by going East. We were going south.

"After we got along quite a ways, I could see the people ahead of me going up to a sort of rainbow or smoky-looking rim. They would go through and it would close up back of them. It seemed once they got through they were safe. Off back of us was the biggest crowd I ever saw. There was something they seemed to be interested in. They would look at us and then back, and they didn't seem to be coming along with us.

"After a while I dreamed that you, Ella, came and walked along with me. That is why, you see, I couldn't tell you at first; you were so sure you would never walk in the same fellowship with me. We came up to the rim of smoke. It was about breast high, about six inches thick. We walked right through it, and after I stepped through, I looked around on the inside and could see people coming through. Some seemed to meet people they were acquainted with and would throw their arms around each other and embrace each other. Others dropped down on their knees and began to pray. Ahead, quite a ways from the edge was a nice grove fixed up like a celebration with a big platform covered with people As I looked at them, they stood up and began to sing:

Lift up your heads, ye heirs of glory,
Cast aside your doubts and fears,
He who called you to His Kingdom
Soon will reign a thousand years."

Emotion choked Winfield's throat as he struggled to continue. "As I heard those words and realized we had got to Zion and Christ would soon reign like the hymn says, I was so over come with such a feeling of thankfulness and joy that I dropped on my knees and began to pray, too, as the others had, and thank the Lord that I was there.[69]

"I realize it was a kind of allegory; as though we were part of the saints from all ages, merging on toward Zion, the goal of the Lord. So it doesn't matter if we see the fulfillment in our earthly lives. As long as we remain faithful and endure to the end, we will take part in that wonderful time as resurrected beings."

"One more assurance," added Winfield, "if there is still any doubt. In Section 64 of the Doctrine and Covenants the Lord said '...be not weary in well-doing, for ye are laying the foundation of a great work. And out of small things proceedeth that which is great.' And in case you feel to judge the human vessels through whom God needs to work, we must realize that He is the Judge. In the same Section he says: 'And even the bishop, who is a judge, and his counselors, if they are not faithful in their stewardships, shall be condemned and others shall be planted in their stead; for, behold, I say unto you that Zion *shall* flourish, and the glory of the Lord *shall* be upon her, and she *shall* be an ensign unto the people, and there *shall* come unto her out of every nation under heaven,

"'And the day *shall* come, when the nations of the earth shall tremble because of her and shall fear because of her terrible ones. The Lord hath spoken it.'"[70]

"Winfield," said Ella, with tears of joy in her eyes, "what a wonderful answer you have given to my question. I will never doubt again and will follow you to the end of the world, if need be. I praise the Lord for you."

For a moment, the years melted away. Winfield was hearing again those divinely spoken words as he knelt on the hill overlooking Silver lake, *"Your companion is honest in heart and she will yet be one with you."* The same wonderful feeling of joy filled his being as he took her in his arms. "The Lord's promises are sure, Ella. Zion will come in the Lord's due time. We have only to be faithful and endure to the end in order to see the glorious consummation."

Epilogue

The story of Winfield and Ella Gould is based on the actual happenings in their lives as given in the family history, written by themselves and some of their daughters. However, in order to tell it in story form, there must of necessity be some imagination used to bring the pieces together smoothly.

I will say, as Mormon said, "If there are faults, they are the mistakes of [the author]." Please don't judge the whole work, by a few ignorant mistakes of hers.

The last chapter of their lives in the city of Independence, is also interesting. They met with disappointments and overcame them. There were times of illness, but there were also many blessings given them. The family remained a closely knit unit, as Hallie, Iva and Gladys never married, but continued to live with their parents and to "work with the priesthood of the church." Hallie wrote many quarterlies at the request of officials of the church. Iva was secretary to the President of the church until her death. Gladys took her sister's place in that office and served faithfully many years. Collectively, Iva and Gladys served as secretary to Presidents Fredrick M. Smith, Israel Smith and W. Wallace Smith.

Frank and Ethel lived on at Deer Creek, in Minnesota, with their two boys, each of whom grew to manhood to become elders in the church. Frank was pastor of the Clitherall branch for many years, with her as helpmate. They traveled the nearly twenty-five miles in all kinds of weather, Ethel teaching children's and women's classes.

Nina raised her three children in her own house, close to that of her parents, with that good association to help. She says in her own story of her life, that four of her uncles built her house. These must have been Clayton Gould, Ret and Lon Whiting, and Art. She worked at cleaning houses, cooked in restraunts, cared for new mothers and their babies to earn money for her household. She taught Sunday school classes, outlined the entire Bible, read all the scriptures to her children. In later years she worked as nurse aid in Resthaven, the church home for the aged, using her free time comforting, writing letters for those incapable and endearing herself to all. Plin became pastor of the branch they all attended, and Maude was the faithful helpmate. They raised, beside Joy, six sons, five of whom became members of the priesthood. Leon raised his large family in Bemidji, Minnesota, and though he separated himself from the Reorganized Church of Jesus Christ of Latter Day Saints, he continued to be a faithful witness for the Lord Jesus Christ, and taught his children so to be.

Winfield received one of his most wonderful spiritual experiences while in Independence, during a time of extreme pain. He was undergoing treatment to remove a tumor from his bladder by electricity. When the pain was so bad he felt he could no longer bear it, he said, "For some reason, I felt to turn my head and look toward the northeast corner of the room, and the walls seemed to have disappeared, and I saw trees and sky and I could see a hill in the distance with a cross standing on it. Then all at once I was out on the hill at the foot of the cross looking up at the Savior. He hung there on the cross, his head hanging to one side. I could see the nails in his hands, and his feet were bent down and a large square-headed iron nail was driven through them. I could understand and feel the pain he had suffered and how much worse pain of mind could be than pain of body.

"Then I heard plainly a voice say to me, 'He that suffers with me shall also reign with me.'"

"Instantly the pain was gone. I looked back at the doctor. I could see the twist he would give to the instrument which before had caused such burning pain, but now I felt only a warm sensation."

July 15, 1898, at the age of forty-six, Winfield was given his Patriarchal Blessing by Presiding Patriarch, Alexander Smith, at Everts, Ottertail County, Minnesota. Among other things, he was told:

"...thy calling is not in the spiritual work to bestow upon others spiritual instruction, but thou art called of God to manifest in thy life that it is easy to serve God, and that by serving God and serving Him faithfully the blessed influence of His Spirit comes and brings confirmation and assurance to him that serveth. Be faithful in the discharge of thy duty, setting a faithful example to thy children and teaching them the principles of righteousness, and a crown of glory shall rest upon thee, and thou shalt be blessed in thy children. Many, many shall call thee blessed, shall remember the blessed influences that flow out from thee because of a life fitly lived among thy fellows, an everyday walk that shall mark to them thou art a child of God."

May the reader judge whether or not he fulfilled that instruction in his life.

As I read the family histories, a pattern emerges. I see my own parents, raised on opposite coasts of the country, drawn together by the hope of Zion. I see in the Whitings, Murdocks, Tuckers, Andersons, Shermans, Flecthers and others, the Lord's hand in leading them to the "land between two shining lakes." And the Goulds, without knowing, followed that inner urge because the Lord knew their potential and needed them to mingle their blood with that of the others He had chosen.

These people set a high standard for those who came after. Their faith, their love of the Lord and His truth, courage in adversity, and ability to endure to the end, are characteristics the Lord needs in His people.

He called on them, as he calls on all, and those who responded are seen as pillars of the Kingdom.

We are a fragmented people. But in each fragment there are those who nourish that faith had by their forefathers—that dream of the "City which hath foundations whose Builder and Maker is God." One day, those with the dream will hear the call the ages have been waiting for, and respond to become "as lively stones...built up a spiritual house—acceptable to God by Jesus Christ." (Excerpts from 1 Peter 2:5)

Who's Who

This genealogy is included to help you identify the people in the story.

Five **Whiting** brothers, sons of Elisha and Sallie Hewlett Whiting, left Nauvoo when the Saints were driven out. Their names were:

> **Chauncey,** head of the Cutlerites who went to Minnesota. His wife was Edith Morely. Their children:
>> *Isaac*
>>
>> *Ann*, who married Cutler Alma Sherman, parents of Effie and Plinnie Sherman
>>
>> *Lide*
>>
>> *Carmeal*
>>
>> *Warren*, photographer, who married Zeruah Sherman, teacher, weaver of cloth, sister of Alma Sherman. Children: Birch, Grace, Ora, Delbert, who married Flossie, daughter of Art Whiting, their children: Harvey, Roderick, who married Gretta Young, Phillip, Laurel
>>
>> *Alonzo*, twin
>>
>> *Lurette*, twin, who married Eleanor "Norie" Gould, children: Cora, Ross, Curtis, Irene, Genevieve—Gladys' special cousin
>>
>> *Lyman,*
>>
>> *Chauncey*, Jr.
>>
>> *Lucy*
>
> **Edmund**, did not stay at Clitherall
>
> **Almond,** "Uncle Al," chair maker
>
> **Sylvester,** "Uncle Vet," store keeper, married Rebecca Redfield. One of their sons, Allie Almond, was Winfield's best man at his wedding.

Francis Lewis, "Uncle Lute," who married Ann Jannette Burdick, "Aunt Net," daughter of Cary and Mary Baker Burdick. Their children:

Emma Locine "Em," who married Edwin Anderson. They had eleven children, including Alice Eugenia, who married Leon Gould.

Lucia Louisa, "Lu," who married Alva Murdock. They had two children: Ralph and Lucia May, who married Harold Black (May Black).

Ella Jannette, who married Winfield Gould, their children:

Leon, who married Alice Anderson, his first cousin, daughter of Edwin Anderson and Emma Locine Whiting Anderson, sister to Ella. Children of Leon and Alice: Alice, Phyllis, Winfield, Lovita, Arlo, Arthur, Darlene, Stella, Helen, Amy, Donavan.

Winfield William, "Winnie," who died at 24, 1900

Lenna Maude, who married Plinnie Sherman, son of C. Alma Sherman. Their children: Winifred Alma, Joy Evelyn, Ronald Gould, Orland, Ormand, Leonard Ornell, Kenneth Maxwell, Howard Winfield, Robert Lee, Willard Warren, Evart Dale

Hallie May

Ethel Jeanette, who married Frank Tucker, son of Abner Spinach Tucker and Emily Murdock. Their children: Frank, Jr., Orison Eugene.

Nina Belle, who married Orison Tucker, son of Abner and Emily Tucker. Their children: Wayne Gould, Joyce Emily, Keith Douglas

Iva Roseltha

Ella Gladys

Arthur Wellington, "Uncle Art," who married Lois Murdock, their children: Flossie, who married Delbert

Whiting, son of Warren and Zeruah Whiting; Floyd, Sadie, Raymond, Della, Violet

Mary Belle, "Aunt May," who married Freeman Anderson, brother of Edwin Anderson, sons of Buckley Anderson. Children of May and "Freem" include Abbie Adell, who married Birch Whiting

Sylvia Cordelia, "Aunt Cordie," who married Orison Murdock, brother of Emily Murdock Tucker, son of Hiram and Rachel Murdock. Their children: Ellis, Jannette—who drank kerosene and was healed,—Marguerite, Ione, Mattie

Francis Lester, who married Effie Kimber, their children: Malcolm, Norma

John Gould and wife, Nancy Fox, came to America from England. Their children:

George who married Amanda Williams. Their children:
George Anthony, "Little George"
Amanda Jane

Amanda died, **George** married Eleanor Colwell Sherman, daughter of Jacob and Rhoda Sherman, sister of Cassius Sherman. Their children:

Roseltha Ann, "Aunt Rosie," who married William Corliss and later Orris Albertson. Children: Minnie, by Corliss; Orris, Nellie, Coral, Earl

Clayton Glacier, who married Delia Sherman, their children: George, Lottie, Etta Fay, Arlo Clayton, Herbert, Minnie

Winfield William, who married Ella Whiting, daughter of Lewis and Jannette Whiting, see children under Ella Whiting, above

Eleanor Rhoda, "Norie," who married Lurette Whiting, "Ret." See Lurette for children

> *Emma Luella,* who married William Oaks, son of Rueben and Eliza Oaks. Their children: Lillie May, Minnie, Harold Tracey, Reuben George, Leon Winfield

Jane

John Gould was drowned at sea when he was on the way back to England. Nancy later married Jacob Wendell who had ten children. Jacob and Nancy had ten more. Among these were:

> *Dr. Jim Wendell,* half brother to Winfield, the one who diagnosed Winfield's aneurysm
>
> *Nelson,* father of Jennie

Jacob Sherman and wife Rhoda were from England This Sherman was not related to Alma Sherman. Their children:

> *Frank*
>
> *Theodore,* who married Sarah. Their children: Rhoda, who married Hugh Hunter, who was blind. They were the parents of Bertha Hunter, Winnie's fiance; Charles, Cash, Anson
>
> *Fred, Levi, John*
>
> *Cassius,* who found the old book in the barn, and froze to death in the blizzard of 1873
>
> *Eleanor,* who married George Gould, see children under Gould
>
> *Jane,* who married Tom Crane, their children: Cora, Tom, George, Ida—married Frank Horne, Ellen—married George Whiting, Walter, Herb
>
> *Mary*

Alpheus Cutler, married Lois Lathrop. He was prominent in the early church. He joined the group of saints in Iowa, believed he had been appointed to reorganize the church. He was leader of group known as Cutlerites until his death, in

Iowa. **Lois** went with the group to Minnesota. When she heard the story of the Reorganized church, she asked the Lord for a sign if it were true. She had, for fourteen years, a bony growth on her finger, which she asked Him to remove as the sign. It was removed and she was baptized when 87 years of age.[71] Their children:

Thaddeus, joined the Reorganization

William, Franklin, Edwin, Louisa,

Lois, who married Almon *Sherman.* Lois was dying of tuberculosis in the home of her parents, Alpheus and Lois Cutler, when David Patten, early missionary, stopped at the house to preach. After the sermon, she asked for administration and was instantly healed. The whole family was baptized the next day.

Cutler Alma, who married Ann Whiting, daughter of Chauncey Whiting. Their children:

Effie, who worked for Ella, and died young.

Plinnie Alfred, who married Maude Gould

Lucy, Mattie, Harry, Roy

After Alma was killed, Ann married William Barnhard. Their children: Joseph Hyrum, Bonnie Belle, Lottie, Grace

Delia Sherman, sister to Cutler Alma, married Clayton Gould. See children under Gould

John Tucker married Abigail. They were from New Jersey of Scotch, Irish, English descent. They were not connected with the Latter Day Saints Church. Their children:

Abner, died in infancy, *Elizabeth, Euphemia,*

Abner Spinach, who married Sarah Emily Murdock. Their children:

Franklin Pierce, who married Ethel Gould

Orison Eugene, who married Nina Gould

Nettie Rose
Frank, married Frances.

Cary Burdick married Mary Baker, of Dutch descent. Their children:

Oscar, Jackson,

Ann Jannette, who married Francis Lewis Whiting—children under Whiting

Jesse, who was among the first group of pioneers to go to Ottertail County.

Daniel Murdock, married Caroline. Their children:

Hiram, who married Rachel Roziela Kelsey. Their children:

Martha Francenia

Charles Ervin, married Anna Sophia Anderson.

Caroline Eliza

Hiram Alva, known as Alva, married Lucia Louisa Whiting, sister of Ella.

Sarah Emily, married Tom Christenson. Their child: Ellis Leroy. After Tom's death, Emily married Abner Tucker. See children under Tucker

Ellen Amanda, who married Jeddidiah Anderson

Diadama Amelia (Aunt Dama), who married Allie Almond Whiting

Lois Mariah, who married Arthur Wellington Whiting "Uncle Art," brother to Ella

Orison Evelyn, who married Sylvia Cordelia Whiting (Aunt Cordie)

Lyman Edward, died at 15 of an accidental gun shot wound.

Almon Lurette, "Let"

Rachel Rozilla, "Aunt Rose," married James Fletcher

Martha, sister to Hiram
Eliza, who married Reuben Oakes
Lyman, who married Elizabeth Kelsey
Emer
Sarah Emily, aunt of Sarah Emily Murdock Tucker

John Anderson, married Lydia Hanks. Their children, thirteen. Listing only those involved in the story:

Buckley, a twin, married Sallie Marie Cutler. His twin was Blakesley. Some of their children:

Jeddiadiah Richmond, who married Ellen Amanda Murdock

Edwin B., who married Emma Locine Whiting. Their daughter: Alice Eugenia, who married Leon Gould

Richard B., who married Eliza Sherman

Freeman Ethan, who married Mary Belle Whiting, "Aunt May," daughter of "Uncle Lute" and "Aunt Net."

The Andersons were prominent families in the church of that time and place. Some left the Clitherall area and moved to Becker County, Minnesota. They were responsible for the "Josephite" missionaries going to the area and were among the first to be baptized. Some later moved back to Girard, east of Clitherall, and took part in the building of the first Reorganized Church of Jesus Christ of Latter Day Saints church building built in Minnesota.

There were many other family names in Old Town and surrounding area, with whom the people in this story had much in common. Some of these are: Lewis Denna, an Indian, who was converted to the church in Nauvoo, and his wife Mary; many Fletchers; Badham; Sperry, Trowbridge, Christenson, Shaw, Taylor and others too numerous to mention. But some of their names are carved on the tombstones on Cemetery Hill, near Old Clitherall, and each played his part in shaping the history of that interesting place.

Reference Notes

1. The date for the organization of the county is given as July, 1868, Centennial issue, "Fergus Falls Daily Journal" dated July 25, 1968
2. *Saints' Hymnal*, #236, Published by Herald Publishing House, Independence, Mo., 1947
3. Acts 20:29, 30 King James Version
4. *History of the Church of Jesus Christ of Latter Day Saints*, Vol. 1, p. 9, Published by Herald Publishing House and Book Bindery, Lamoni, Iowa, 1911
5. Mun-dam-in, Chippewa word for corn, *History of the Ojibways*, by W. W. Warren p. 97, Minnesota Historical Press, St. Paul, 1984
6. Akik, Chippewa word for kettle. Manomin, rice. Makuk, birch bark container. I'ckode', fire. *Chippewa Customs*, by Francis Densmore, Minnesota Historical Society Press, 1979, pp 16, 17
7. 1 Nephi, 5:10–12, Book of Mormon, 1908 Edition, Herald Publishing House, Independence, Mo.
8. Ibid 5:70, 71
9. Ibid, verses 157, 158, 159, 163
10. Ibid, Jacob 2:33, 34, 36
11. Ibid, Mosiah, 11:156–157
12. *The Treasury of American Poetry*, A Collection of the Best Loved Poems By American Poets, Selected by Nancy Sullivan, Dorset Press, New York, N.Y. Note: Selected verses from the poem Snowbound, by Whittier.
13. Psalms 1:1–6, K.J. Bible
14. Title page, Book of Mormon
15. Ibid, 1Nephi 3:146–150
16. *America's God and Country Encyclopedia of Quotations*, by William J. Federer, p .113. Federer gives the reference as coming from *Life and Voyages of Christopher Columbus*, by Washington Irving.
17. K.J. Bible, John 10:16, emphasis added
18. *History of the CHURCH OF JESUS CHRIST of Latter Day Saints*, Herald Publishing House and Book Bindery, Lamoni, Iowa, pp 11–16
19. *The American Heritage Songbook*, by the editors of "American Heritage," the Magazine of History, Words and Music by the Hutchinson Family, p. 106
20. Genesis 49:22, 26, K.J. Bible
21. Doctrine and Covenants, Section 111:2b, Herald Publishing House
22. *The Story of the Church*, by Inez Smith Davis, Herald Publishing House, 1943, p. 404
23. Doctrine and Covenants, Section 1:3, a, b, d; 4,
24. Acts 2:38–39, K.J. Bible
25. Book of Mormon, Moroni 8:8, 9, 11
26. Doctrine and Covenants, Section 68:4a
27. Ibid, Section 1:3d, e
28. K.J. Bible, Genesis 5:24
29. Genesis7:20–25, 76–78, The Holy Scriptures, Inspired Version, Herald Publishing House, first printing 1867
30. Ibid 7:70–72
31. Ibid, Isaiah 11:12
32. Ibid 2:2–3
33. Book of Mormon, Ether 6:2–3
34. Doctrine and Covenants 65:1, d, e
35. Genesis 9:22, I.V.
36. Book of Mormon, Ether 1:31, 32, 35
37. Doctrine and Covenants, Section 57:1, a, b
38. Micah 4:4, I.V.

39. Doctrine and Covenants 42:12b
40. Ibid, 101:2, f, g
41. Ibid, 83:3
42. *Story of the Church*, by Inez Smith Davis, pp 398–399
43. Revelations 1:18, I.V.
44. John 5:25, I.V.
45. 1 Peter 3:18–19; 4:6, I.V.
46. Section 108:10 Doctrine and Covenants
47. Acts 24:15, I.V.
48. Rev. 20:12, I.V.
49. Doctrine and Covenants, Section 76:4, g, h
50. Ibid, 6:3, a, b
51. *Bury My Heart at Wounded Knee,* by Dee Brown, pp 413–418; U.S. Bureau of Ethnology Report, 14th,1892–1893, part 2, p. 885
52. Book of Mormon, I Nephi 3:150
53. II Nephi 12:81–84
54. Section 76:5a–d, k, Doctrine and Covenants
55. From the poem LINES, composed a few miles above Tintern Abbey, on revisiting the Banks of the Wye, during a tour, by William Wordsworth.
56. Doctrine and Covenants, Section 85:2
57. *Literature and Life,* Book Four, by Greenlaw and Miles, Scott, Foresman and Company, 1929, p. 665
58. Doctrine and Covenants, Section 1:6, a, b
59. Journal by Ethel Jeanette Gould (Tucker*), MINNESOTA PIONEERS,* A History of the Founding of Ottertail County and Families of Gould, Sherman, Tucker, Whiting and Others," Compiled by Frank and Norma Tucker, 1975; updated by Velma Sherman, 1992
60. Doctrine and Covenants, Section 101:2c
61. Ibid, 59:3, 4, 5a
62. Exodus 28:1; 29:9; Hebrews 5:4, I.V.
63. Doctrine and Covenants, Section 104:1
64. *The Story of the Church*, by Inez Smith Davis, p. 256–257
65. Ibid, p. 398
66. *MINNESOTA PIONEERS*, A History of the Founding of Ottertail County and Families of Gould, Sherman, Tucker, Whiting and Others," p. 41
67. Delbert Whiting's Testimony, Ibid, p. 413
68. Winfield Gould's Story of His Life, Ibid, p. 57
69. Ibid, p. 72–73
70. Doctrine and Covenants, Section 64:6c, 8, Emphasis added
71. *Saints Herald,* Volume 25, page 172 Herald Publishing House, Independence, Mo

Errata:

page 123, 7th line down, and page 214, 3rd line from bottom. In both instances the text reads *Oliver Cowdry*, but should read *Sidney Rigdon.*

Page 104, 2nd line from top, the date *1970* should read *1870.*

Page 189, 14th line from bottom the word *also* has been omitted. The reference should read *For Christ also once...*